THE WILDERNESS OF RUIN

ALSO BY ROSEANNE MONTILLO

The Lady and Her Monsters

THE
WILDERNESS
OF RUIN

A TALE OF MADNESS, FIRE,
AND THE HUNT FOR AMERICA'S
YOUNGEST SERIAL KILLER

ROSEANNE MONTILLO

wm

WILLIAM MORROW
An Imprint of HarperCollins*Publishers*

HarperCollins books may be purchased for educational, business, or sales promotional use. For information please e-mail the Special Markets Department at SPsales@harpercollins.com.

FIRST EDITION

Designed by Jamie Lynn Kerner

Library of Congress Cataloging-in-Publication Data has been applied for.

ISBN 978-0-06-227347-5

15 16 17 18 19   OV/RRD   10 9 8 7 6 5 4 3 2 1

Dedicated to my family

CONTENTS

THE WILDERNESS OF RUIN

PROLOGUE

O Boston, city of our Pride!

O Massachusetts, our loved State,

Thy faults we ever seek to hide,

We for thy perfect glory wait!

—POEM READ BY REV. MINOT J. SAVAGE AT THE
DEATH OF GOVERNOR WILLIAM GASTON

In the early hours of Thursday, August 1, 1929, crowds formed in front of the main gate of the Massachusetts State Prison in Charlestown, a sprawling compound of brick and granite encircled by a tall, wrought-iron gate. It was a warm morning and would become even more so as the temperatures reached as high as ninety-five degrees. Young mothers had risen early so they could make it to the prison, dragging their children along with them. Workers from the nearby factories had taken the day off, and the elderly men who had followed the notorious case for more than fifty years were lined up along the streets. Standing next to them on the sidewalk were numerous reporters from across the country, who did not seem to mind the heat. All of them had been drawn there by the fermenting curiosity of years past and by more recent tantalizing articles.

For days newspapers in the region had been speculating about whether the people of Boston would get the chance to see Jesse Harding Pomeroy again. Or, as the *Boston Daily Globe* wrote, would Pomeroy "have a glimpse of the world denied him for 53 years." In recent days those residing near the prison, and in the city at large, had been waiting to hear if Jesse Pomeroy would be transferred from the state prison to the Bridgewater State Farm, nearly two hours to the south of Boston. Originally built to house "paupers" from the state hospitals, the Farm had now become a warehouse where hospitals, prisons, and other institutions dumped their so-called undesirables, those who could not be helped by routine treatments. On the evening of July 31, special editions were printed with headlines screaming that indeed, it would be so: he would go on the following morning.

Sixty-eight-year-old Pomeroy was not happy about his transfer. He had entered the Massachusetts State Prison—or the Massachusetts Bastille, as it was often referred to—when he was barely a teenager, and his cell, Number 19 in the South Wing, had become his home. He knew where each brick had a line running across it, most likely because he had chiseled it there himself. He had felt every wedge or crack the walls possessed with the tips of his aging fingers. He knew where his old cot sank beneath his weight, where his pillow had come loose at the seams; he knew which of the officers would be bringing him his meal simply by the distinct way that person had of jingling his key into the door. He knew what that meal consisted of, and how many minutes before the appointed hour it would arrive. Now he would have to leave it all behind in favor of a place where people donned not guns, as was customary, but white uniforms, as white as his eye.

Jesse was adamant that he deserved a full pardon and had not wanted to leave until it had been granted. He felt so strongly about it that, as a final act of defiance, he'd even refused to pack his few belongings until a guard had made him do so—first gently, then with a little more force. Jesse's attorney, John Daly, had fought a valiant fight. He ardently believed that Jesse deserved to be pardoned because if he had been tried today instead of the 1870s, he would have been sent to a hospital for the mentally "unsound," and not to the state penitentiary.

"He was a victim of circumstance," Daly argued before those members who had agreed to hear his plea. He proclaimed that Pomeroy's sentencing had occurred "during an era when insanity was not considered to the degree" that it was now. Daly was also in agreement with Pomeroy that he needed to be pardoned. He was so convinced of his argument that he'd even taken the liberty of coordinating with the Salvation Army, who had assured him a home would be provided for Jesse upon release.

But something in Daly's eagerness and choice of words had unwittingly irked those on the panel deciding Jesse's fate. At one point, Daly had described Pomeroy's murderous actions as "getting into trouble," which had seemed to trivialize the offenses. Daly's summations had also seemed to imply that the state owed Pomeroy not only his freedom, but an apology, which Jesse had been requesting for years. When the committee released their decision, they gave no validation to what Daly had expressed. If anything, the men felt that too much grace had already been extended on the prisoner. Pomeroy would not be pardoned; instead he was being transferred.

On this August morning, Pomeroy shed the prison uniform he had worn for fifty-three years and changed into a borrowed suit, dark in color and two sizes too big. It hung ungainly from his body, the fabric alien on his sagging skin. In his pockets, he carried a dollar and sixty-six cents, part of his earnings from legal speculations with the stock market, and when he spoke to the minister, his breath smelled of hot beef hash and coffee, which he had consumed as his last meal on the premises.

With the paperwork taken care of, the door to his cell opened and he was escorted into the corridor. It must have seemed odd that with a few twists of the key, he was able to step beyond the threshold of his cell, beyond the steel bars he had often tried to dislodge with contraband weapons. He walked slowly down the South Wing of the prison and followed the hallway that led to a large rotunda, where a guard post was located. He looked up and saw the cells arranged in a circular formation, heard the shouts from the prisoners that in isolation he had never heard before, the ding of steel bars as they opened and closed. On entering the prison, some visitors compared the institution to a busy beehive. And so it must have looked to Jesse when he stared upward.

As he walked out, he did not offer a thank-you, a salute, or any kind words to the warden, James L. Hogsett, or to the officers who had taken care of him during the past years. He merely pushed the tip of a newsboy cap over his eyes and readied to walk outside, where the crowds awaited him.

Guards posted near the prison's front staircase stared as the people surged forward by the locked gates; these officers patrolled the area holding bayonets and wooden clubs, making certain that a riot would not ensue. Taking drags from their cigarettes, reporters stood in the sun with pencils at the ready. "It was a morning of tense silence," an editorial in the *Boston Evening Globe* stated later that evening, describing the moments prior to Jesse's arrival. Most of those who idled by the curb had been youngsters at the time of Jesse's roaming, protected by their mothers, whose fears had overwhelmed them. Along with them there were now young mothers, sisters, and some much older individuals who had been Jesse's schoolmates.

For the most part, they remained calm and quiet. The only sounds

In 1634, the governor of Massachusetts, John Winthrop, ordered Castle Island in Boston Harbor to be used as a prison fortification. It was in 1803, following a series of highly publicized breakouts, that the Massachusetts Senate passed a bill to close Castle Island and build a new state prison on five acres of land on Lynde's Pond in Charlestown. Built entirely of granite, and surrounded by tall barbed-wire fencing, Jesse Pomeroy went on to spend more than half a century within it, becoming one of its most famous inmates. (*The Charlestown Historical Society*)

they heard were the dings and whistles from the elevated trains running nearby, and the shouts of dogs in the distance. Occasionally a murmur arose when they thought the approaching hour was at hand, until it got louder and louder when from "behind that big door arched as cathedral window set down the center . . . was the answer to our gathering," continued the *Boston Evening Globe.*

Warden Hogsett emerged from the main door, looking serious and pale, and began to chat with several of the uniformed guards. As a group, they moved toward the gates and eyed the crowd. Moments later, from behind them there appeared several more guards holding rifles, followed by two other inmates also being transferred, their shackled feet clinking as they walked forward.

Jesse Harding Pomeroy left the Massachusetts State Prison at precisely 11:33 A.M., the rattling of his chains announcing a reemergence into the sunlight. Although the sun was blinding, as he moved toward the car he saw the outlines of those who had come to see him and heard the shouts coming from their direction. He did not acknowledge their presence or the words they were hurtling toward him. Instead, he lifted his eyes toward a hot and unfriendly sky. He blinked several times, then headed toward a black sedan enlisted for the occasion and took a seat between the two other inmates, Daniel Watts and Giuseppe Malavia, also headed for Bridgewater. William I. Robison, from the Parole Office, drove the car, while Joseph O'Brien, another state official, sat in the passenger's seat. A second black sedan followed them, carrying three more inmates to Bridgewater.

As the people dispersed in the hot haze, they realized that something was amiss and anticlimactic in the way Jesse had been returned to them. From its very beginning, the newspaper articles had described Jesse as a beast, the devil, a larger-than-life individual lurking among the streets of Boston and leaving havoc and death in his wake. That's what the crowd had come to see, what the people had expected. But the man who had left the prison seemed shriveled and desiccated by time, not even of average height, a long mustache hanging limply by his cheeks, bearing the whole of his life under his arm in a small package wrapped in old newspaper and tied with butcher's string, like a Sunday roast. The person he had become had stunned them into silence, and as the sedan became a speck of black on the horizon, they quietly returned to their lives, to the breweries and the factories making buttons, to taking care of their children, and to their games of baseball in the nearby park.

During the ride to the Bridgewater State Farm, Jesse remained quiet, almost solemn. As they moved from the prison grounds toward the Charles River, he looked out at the city that had developed during his absence, the buildings that had risen at the banks of the river. While in prison, he had been allowed to pass the time reading books and newspapers, and had memorized poems, sonnets, languages, geographical locations, historical facts, maps, and figures in order to keep up with the world. But now, looking out from the window, it seemed as if the speed in which the world in general had progressed in the previous fifty years had been faster than Jesse's reckoning. What he had not been a part of for more than fifty years now revealed itself, on August I, 1929.

Indeed, it was the type of world his books and newspapers had described in detail yet reality had not prepared him for: bright, breezy, crowded, noisier than he recalled. There were no horses on the cobblestone streets he had trod upon as a boy. The click-clacking of hoofs had been replaced by the honking of automobiles whizzing by at the dizzying speed of twenty or thirty miles an hour. A grinding noise alerted him to an alien creature flying toward soft cumulus clouds, and looking upward he saw the wings of an airplane gliding across the blue expanse, machines unheard and unseen during his time.

Trains lumbered across bridges extending from Boston to Cambridge, seemingly gliding over the waters of the Charles and carrying hordes of people through the city in a matter of minutes. Some rushed to work, their movements swift as they walked forward together, members of a group he had never joined. Others, in the midst of a recreational day, were making their way to Fenway Park, where the Red Sox were hosting the Cleveland Indians. (The Red Sox would go on to lose the game 10–3, one of many losses in 1929, a particularly ugly season for them.) The river flowed lazily from Charlestown to Boston, and on its banks were moored ships and small vessels of a practical nature, as well as tiny pleasure boats. And what to say of all those wooden poles erected everywhere, from which power lines were strung like Christmas ornaments.

In Washington Irving's "Rip Van Winkle," written in 1819, the titular character awakens from a twenty-year sleep and finds himself in a world that has drastically changed. "There were rows of houses which he had never seen before, and those which had been familiar haunts had disappeared. Strange names were over the doors—strange faces at the windows—everything was strange." So it was for Jesse, and reporters who described this day's event called on Irving's story and its parallel with Pomeroy's. The prison warden also recalled the famous tale while describing Jesse's new adventure.

On the next day, August 2, nearly every newspaper in the country, large and small, printed a story about his release. Connecticut's *New Britain Herald* was one of them: "Pomeroy in his youth clearly had a defective mind; yet today he insists he is sane. Had he not been a youth himself, he probably would have been hanged for his crimes of 53 years ago; but this very fact that he was a youth at the time and has spent so many years in prison . . . makes the case one that has attained world-wide interest," the editorial stated. "Many agreed that life in prison had not been enough. . . . But, if the mere process of breathing, eating and sleeping—merely existing amid concrete and steel cells—is preferable to death, than [sic] there is a difference in degree of punishment between such a term for life and execution. But life as we understand it and what we expect of it surely amounts to more than this. Pomeroy in effect has been dead for 53 years, he has suffered the pangs of remorse, the stir of conscience and the pain of thinking about what might have been."

But had he done any of those things? Had he become remorseful, felt his conscience stir, or thought of what might have been? Perhaps he thought of what might have been, most especially as the car left the courtyard of the Massachusetts State Prison for its one-hour-and-forty-three-minute drive to Bridgewater.

As they drove ahead toward his final destination, one cannot help but think, his mind must have traveled back to the time when the streets were muddy and overrun with omnibuses. To a time when he ran atop the bridges away from his home and toward the waters to watch the fishermen dig their clams. To a time when the bakeries sold their sweets for a penny, buns he coveted even from his neighbors. To a time when his mother and his brother were still very young, and he was just a boy of fourteen, exploring as he had done many times before the crooked streets of his new home, in South Boston.

To a time when the children laughed as innocently as he had never done.

CHAPTER 1

THE INHUMAN SCAMP

The Sandman's coming in his train of cars

With moonbeams windows and with wheels of stars

So hush you little ones and have no fear

The man-in-the-moon is the engineer

—"THE SANDMAN"

In the spring of 1872, a twelve-year-old boy scurried across the bridge that led from Charlestown into the city of Chelsea. He had made his way across the wooden planks before, running southward along Bunker Hill Avenue and leaving behind Lexington Street, where his family had once lived and where he had been born on November 29, 1859. His mother had despised that apartment and the sheer smallness of it, despised the muddy streets that flooded with muck from the rain and the horse excrement from the animals passing by; despised the scum that collected at the water's edge from the factories nearby, and the stench that arose in the summer from the tanneries doing business across the bridges. Still, the boy had enjoyed the closeness to the stagnant river.

Their new home, on 78 Bunker Hill Avenue, was slightly larger. It was located just steps away from the Bunker Hill Monument, which recalled the opening battle of the American Revolution. That battle had occurred on June 17, 1775, on Breed's Hill, where troops led by Colonel Prescott, General Putnam, and Major Brooks had fought against the British. It was also there that General Putnam uttered the infamous words "Don't fire until you see the whites of their eyes!"

The monument was completed in 1845—well before the boy's birth. President John Tyler attended the opening celebrations, while the famed Daniel Webster had given a stirring oration, imparting such inspirational words as "Let it rise, till it meet the sun in his coming, let the earliest light of the morning gilded it, and parting day linger and play on its summit."

People who visited the area on quiet afternoons were often struck by the monument, an obelisk of Egyptian-inspired design with a gilt urn pointing skyward.

But living in the shadows of such a historical marker meant very little as far as the boy's mother was concerned; it was the actual space of the apartment she was worried about. The boy cared even less. For him it was the proximity to the bridge that mattered, as it linked Charlestown to Chelsea.

Not far from his own home, the boy came across the Navy Yard, a sprawling compound occupying nearly one-eighth of the land in Charlestown. As busy as some of the navy yards in larger cities, it made a brisk business of building and repairing boats and ships and employed thousands not only from Charlestown but also from the surrounding areas. Every day these men could be seen hurrying to and fro on landings for transatlantic steamers such as the Warren Line, which traveled from Boston to Liverpool, England. But workers were also hired at several distilleries, their fumes emanating from long smokestacks by the wharves day and night; at the state prison, that large and imposing institution that swallowed up the better part of the Charlestown landscape; and at the McLean Asylum for the Insane, which had opened its doors in October 1818.

Near the Navy Yard there existed one of the few empty plots of land that opened out into "pasture" land, as it was called, which backed up into a dilapidated warehouse called Moulton's Hall. This stretch of land had a very low beach ringed by willow trees, and in the summer the children of the area scampered there with lunch pails and long fishing poles. The boy had gone there many times before with his brother, Charles, when they were much younger. But now Charles no longer cared for fishing. Twenty months the boy's senior, Charles had lately taken more of a shine to the neighborhood girls, even trying to grow a faint mustache to impress them.

Though it was already spring, that day of 1872 had dawned gray and sleety as the boy crossed the Chelsea Bridge. He could detect the delicate smell of confections and bonbons emanating from Schrafft's

Candy Company mingling with the strong scents coming from the nearby factories brewing ale. He did not stop to glance at the lead-colored waters of the Mystic River rushing below him, which bordered Charlestown to the west, but instead he held on tightly to the white-handled pocketknife, several yards of rope, and a tight bundle of fabric he had brought along with him.

Any businessmen on their way into the city would not have paid any attention to him as they passed one another. Prior to the bridge's development, the trip from Chelsea into Boston had been a roundabout horse ordeal that took the better part of two days. When the ferry service was started in 1631, the first of its kind in the country, it made the ride across the Mystic much shorter, albeit more dangerous. But the bridge, built in 1803, gave Chelsea new life.

Crossing it from Broadway in Chelsea into the lower end of Charlestown now took only a short while, and farmers and business-men could come and go freely carrying their products: fruits, vege-tables, meats, milks, eggs, and cheeses to sell to grocers in the city. Though the bridge was now old and would soon require a great deal of refurbishing, the city of Charlestown was still in charge of paying nearly two-thirds of its upkeep. But commercialists didn't care about such details. Those who were busy with such matters of commerce and opportunity would not even notice a boy's comings and goings. He became part of the landscape.

Quiet and pleasant in the early 1800s, that area of Chelsea, even its waters, held beauty and tradition. It was not uncommon for the Baptist Society to hold its Sunday baptismal ceremonies in the Mystic River, groups of families gathering at its banks wearing their Sunday best and looking on as a minister dunked a small child into the chilly waters.

But that ended with the advent of the ferry, and more important, with the bridge, as the area around Chelsea's waterfront began to de-velop, industrialists eyeing not its charms but how cheap and conve-nient it was.

Most of the people in town had been happy to see Chelsea grow.

But the wealthy, those who had summered on the waters and who had mansions located in and around the waterfront, found the new changes deplorable. Factories began to sprout: coal, from the Campbell & Company Coal Wharves; wood, from George D. Emery Enterprises, whose mahogany was shipped all the way from South America. James S. Green even opened a stable for horses, not only selling them but even lending them out, the stable becoming larger and larger with each passing year. The factories fronting the river turned their backs to the mansions, their smoke and soot obscuring the water's views. And as more opportunities arrived, so did more people.

The stately homes were replaced by cheap lodging for the factory workers and everything else that was needed for their care and entertainment: a ramshackle doctor's office, a small grocery store, even a tavern and a vaudeville theater. Where once there arose the fragrant smell of blooming gardenias, now residents had to accept the pungent odor of fresh horse manure littering the streets. Eventually the wealthy left the riverfront and gravitated inland, and without their money to keep up the area's physical appearance, it took on a dingy look that reeked of despair.

It was here that the boy from Charlestown headed.

EIGHT-YEAR-OLD ROBERT MAIER WAS the son of local factory workers who made their home in Chelsea and had lived there for several years. As they did for all the other children of the area's factory workers, the streets had become Robert's playground. These were now a plethora of untidy backyards, broken porches overgrown with leaves and refuse, and mangy dogs scavenging for food and chasing after rats. On this day Robert was spending a late afternoon flinging pebbles across his small messy garden, as he had done many times before. It was a cold day, the brisk wind carried off from the Mystic River banging the shutters of those homes nearby.

Not long after he began his game, a boy he did not recognize, a bigger boy than himself, approached him. Of course, Robert's parents had told him to stay close to home and speak to no one. But this bigger boy smiled as he neared Robert. He seemed friendly and, besides, Robert reasoned, he was a boy like himself. He was much taller than Robert and had to bend over substantially to collect several rocks from the mound Robert had gathered on the ground. The big boy quickly aimed the rocks at a gate nearby and at a window, loudly shattering it, until soon he became bored. He told Robert they should take a walk.

Remembering his parents' words, Robert hesitated, and in sensing his misgivings, the boy from across the river told him the circus had arrived in town and wouldn't he like to go and see it.

In 1872, P. T. Barnum's Grand Traveling Museum, Menagerie Caravan and Circus train began to travel the country's railways, stopping at the many industrial communities. Like all the other children, Robert had heard about the penguins from Antarctica and the lions from the savannas of Africa, how conjoined twins twisted their limbs like pretzels and about the ladies with long beards they groomed like men's; he'd also heard about the armless women who knitted fancy wear with their toes; and the ancient mummies arising from sarcophagi, and the vivisected animals, and the freaks of all kinds. Robert had never seen any of the wonders the big boy was describing, but they seemed fun. A curious boy, he could not refuse such an enticing invitation.

As they sauntered away from Robert's street, suddenly the big boy turned away from the main road and followed a quieter one, leading not toward the town's center, where he had told Robert the circus had set up its tents, but into a more rustic lane that led forward onto Powder Horn Hill. In 1634 an attorney named Richard Bellingham had moved from Boston, England, to Boston, Massachusetts. In his new home, he had ascended to the ranks of lieutenant governor, and although he had made his permanent home in Boston, he had also purchased an expanse of land in Chelsea, where he had built a large estate on a slope he had named Powder Horn Hill. From there, he said, if he stood on the summit, he could see across all the way to Boston, and if he stretched far enough, perhaps to his childhood home of Boston, England.

But that was many years ago, and the grandeur of the estate and of Powder Horn Hill had now disappeared and only decaying shacks remained, those that had once belonged to servants. One could still see the city, but the hill had become lonely, isolated. Nearby swished a small, murky pond where dead leaves floated in winter and tiny inedible fishes swam in the summer.

Whether or not Robert worried about the boy's change of direction is uncertain, but he became aware of his intentions soon enough, when the boy unexpectedly lifted him off the ground and catapulted him into the pond. Robert struggled to get back to the pond's edges, but the boy pushed him underwater, as if wanting to drown him. Moments later the boy lifted him out, and though Robert tried to free himself, he could not, because the big boy was very strong and held on firmly before shoving him to the ground. That's when Robert felt something heavy land on the back of his head; he blacked out.

Robert woke up as tiny flashes of light crossed his eyes and pain riddled his body. He was being dragged by his neck along a quiet road that felt bumpy against his aching limbs. He and the boy arrived at a small and dilapidated outhouse on top of Powder Horn Hill. Its smell was so rotten that Robert nearly gagged. Though he tried to scream, the boy quieted him by pushing a piece of rag into his mouth. The boy ripped the clothes from Robert's body, stripping him completely naked until he shivered. Then, using the rope he had brought along, he fastened Robert to a wooden beam. The rope cut deeply into the little boy's flesh.

Robert was now fully conscious and could hear the boy's giggles as he danced around him, laughing and jumping back and forth, spewing out lewd words, over and over. Frightened, Robert watched as the boy crossed the small space and picked up a wooden stick. He then neared Robert and like a dog sniffed him; the terror he noticed in Robert seemed to thrill him, for with a smile, he landed the stick over his body, hitting Robert across his chest, his legs, and his genitals. The rag in his mouth prevented Robert from screaming, but he could feel the pain intensely. Moments later, the boy took the rag from his mouth and told him not to make a sound, and simply to do what he was being told. Robert nodded. Then the boy told him to repeat the words he said, foul words Robert had been told never to whisper out loud.

Profanity was not allowed in Robert's home, and his parents punished him and his siblings if they ever heard them whisper such things. But the boy was big and bad, and the wooden stick painful, so Robert did as he was told. And as he repeated the words, he noticed something peculiar: although his parents didn't approve, the boy seemed to like them very much. The louder Robert uttered them, the giddier the boy became. Soon even the boy's breathing changed. Robert saw that the boy now inhaled very sharply. He even roughly unbuckled his belt and began groping inside his pants. Robert didn't understand but said the dirty words over and over, louder and louder, until the boy screamed, closed his eyes, and fell to the floor in great spasms.

Sometime later, a man walking through the area became aware of a strange moaning. The sound seemed to come from up high in the hill, but it could easily have been the wind rustling through the empty interiors of those abandoned houses or from any of the small animals that had found shelter there for birthing their litters. But as the murmuring became more insistent, the man rushed toward it, leading him to the outhouse, where he found not a cat in labor, but a numbed little boy hanging from a rope tied around the center beam, his naked body limp and bloodied and covered in bruises, his lips a peculiar shade of purple due to the cold spring air that entered through the wood's opening.

THE CHELSEA POLICE WERE shocked, but not entirely surprised to find Robert in such brutal conditions. Lately there had been a "regular epidemic of crime . . . in which little children figured as the victims." Someone had been lurking along the Chelsea waterfront and luring little boys away from their families. The city marshal, Mr. Drury, had already issued a warning. On February 21, prior to the attack on Robert, another boy, ten-year-old Tracy Hayden, had also been induced to follow an older boy to Powder Horn Hill, where he had also been stripped, whipped, and manhandled. But in that case, the big boy, as Tracy had called him, had shown some measure of consideration after he was finished with his doings and had rearranged Tracy's clothing and walked him back to his neighborhood. Tracy had not been able to provide a detailed description for the police. He had simply stated that while playing in the streets, he had been approached by a boy he had not recognized, a boy he recalled as being older, bigger, and taller than himself.

And even before that, on the very day after Christmas 1871, a younger boy, Billy Paine, had been subjected to a similar attack, then found suspended from a roofbeam, his hands coiled with a rope and crying like a newborn kitten.

In Robert's case, the demon—as the boy was nicknamed after the spring ordeal—had followed more or less the same routine: he had approached him and befriended him in a soft and somewhat friendly manner; he had told a convincing story, in this case using the arrival of the circus in town; he had then directed the little boy to an abandoned shack no one would go to if not on purpose; there he had beaten him, laughed at him, become sexually excited, and used profanity. But this time he had not taken him home and instead had abandoned him to the elements.

Robert, Tracy, and Billy were the latest in a long string of assaults. The torturer's ruse had worked on several others, who instead of money, sweets, and visits to the circus had been met with vicious beatings. Police and the general populace speculated as to how the demon had managed to retreat so noiselessly into the shadows without anyone observing him. Some even suggested that he had melted into Chelsea's back alleys like the fog brought forth from the river. Perhaps he had been concealed by the general gloominess of the area, they reasoned, or the intertwining roads that led him far from the spot.

More likely, the police believed, it had simply been his age that had allowed him to go unnoticed. Who would think a boy capable of such horror? Local parents were as stricken as they were horrified, and together with neighbors formed a vigilante group. Arming themselves with wooden clubs, firearms, and even knives, they began to patrol the area, intent on bringing the fiend to justice. They also placed a five-hundred-dollar bounty on his head, knowing that the prospect of money would now unleash a hunt upon the newly rechristened *Boy Torturer.*

SOME YEARS BEFORE, IN 1867, Boston had commemorated the end of the Civil War with the National Peace Jubilee. It was such a success, they decided to celebrate the end of the Franco-Prussian War in 1871 with the World Peace Jubilee and International Music Festival. The man behind the festivities was an Irish bandleader named Patrick S. Gilmore, a man who believed that music could bridge a gap not only between nations but between people. The city agreed, and for months prior to the event, set for June 1872, Bostonians readied themselves almost without regard for anything else.

Mayor William Gaston knew that the country and the world at large would be descending upon Boston, and he warned that the city had better prepare for the inundation of strangers as well as the influx of commerce it would bring about. Gaston had been in office since 1871, and although well liked by Bostonians, he was not revered. He had been admitted to the bar in 1844 and opened his first law office in 1846 in the Roxbury district of Boston, where he had continued to practice law until 1868, when he was elected to the state senate.

Despite his obvious intelligence, people couldn't help but remark negatively about certain of his traits that were deemed "almost feminine." He was too kind, they said; too courteous. While men admired those gifts in a wife, in a public official they were dishonorable. Gaston was also often accused of being withdrawn, particularly when the occasion called for his total presence. But his personal reticence belied a nature that was far more humorous and curious than people gave him credit for. He was also known for a lack of decisiveness, but when it came to the Jubilee, that aspect of his character was nowhere to be found. He immediately put people to work and stunned the locals.

A spectacular structure called the Coliseum was built in an empty lot in the Back Bay. Architect William G. Preston wanted the amphitheater to rival the original Roman structure, the Colosseum, and though it did not, some felt it came close, managing to hold more than 100,000 attendees, nearly 2,000 musicians, and even 20,000 singers. Of particular note was Johann Strauss, who had become acquainted with Gilmore on a previous trip and agreed to come to Boston. His rendition of "The Blue Danube" enraptured those in attendance, and even brought tears to those listening from afar, as young boys had made swift business of selling ear trumpets to little old ladies who could not make it to the Coliseum.

Along with Strauss, the Boston firemen took center stage, 150 of them donning red shirts and hammering out a tune on their anvils, which allowed them to garner the name of "Anvil Chorus." Streamers and confetti floated in the air as children ran after them and adults tried to keep up with the choir.

Those in attendance couldn't help but remark about the freshness of the air being pumped into the structure, which they deemed "almost perfect." Ice water was freely handed out to anyone in need by the Young Men's Christian Association, whose stall became the most popular, while others hurried to try what was being called a "cocktail," a blend of spirits introduced to the public for the first time, further adding to the giddiness attendees were experiencing.

Among the crowds were also con men, thieves, and pickpockets of every sort who had elevated the trade to an art, all of whom Chief of

Police Edward Hartwell Savage had expected and prepared for. Having joined the force in 1851 and quickly moved up the ranks to become chief in 1871, Savage had earned the city's respect, for all knew there was nothing of mischief he could not handle, having already apprehended many of these criminals.

Although not a commercial success, the World Peace Jubilee was a triumph in other ways. It began on June 17, Bunker Hill Day, with ceremonial speeches atop a bedecked stage by the mayor as well as prayers from Reverend Phillips Brooks, of the Trinity Church. It ended on the Fourth of July, with dozens of newspaper articles detailing and commemorating the event. The Coliseum officials had arranged for a portion of space with writing desks, more than a dozen telegraph lines, and steel pens so reporters could have free access to the events. It was well furnished, well lit, and secure, and many reporters found their temporary workspace more appealing than their home offices. Grateful, they showed that gratitude in their reports.

One particular reporter, feeling especially solicitous toward Bostonians, concluded that next the city should hold the Universal Jubilee in 1875, for now Boston had become the "hub of the universe," he decided, "and no other city is to be thought of as a location." Yes, in his mind Boston deserved to garner universal limelight, or, at the very least, national attention. Unbeknownst to this journalist, the city would do so very soon, though not for the reasons he anticipated.

As summer progressed and the memory of the Jubilee faded, other concerns began to preoccupy the city. It was not long before words of the Boy Torturer's deeds in Chelsea drifted over the Mystic River and reached the city proper. The *Boston Globe* became aware of them and, on July 28, 1872, printed an article that wasn't long, though it certainly struck its readers with its description: "A Fiendish Boy: the public are considerably excited—and it is a good thing for the inhuman scamp that his identity is unknown just now." With its dramatic flair, the author's words hit a chord, and it caused the suspect to become known, at least for a while, as "the Inhuman Scamp."

CHAPTER 2

THE BRIDGE

Yet whenever I cross the river
On its bridge with wooden piers,
Like the odor of brine from the ocean
Comes the thought of other years.

And I think how many thousands
Of care-encumbered men,
Each bearing his burden of sorrow,
Have crossed the bridge since then.

—HENRY WADSWORTH LONGFELLOW, "THE BRIDGE"

Just as the July 28 article made its way across households all over the state, the big boy's mother, Ruth Ann Pomeroy, stood at the window of her Charlestown apartment and looked across the Mystic River toward Chelsea, the city described in the story. It was only a few miles away from her. The landscape had changed greatly just in the time since she'd moved to the area. Her view was now filled with the tall smoke-stacks protruding from innumerable factories.

Ruth Ann was small-boned, with sharp facial features and gray eyes that were very difficult to see beneath heavy lids and even heavier eyebrows that arched upward. She always seemed to carry about her a look that combined a haughty contempt for those she came in contact with, along with a good dose of sorrow for the way life had treated her. She was often heard cursing the misfortunes that had befallen her—or the fortunes that hadn't. But she felt that deep down the primary reason her life had gone astray was her husband—her now ex-husband, Thomas Pomeroy. As she often stared at the dingy furniture occupy-ing the equally dingy apartment she didn't even own on Bunker Hill Avenue, she couldn't help but blame all of her problems on him.

Divorce was nearly unheard-of during the 1870s, but Ruth Ann Pomeroy had taken these drastic steps to dissolve her marriage. She al-leged that her husband had, among other things, "contracted gross and confirmed habits of intoxication" from the moment they had gotten married until the day of their separation; that he was physically abusive toward her and her sons, most especially her younger, Jesse; and that he didn't like to work. The papers describing this pattern and his many shortcomings were detailed and engaging, and it was not difficult to see why a divorce was quickly granted.

Thomas and Ruth Ann had married on September 12, 1857, in Charlestown. He was a twenty-two-year-old man who already had a propensity for liquor, and she was a seventeen-year-old girl who was already far too disappointed with her life and surroundings. From that day forward, Ruth Ann always maintained, she had not complained about his drunken binges or the rages that followed. She had not spoken out—at least not too much—about his lack of initiative when it came to work. She had not nagged him about the other women she believed he kept on the side, nor over his endless whining about the headaches she did not believe he really suffered from. But she could not tolerate the beatings he inflicted on the boys, especially on Jesse, the rowdier of the two. She would never tell her son this, but it had been an incident involving Jesse that had caused her to seek the divorce from Thomas.

Some weeks earlier, when she returned home from her errands, neighbors had told Ruth Ann that Jesse and his father had become embroiled in a fight. They had watched as Jesse stormed out of the apartment and ran toward the river, with a drunken Thomas Pomeroy following quickly at his heels. Moments later, the two had returned, Thomas dragging Jesse by the collar, his young body seemingly no more than a sack of grain as it bounced over the muddy road.

Jesse later admitted to his doctors that his father had made him go to his room and strip totally naked, whereupon Thomas had proceeded to lash out with a leather belt, the blows raining down on Jesse's body with that whistle sound the leather made. Jesse recounted that as he cried, as the welts sprang out over his skin, he realized the beatings, although malevolent, were not that bad, not nearly as horrific as the relentless pummeling he had received almost four years earlier, when his father had taken Jesse, just eight years old, to an abandoned shed in the woods. There Thomas had become so enraged that the blows from a horsewhip had nearly killed his son.

Jesse may not have thought the beatings were so terrible, but Ruth

Ann Pomeroy had had enough. When she returned and found her son curled upon himself in a corner of the living room, his skin raw and beaten, she was overcome by a rage that propelled her forward toward a stack of knives she kept on the kitchen counter. Taking hold of the largest one, she lunged at her husband. Though very drunk, Thomas Pomeroy had been quick. He managed to run out of the house toward safety. Ruth Ann later said she regretted she missed and wished she had butchered him. When she couldn't do that, she served him with a copy of a divorce certificate and ordered him to appear in court, daring him "to show cause why the prayer of said libel should not be granted." The marriage was severed, and soon Ruth Ann found herself a single mother of two, Charles and Jesse.

Jesse was a strong-willed boy, Ruth Ann always claimed, and though Charles was helpful around the house, a steady, working boy, respectful to both of his parents and to his teachers, it was Jesse who was her favorite. She had been aware of Jesse's adversities from the start. She knew his classmates thought him odd, a boy larger than they were, with a head that seemed too big for his frame and a white blotch covering his right eye. The children were surprised when he retaliated for their jeers, so much so that in primary school his teacher, a Miss Abby Clark, had told Ruth Ann the other youngsters were frightened by Jesse's "deformities." Ruth Ann had not believed her, but the teacher insisted that Jesse was unmanageable and did not get along well with the other pupils, and that he made no effort to follow her lessons, preferring instead to distract the other children by making faces at them.

Miss Clark did not say why the children jeered at Jesse to begin with. Perhaps, Ruth Ann had told the young teacher, the other children should be disciplined so the jeering would never happen. Had their parents been summoned to school like she had? She suspected they hadn't. Miss Clark also told her she'd noticed that Jesse had become a constant reader of those cheap little novels now being published and that he kept them hidden within the pages of his schoolbooks while pretending to do the required work. All of Jesse's teachers had come to believe that his newfound penchant for deviltry was inspired by these books. The pattern of bad behavior had continued for months, and Ruth Ann was being called to school so often she was eventually advised to remove her son from primary school altogether.

Those who lived in the vicinity of Ruth Ann's apartment later recalled an episode when Jesse was a young boy that had caused them to be concerned about him even further. Before Jesse's removal from primary school, when he was still a small child, a neighbor learned that Ruth Ann had purchased two small yellow canaries to cheer up her home. This did not surprise the neighbor. Often, when she returned to her house, Ruth Ann was reminded of the dreariness her life had taken on. Charlestown was then a cluster of tightly constructed row houses that seemed to lean atop one another as if for support. These apartments were not far from the large Massachusetts State Prison, which she could see out her window.

Charlestown was founded in 1629 and was nearly burned to the ground on June 17, 1775, by the British general Thomas Gage. All along the shores and docks had sprouted distilleries and warehouses, those buildings involved in the business of ship and boat building, and others dealing with copper. Business was good, and those who had made this nook of the city their home lived in dwellings a quarter of a mile inland from the docks.

Finally, in 1777, people started returning to Charlestown, and by 1783 new homes and warehouses had arisen. But the bridges were what truly made the difference. When the Charles River Bridge opened, connecting Charlestown to Boston, it provided a footpath to the city proper. Made of wood and incomparable to those of better quality, the rickety and splintered bridge appeared almost flimsy in nature, though its tangibility provided a link to the city not only physically, but morally as well. Other bridges soon followed: in 1787 a short one connecting Charlestown to Malden was built, and in 1803 the one to Chelsea.

Aside from the bridges, the Massachusetts State Prison was one of Charlestown's greatest accomplishments. Soon after it was built, it quickly filled to capacity and talks erupted that perhaps it would be best to relocate it from its present location, but nothing had come of it. People yearned for that day, for they had been complaining that the area around it was foul, and so was its drainage system, which dumped all of its refuse into the waters and small streams emptying into the Mystic River, allowing it to slosh by the riverbanks and to collect in stagnant pools nearby. Other sites had been spoken of, such as Concord, Worcester, and Auburndale, but no more news had come for months.

The prison had also brought with it a new railroad station. When the lines were built, they also introduced even more business to Charlestown, as well as traffic. A line extending to Lowell opened in 1835, and in 1836 the Charlestown branch was built not a mile away from the McLean Asylum, owing to a bridge from the direction of the prison named Prison Point, eventually linking the asylum to the jail.

Like others in the area, Ruth Ann often heard the sounds coming from behind the prison's tall walls and locked gates. She heard the stories of those audacious prisoners who had cleverly scaled the prison walls and made it all the way to the river, striving for freedom in the city. All in all, it was a dismal area, often suffused by the "villainous stench" permeating the air and coming from the nearby slaughterhouses, tanneries, bone-boiling establishments, all collecting into pools of filth around the riverbanks. The filth that was dumped along the tributaries then made its way to the river proper and to the cities and streets nearby, announcing itself with a nauseating stench that "prostrated" those walking by. In the summer months, the choice had to be made between suffering the heat inside one's home or opening the windows and waiting for the vomit to rise in the stomach.

Although everyone who lived near the prison and the river suffered the same indignities, it seemed to Ruth Ann that her desperation was greater than theirs. The arguments she had with her husband sounded louder and more ferocious; she looked with envy toward those women whose spouses left for work in the morning and returned late in the evening. The rent collector never visited other people's apartments as often as he did hers. Even the neighboring children appeared more well-behaved and studious than hers. No one was surprised that Ruth Ann's anger seemed not only to ooze out from her pores but to drip off the very walls she inhabited, a sort of dirty scum similar to the one that often floated on the nearby river.

She had bought the yellow canaries to bring some pleasure to an otherwise squalid environment. As such, she had placed the chipper birds in a small wooden cage in the kitchen, and as she prepared the evening meals, she listened to them. She enjoyed returning home to the birds' welcome, until one afternoon she came into a house that was strangely quiet and unnaturally empty. Her husband had found work and was nowhere to be found and the children were playing outside in the street; the canaries should have welcomed her, yet she couldn't hear them. She neared the cage, expecting to see the small birds swinging on their little wooden sticks, only to find them dead, their necks wrenched off their bodies.

Perhaps she should have known better. Prior to the bird incident, a neighbor, Mrs. Lucy Ann Kelly, had come to call on her one day when a kitten of hers had gone missing. The neighbor suggested that Jesse had stolen the kitten. Though Ruth Ann refused to believe such a thing, she had to admit the obvious when Jesse was later found wandering aimlessly in a nearby street, the dead kitten hanging from one hand and a kitchen knife in the other. The neighbor had been horrified.

Time had passed, but Ruth Ann recalled those incidents vividly. The heat of that July 28, 1872, came pouring in as she opened her windows, and it would remain that way for weeks to come. July was always one of the hottest months in the commonwealth, and 1872 proved to be no exception. The afternoon sun beat mercilessly on the dusty streets. Not a breeze blew from the river, yet the water's foul stench arose from it and wafted all the way toward her windowsill and into her home. She could not hear the usual cries of the neighborhood children, who might have gone home for a rest. Even the flies seemed to have stopped their buzzing, too hot to bother. As she read the printed articles, she felt inexplicably chilled.

The papers detailing the Boy Torturer's deeds had only a faint description to go by: a large boy. Of course, other people had added that the boy seemed to have long and sharp fingernails. Despite his age, someone else had said, he had a beard that was pointy with a rusty hue that matched his hair. Everyone agreed these details were implausible, and even local police agents said they sprang out of the realm of the imagination rather than reality. Nonetheless, they pointed to the torturer's new moniker: the Red Devil.

For days reporters had speculated about the Red Devil, giving him powers reserved for the creatures of hell rather than to humans. That he had not been apprehended showed not only a cunning personality and intelligent nature but a mind that was beyond the mere mortal, or so some of the readers assumed. But there were those of a more practical nature who disagreed with the reporters, and felt that nothing superhuman at all was happening

The practical-minded folks knew that the lashes on the little boys in Chelsea had been inflicted by the hands of a human, albeit a young one. They never doubted that he was a very earthbound entity, not one with supernatural powers. Granted, Boston was, after all, a deeply puritanical place, located only some twenty miles south from where several men and women had been stoned and hung to death in the late 1600s because the people of Salem thought they were bewitched by the devil.

One practical-minded man who had noticed this turn toward the supernatural was Boston fire chief John Damrell. Lately he had heard more and more mentions of the devil, and evil in general, while he went about in his work. It had begun, he realized, the previous fall, when the news of the great fire in Chicago on October 8, 1871, reached Boston. The fire had been deemed a "national calamity," and people across the country, including Bostonians, were trying to find meaning in the flames. From the crowds, pulpits, and printed pages, the answer had not been hard to come by, and according to many, it was one of biblical proportions: Chicago was a large city of "loose morals," a virtual Sodom and Gomorrah, and the fire that nearly destroyed it was the hand of God striking down on it.

The flames first ignited in the southern point of Chicago, in an area of the city where homes had been built primarily of wood. Then the fire moved northward with a speed and rapidity that surprised everyone. Newspapers told the stories of those who hurried to save what they could: slightly singed clothes and drawers full of smoky undergarments and ripped stockings; an ironing board; mattresses and pillows; a large cabbage, a lonely slipper, spools of knitting wool, and those sentimental trinkets that seemed to hold no particular value at all.

In Boston, Chief Damrell was asked what he thought had caused the Chicago fire, and as always his explanations focused on a number of tangible clues and dismissed any otherworldly worries. His nature was always to provide practical answers, even if that was not always appreciated.

The Boston Fire Department, of which he was a part, was under the charge of the City Council, which was composed of two distinct bodies, the Board of Aldermen and the Common Council. Chief Damrell had been born in the city's North End district in 1828, to a family of "humble circumstances." Before he was even ten years old, he was sent to work on a farm in Haverhill, Massachusetts, and at the same time he began an internship with a carpenter in Cambridge, thus splitting his time between the two cities. In addition to farming, he learned how to build winter sleds for little boys, which gave him quite a fruitful side business.

In 1850 he married a young woman he met in Cambridge named Susan Emily Hill, and she eventually bore him three daughters and two sons. At the same time, he also began to desire a career in the fire department and joined the Company Cataract 4. By 1856 he had earned the distinction of being named foreman of Cataract 4, and in 1858 he was moved up to assistant engineer. His quick ascent through the ranks continued and led him to the post of chief of the whole Boston Fire Department, a job he assumed in 1868.

In addition to being a hardworking and practical man, he was also a somewhat obstinate one, which members of the City Council soon learned, and even before the fire in Chicago he had been making a nuisance of himself with the Boston aldermen by repeatedly drafting memos about the city's outdated equipment and lack of fire hydrants. He warned that if a fire broke out in Boston, whose population continued to grow, the combination of insufficient apparatus, the condition of the aging fire hydrants—which were as old as the city itself—and a scarcity of funds allotted to his department could be calamitous, even worse than what happened in Chicago.

Years earlier, Boston had been devastated by fires. In 1679 an arsonist set flames that destroyed eighty buildings by the Boston waterfront. A Frenchman was found guilty of the crime, and as punishment, both of his ears were lopped off, and he was made to pay fines to the lawyers who argued his case, as well as to those people who lost businesses and merchandise in the blaze. He was kept in jail until all the requirements of his sentence were fulfilled.

Chief Damrell also knew about the 1711 fire, which had burned through the streets of Boston, this time destroying not only retail shops, but the famous First Meeting House. Several residents and local mariners had died in this blaze, while a number of other inhabitants were left homeless.

Damrell had even suggested to members of Ward Six that running a main of salt water from the Boston Harbor underneath the city could be useful in fighting fires. This could, in theory, have supplied water to each of the main pumps located across the city. But his suggestion had not been taken seriously, and he had been rebuffed.

In October 1848, the General Court had allowed Boston to bring water into the city from an aqueduct on Lake Cochituate to use for fighting fires. The project had been planned by well-known civil engineers, such as James Fowler Baldwin, and continued to serve Boston until other reservoirs were found to be more adequate. Many Bostonians had not supported this solution, but as the water was piped along predetermined sections of the city and eased the firemen's burdens, even those councilmen who had opposed the measure saw its benefits. But now the city was growing, and this method seemed inadequate, since it was antiquated.

Soon after the Chicago fire, Chief Damrell visited that city and studied how the fire had spread, as well as the route it had taken, the flames moving from south to north like a snake tracing a path through blades of grass. He heard of the various acts of heroism as well as the many stories about looting. He was told about the tragic damages, the millions of dollars' worth of ruined homes, crumbled walls, and destroyed churches. He learned quite a bit about that particular section of the city to the south that prior to the fire had grown congested. All in all, he was struck by the remarkable similarity between the blueprints for that section of Chicago and the downtown area of Boston.

While Chief Damrell spread Chicago's city maps atop a table and stared at the lines where the fire had burned, the charred remains of the city lay before him, and in their ghosts, he caught a glimpse of the future: looking at the charts and blueprints of Chicago, he could see his own city. The buildings in both Chicago and Boston had been constructed so close to one another that sometimes not even a knife could pass between them. And what to say of the cheap wood that had been used for the structures, and those mansard roofs everyone was so fond of; the steep, double-sloped roofs had no real purpose other than being aesthetically pleasing, but Bostonians appreciated the touch of European elegance they imparted to their buildings. It didn't take long for Chief Damrell to figure out that should a kindle burn in downtown Boston and spark a fire, they would be faced with the same problem Chicago had had.

As Chief Damrell thought about Boston and the fire that had occurred in Chicago, he realized that it had not been, as the newspaper *Zion's Herald* had declared, Chicago's "bar . . . the beer cellar, the brothel . . . its most popular and profitable haunts" that had caused the city to burn. Nor had it been its theaters luring the boys of the city astray and the immorality of city life. None of those things had made the fire so devastating. Chief Damrell, studying all that had been made available to him, came to realize that building construction, coupled with a lack of manpower and old hydrants, had gathered at a perfect moment in time and caused a catastrophe of unimaginable proportions. He feared now, more than ever, that such a calamity would occur in Boston.

He was not a superstitious man, yet the signs were all there, and they had nothing to do with a young red devil walking the streets of Boston at all.

Ruth Ann Pomeroy also saw the signs of something happening nearby, and she also knew they had nothing to do with a supernatural red devil. Like every mother in the Boston area, she thought of her children, and of Jesse, in particular. But unlike those other parents, she doubted that either of her boys would meet his demise at the hands of the fiend, or red devil. She had no family in the area and no neighbor to whom she was attached; those living close to her would later describe Ruth Ann as not possessing the natural social graces that invited companionship, much less intimacies of a more personal nature. She also didn't own much, for that matter. She reread the *Boston Globe* article of July 28 and the descriptions that followed and knew what she had to do.

She hastily packed her belongings and those of her sons and on August 2, 1872, Ruth Ann Pomeroy and her boys found themselves in South Boston, starting life anew.

CHAPTER 3

THE MARBLE EYE

One adequate look at the face conveyed to most philosophical observers a notion of something not before included in their scheme of the universe.

—HERMAN MELVILLE, *PIERRE*

A junction not far from Dorchester Avenue and Forest Street in Boston had been given the benign name of Glover's Corner, though it had quickly acquired a disreputable reputation and was nicknamed Sodom and Gomorrah. It was an area teeming with taverns, billiard parlors, houses of ill repute, and gambling shacks. Sailors who found themselves on land for a few hours sought Glover's Corner and the willing arms of the prostitutes who arrayed themselves at its perimeter like rotted fruit.

Glover's Corner was not a place for the children. Instead, they headed to Savin Hill, a rocky outcrop near the beach. From there they could watch the boats and the doings of the Tuttle House, the first seaside motel in the area. Its owner, Joseph Tuttle, had renamed the place Savin Hill because of the many juniper (savin) trees that grew nearby. He thought its previous name, Old Hill, was not descriptive enough. But the trees weren't what drew the children to the spot. They went there for the beaches, where they could splash in the waters or stroll along the banks.

On August 17, 1872, a very hot day, seven-year-old George Pratt walked leisurely across a small sandy patch of land bordering the waters. He was an unusually pale boy, and so small for his age that his mother often worried about letting him out on his own. It was so quiet that day that George thought he was alone as he began to meander near the water's edge, stooping down every so often to collect shapeless pieces of driftwood that had washed up with the tide, shiny rocks for his collection, and empty seashells. He was so involved in his treasure hunt he did not notice the tall shape of a boy overcoming him until it was too late.

Some hours later, the authorities and local newspaper reporters picked up the story, as it had a ring of the familiar to it: the Boy Torturer had struck again, but he had not used a wooden stick to beat up his victim, as he had previously done. On this occasion he used a long sewing needle and had pierced the little boy's limbs and genitals, drawing blood. Worse still, as the little boy pointed to his backside, the police noticed something even more disturbing: the Boy Torturer had bitten off a chunk of flesh from George's buttocks and poured fresh seawater on the open wound; this had been done, the officers reckoned, in order to inflict additional stinging. And though he had followed his same routine, more or less, this assault was quite different because a geographical shift had occurred: it had happened not in Chelsea, as the earlier ones had, but on the beaches of South Boston.

But it was the torturer's next victim that would give detectives the first clue into the assailant's identity. Even though five-year-old Robert Gould was terrified during questioning, he still managed to recall something peculiar about his attacker: the big boy had a "funny" eye, he told the detectives. Funny, and as white as the marbles he played with.

JESSE DIDN'T KNOW WHAT had caused his marbled eye. He often blamed a bad batch of childhood smallpox vaccines, while Ruth Ann insisted he had suffered an infection when he was just a toddler. Either way, when strangers saw the whitish film over Jesse's eye, they often reacted with repulsion. Some thought there was a "white lace curtain" covering the pupil, while his own father, Thomas Pomeroy, had taken such an aversion to the boy's eye albinism that he often recoiled at his son's face. Ruth Ann also mentioned that Thomas eventually thought of it as "the evil eye" and used his belt in an attempt to drive the devil out of Jesse. Many of the neighborhood boys and even the ones Jesse went to school with often mocked and teased him for it.

As a result, he had had very few friendships when the family lived on Bunker Hill Avenue, and that didn't change when they moved to South Boston. Part of it was Jesse's own fault. By age twelve, he had become so intensely withdrawn that he did not join the local games, nor did he make an effort to get to know those children beyond his own new neighborhood. Sometimes he silently appeared by the playground, as if he wanted to partake in the other kids' games. He would mill about for a few minutes, then stare at the boys already playing an impromptu game of baseball until he finally shrugged his shoulders and, with a book in his hands, moved away to find a place of his own.

A local boy named George Thompson later acknowledged that Jesse did occasionally stay behind. He even took part in the "extravagant talk" the boys indulged in, talks of blood, scalping, and the roasting of Indians like "venison." Thompson said the children talked in this manner because at the time Boston was in "a sea of excitement" over the awful deeds someone was perpetrating on little boys in Chelsea and South Boston. Neighborhood boys had heard the stories about the little boy who was beaten on Powder Horn Hill and another boy on Savin Hill Beach, who was mauled and tied up to a telegraph post. Their mothers had warned them to be especially careful of a man with "red hair and beard." In the fading twilight of summer, they spoke of this fiend as years later they would speak of the doings committed by Jack the Ripper, comparing the merits of their own monster to that of London.

But Jesse never contributed much to the conversations, his neighbor later recalled. For the most part he only listened. Nonetheless, one thing seemed to cheer up Jesse: a game of Scouts and Indians. He would stare spellbound as the boys took on their guises of Wild Bill, "who had killed thirty-nine Indians," Buffalo Bill, Charlie Emmett, Texas Jack, Squirrel Cap. The Indians were often portrayed by the smaller and more defenseless children, those whose demeanor, Thompson went on, "generally deserved nothing but a good thrashing."

Jesse looked on as the Indians were always the ones to die, once telling a Scout that the Indians should revolt, kill the Scouts, and become victorious. "He seemed to think more of the Indians than he did of the Scouts," Thompson told the *Boston Globe*. "I guess that was because he was such a novel reader. He always had a brick-colored 'Beadle' or a white-colored 'Munro' in his back pocket."

The novels Jesse read, commonly referred to as dime novels, didn't have much to offer in terms of a plot or a narrative thread. Instead they were heavy with sex and bloodshed, abounding with characters who were always a step ahead of the law and who indulged in a lot of sex with prostitutes, who invariably possessed a heart of gold. They fought duels in the heat of high noon, butchered dozens of Indians, and scalped a few heads for trophies. The savagery had been imposed on the characters by society, the novels implied, and had not been sought for the mere fun of it. They fought injustices, whether real or imagined, and did so to save their honor and their family. But always, they got away with their crimes.

The success of the dime novels did not please everybody, of course, particularly those writers who were trying to bridge the gap between popular and critical writing, such as Nathaniel Hawthorne and Herman Melville. Their works managed to sell only a few thousand copies, a matter that irked them, particularly when a dime novel such as the one titled *The Privateer's Cruise and the Bride of Pamfort Hall* outsold them by the thousands.

In a letter Hawthorne wrote to a friend, he could not help but bemoan "America is now wholly given over to a damned mob of scribbling women, and I should have no chance of success while the public taste is occupied with their thrash—and should be ashamed of myself if I did succeed. What is the mystery of these innumerable editions of the 'Lamplighter' and other books neither better nor worse?—Worse they could not be, and better they need not be, when they sell by the 100,000." He used the letter to touch upon several issues, even noting that many of the dime novels were written by women.

Beadle & Adams Publishers were initially responsible for this publishing trend, though soon, other publishers began to release similar books, including books by the publisher George Munro, whose versions of the dime novels skyrocketed their popularity. And while boys loved them, critics began to see in them nothing more than cheap filth that would corrupt the youth of America. One such critic was Anthony Comstock, secretary and special chief agent for the New York Society for the Suppression of Vice, and a post office inspector.

In a book he authored in 1883 titled *Traps for the Young*, Comstock defined dime novels as "vile books and papers . . . heated in the fires of hell, and used by Satan to sear the highest life of the soul." He went on to add that "good reading refines, elevates, enables and stimulates" one's mind and purpose. But he said dime novels were "evil reading" that "debases, degrades . . . and turns away from lofty aims to follow examples of corruption and criminality." He believed the "sexual purity" of young individuals became corrupted by reading these books because the scenes depicted in them managed only to "sow the seeds of lust."

In 1872 the first *Fireside Companion* was published, changing the cowboys-and-Indian motif to that of detectives. For the first time the word *sleuth* was used, forever associating it with detectives. For an even younger audience, Frank Leslie's *Boys of America*, first issued in 1873, became fashionable. Mostly aimed at a readership of very young boys, the stories often had unrecognizable foreign landscapes as settings, amoral characters, a thirst for blood and guts, and a heightened sexual tone. They were serialized to last several months, and boys saved their pennies in order to run to the bookstalls as soon as the next installment came off the press.

It was believed that the violent, intense, erotic depiction of sexual encounters in dime novels inflamed the immature imaginations of these boys. Those endowed with a morbid imagination to begin with would have their festering sadistic fantasies ignited, which would escalate with every rereading or every new novel. Critics feared that the boundary between fantasy and reality became blurred. A natural out-come of that, Comstock and others like him alleged, would be the im-moral vice they were already witnessing and which was causing a spike in insanity cases: a frantic need for masturbation.

Whenever Jesse was not reading one of these novels, he often stood on the nearby pier watching the waters of the Atlantic, the rickety fishing boats bobbing and retreating into the harbor, and the weather-beaten sailors mending nets and patching sails, or smoking pipes. These old men were not unlike his paternal grandfather, his namesake, Jesse Pomeroy.

The elder Jesse Pomeroy was now seventy years old and living near New York City, though he originally came from the northern part of Maine, near the Canadian border, where he made a living as a ship-builder. When he was still a youth, the call of the sea brought him to Massachusetts, presumably to work as a carpenter or as a boatbuilder. He had settled in a town south of Boston called Hingham, where he found lodging with a woman who had provided him with not only food and shelter, but also a pretty, young, and unmarried daughter. The elder Pomeroy married the girl, later going to live in Charlestown, where Thomas, Jesse's father, had been born. But Grandpa Jesse Pome-roy had a history of maltreatment toward his wife, and subsequently they divorced. After the divorce, the elder Pomeroy went on to marry a woman much different from his first wife, someone who was said to be now maintaining "her position as mistress of the situation," ruling the house and her husband with an iron fist.

Now young Jesse Pomeroy often watched the waters and the boats and the ships similar to the ones the old man might have built, or something akin to them. Oftentimes he merely sat on the sand, the beach offering a respite from his crowded neighborhood and allow-ing him to daydream about life at sea, his eyes scanning the horizon as he carelessly stuck a knife deep into the wet sand. In and out, he later stated, in and out, deeper and deeper he drove that knife into the moist, soggy sand.

ONLY A FEW HOMES were erected by the seashore during the early 1870s, though when the Old Colony Railroad was founded in 1844 and its trains began to rumble nearby in 1862, linking Boston proper from its terminal on Kneeland Street to its South Shore communities, those searching for wider spaces and an easy commute made their home in South Boston and the Dorchester village.

In 1630 the area was settled by the Puritans, arriving from England, and by 1635 Rev. Cotton Mather followed suit, landing on its shores with several hundred of his followers, all of them bringing cows and livestock, which were let loose upon the pasture they eventually named Dorchester Neck. Later still, the Neck evolved into South Boston. The spot now had a pleasant view of Boston, easy access to the city, good neighbors, and delightful salty ocean breezes in the summer.

On September 11, 1872, a group of railroad workers inspecting the line running along South Boston discovered the naked body of a five-year-old boy tied up to a telegraph post. Like others before him, Joseph Kennedy had been lured to a local boathouse, made to strip, and beaten viciously. And, like the previous victim, Kennedy had also noticed something not quite right about the assailant: he had a "queer" eye. Although badly frightened, Kennedy agreed to help track down the big boy. After all, officers wistfully told one another, how many big boys could there be who sported a massive head, a heavy jawline, a downturned mouth, and a peculiar white eye? That's how Kennedy had described the assailant.

The case was assigned to Officer Bragdon, of Police Station Six. Given that the assailant was thought to be an older boy, the officer decided early on that perhaps he was a student at one of the upper schools in the neighborhood. A few days after the attack on Joseph Kennedy, Bragdon took the boy by the hand, and together they went to various classrooms in the area, particularly of those schools located in the vicinity of the harbor, hoping to find this white-eyed fiend. By noon they made their way to a Mr. Barnes's classroom, at the Bigelow School, located at the corner of E and Fourth Streets.

Jesse Pomeroy had been attending Mr. Barnes's class since the family's move to South Boston. When Officer Bragdon, accompanied by young Kennedy, entered the room, Jesse panicked. He feared the little boy might single him out from the rest, so he lowered his head and pretended to be reading. But as he waited to be discovered something happened, or rather did not happen: Joseph Kennedy didn't see him. The little boy shook his head and told the officer that the milky-eyed fiend was not there.

As the bell signaled that the day's classes were over, it became obvious that Jesse Pomeroy had escaped detection. However, while strolling down the street, he felt an urge he could not deny, nor would he be able to make sense of it then or afterward. He passed by Police Station Number Six, located at 194 West Broadway, near C Street, a building made of brick and granite, and walked through its main doors. He had not been prompted by guilt to walk inside and take a peek at the establishment, as officers later assumed. Rather, Jesse eventually confessed he had done so "out of mere curiosity." Whatever the reason, it no longer mattered. As soon as he stepped inside the door, the first people he saw were Officer Bragdon and Joseph Kennedy. It was too late.

Bragdon heard the main door open and a shuffling occurring by the foyer. A young boy had entered, he noticed, though when he looked at him, the boy didn't move. Bragdon stared at him and then noticed the albino eye. Turning toward Joseph Kennedy, Bragdon saw the little boy pointing toward the boy loitering in the doorway, It was then that it all came together: the Boy Torturer, the Boy Fiend, the Inhuman Scamp, the Red Devil had been caught.

To the astonishment of all, Jesse Harding Pomeroy was barely more than a child himself: twelve years old; four feet nine and a half inches tall, and weighing in at approximately ninety pounds.

Those who examined Jesse immediately saw something "defective" in his nature and appearance. His lack of fear, guilt, or remorse over the deeds he was being accused of seemed unusual for a boy his age, as did his lack of empathy for the boys the police said he had maltreated. In looking at him, the doctors also assumed that his large cranial structure and white eye correlated to abnormal traits of character. Such an idea had been first given credence by phrenologists, who had made a business of palpating patients' faces and skulls to determine character traits, good and bad. "Your head is the type of your mentality," read the first page of the Fowler Brothers' *Illustrated Self-Introduction on Phrenology and Physiology*, published in 1852. The book was a training manual for those who wanted to learn how to distinguish mental and moral traits simply by feeling the cranial structure with their fingertips. Although phrenology was all but discredited in the 1840s and 1850s, the fad continued to have its followers for decades afterward.

Criminologists followed along the same lines as the phrenologists, including Cesare Lombroso, an Italian physician, criminologist, and anthropologist, who expanded on this idea even further in his groundbreaking book *L'Uomo Delinguente* (The Criminal Man), published in 1876. Based on years of case histories, many of them his own, he determined that criminals were actually a distinctive species altogether from their brothers. They had not evolved like the rest, he said, and that could be seen in their facial and cranial features, whose detailed studies revealed criminal tendencies. Although the book made quite a stir in criminology circles, it was later criticized because not all criminals have distinctive features, and those who have such features are not always criminals.

Despite the backfire, Lombroso still adhered to his theories on crime and called this penchant for cruelty he noticed in certain people the *stigmata of degeneration*. The biologist and social scientist M. F. Ashley Montagu also took up Lombroso's idea and in his own book, titled *The Biologist Looks at Crime*, published in 1941, he said, "in almost all cases, it is not the unfavorable environment which led to the commission of crime, but the biological predisposition to commit it, externally advertised by the presence of stigmata."

Ruth Ann Pomeroy did not feel there was anything amiss with Jesse: he was a young boy and young boys were known to misbehave.

Yes, when questioned she admitted that Jesse had been cruel to animals and even very young children while at school, but to her those seemed the natural responses from a boy who had been bullied and tortured himself. If officials wanted Jesse to stop what he was doing, Ruth Ann reasoned, then perhaps punishment should also be extended to the boys who had been making his life miserable, taunting him about his white eye. She had made the same argument with Miss Clark at the primary school in Charlestown. She also did not find his reading material unusual; didn't all boys at one time or another read those lurid novels her son enjoyed?

Perhaps, Ruth Ann suggested, the fever he had suffered when a child had left some residual effect on him, some brain inflammation that had caused him to act the way he did. Brain fever, doctors had called it, which he had not only suffered from but nearly died of at the age of three.

Indeed, brain fever was often associated with some kind of brain inflammation and had been recognized as such in the eighteenth century, when the malady had evolved from "phrenzy." This had occurred in 1781, when the physician William Cullen came to believe that this was some kind of "acute paroxysm," which had as its symptoms "a violent headache, a redness of the face and eyes, and impatience of light and noise, a constant twitching, and a delirium impetuous and furious."

Taking a cue from Cullen, in the 1850s James Copeland evolved its symptomology and described brain fever as an "acute pain in the head, with intolerance of light and sound; watchfulness, delirium; flushed countenance, and redness of the conjunctiva, or a heavy suffused state of the eyes, quick pulse; frequently spasmodic, and complete relaxation of the limbs."

Jesse was now twelve years old, and although he often complained of pains in his head, just like his father had, he had none of the other symptoms usually associated with brain fever. Though they might have troubled him as a toddler, doctors reasoned he had now grown out of them.

On September 21, 1872, after relentless questioning, his brother's lamenting, and his mother's assurance that he was a "good boy," Jesse Harding Pomeroy admitted to being the Boy Torturer. The children who had come to testify against him included several from Chelsea and the latest victims from South Boston. Pale and trembling, their scars crisscrossing their faces, they pointed their fingers toward Pomeroy as they recounted how they had met him and how they'd been lured away from their respective spots: he had promised them small sums of money, handfuls of sweets, and visits to the circus. Their stories were remarkably similar, pitiful, and startling unimaginative, the very scenarios their mothers had warned them against. Because Jesse was a minor, Judge William G. Forsyth confined him to the House of Reformation at Westborough, where he would be monitored for "the term of his minority," six years.

But as Jesse stood in the courtroom staring straight ahead, noticing and not noticing the crowd of onlookers who had come to view the ordeal, the police officers detected something odd. Jesse seemed completely indifferent to the suffering of his victims and untroubled by the sentence. There was no special nervousness about him, nor the fear one would expect from a boy his age at the prospect of being sent away for an extended period of time. He also did not express any sorrow, either. There was no crying out toward his mother or an embrace for his brother. There was only an eerie calmness about him, a calmness that the officers thought was extremely out of place.

THE STATE REFORM SCHOOL was located on the top of a verdant hill adjacent to a calm and glassy lake, not three miles away from the city of Westborough, which was nearly thirty miles west of Boston proper. The views from the school were of the spectacular outlines of the Wachusett Mountains, behind which grew woodlands, ponds, lakes, and smaller villages. The nearby grounds were lined with numerous streams and small rivers, where the inhabitants flocked every summer for fishing expeditions.

In the early days of Westborough, the territory was under the tutelage of two Native American tribes: the Nipnicks and the Wannesits. Chancey Pond, or Lake Chancey, one of the most popular in the area, was known to these tribes as Naggawoomcom, or Great Lake, and was believed to be inhabited by beasts that demanded reverence and obedience. But by 1846 the tribes were gone, as were the beasts of Lake Chancey. Whatever supernatural creatures had been there were replaced by the State Reform School and its band of unruly youths.

By the time Jesse Pomeroy arrived at the school, it had grown to nearly three hundred boys, ranging in age from six to twenty, all confined there by the law to prevent them from harming others, as well as themselves. Established in the mid-1840s by the Commonwealth of Massachusetts as one of the country's earliest reform schools, it had come into being partially as a response to the many petitions by the state's chief justices, who lately had noticed a great rise in juvenile crime and juvenile delinquents roaming the streets of their beloved cities. The justices wished to have "a well-regulated home—order, neatness and harmony, within doors," and outside "the beautiful sights and sounds and heartfelt influence of nature."

Upon its completion, the school was made up of a three-story structure with deep gray walls more reminiscent of a lunatic asylum or, worse still, of a prison, holding within its embrace several large dormitories with beds bolted to the floors, and eight of the infamous "punishing cells," where the boys were locked up for misbehaving. They were isolated from any outside interference, and all the dining and bathing facilities, as well as the play areas, were encased or flanked within the walls and thick barbed wires.

It was one of the country's first reform schools to use the "parens partial system," a regulatory method with the school system "serving as parents to its dependent and delinquent children."

The school prided itself on reforming the minds and actions of youthful offenders, but it was far from perfect. In 1858 an eleven-year-old boy named Daniel Creedon, unhappy at having been sent to the reformatory for the next ten years, rebelled by setting what he believed would be a small fire. But the blaze that rose from the bushes became so tall it eventually destroyed several of the institution's wings and prompted the governor to visit. Creedon's act turned out to be a blessing for the boys locked in the school because the governor noticed the prisonlike environment they were subjected to and ordered the drafting of new regulations. In his opinion, the school, which had started out with such benign intentions, had become an utter "failure," and its internal structures needed to be reevaluated.

It was not uncommon for many of the boys to make a run for the gates, and of those who escaped, several were never caught. Stories persisted for decades that these missing boys had not run away at all but instead had been killed by the school's guards and officials while undergoing punishments, their bodies later buried in the swampy lands that surrounded the facility.

JESSE WAS DELIVERED TO the reform school as others before him had, and most likely he was treated to the same entrance routine every boy before him had undergone: in front of a disenchanted guard, he had to strip and relinquish not only his clothing but the few personal possessions he had brought along. These possessions would never be returned. The school's philosophy held that these boys would grow into adulthood within the confines of the institution, and what they wore and brought with them upon entering would not be needed when they left.

After stripping, as the chill of the large and empty room entered the naked skin, he was directed to the wooden washing tub and watched over as he sponged his body with a piece of frayed cloth dipped into tepid water. For most of the boys, this humiliating and demoralizing act caused them to loathe the guards from the very first day. Then Jesse was handed his new uniform: boots, blue pants, a long shirt, and cap. There was no underwear: the shirt was long enough to offer some coverage for the private areas. Suspenders were given to those whose trousers fell to the ankles. Finally, all new inmates were required to cleanse their souls by confessing their crime and sins to the chaplain.

The officers' official impressions of Jesse were recorded in a file that kept record of his doings and progress: "The boy pleaded guilty to several assaults," the record began. "The statement given at the hearing by the Austin boy was that the Def. met him on a street in South Boston and induced him by offering a small sum of money to go with him under a rail road bridge in So. Boston, and when they arrived there the Def. stripped all the clothing of the Austin boy, and with the blade of a pocketknife stabbed him several times between the shoulder blades, under each arm, and in other places. The Dr. stated that he examined the Austin boy Sept. 5—the day the assault was alleged to have been committed—and found wounds like stabs made by some sharp instrument between the Austin boy's shoulders, under each arm, and penis half cut off."

The report continued in even more detail. "The statement given by the Pratt boy was that the Def. induced him by the offer of money to go with him to a beach and boathouse in So. Boston, that the Def. took all of the Pratt's [sic] boy's clothing off, and then tortured him by sticking pins into his flesh. The statement made by the other two boys (Kennedy and Gould) were [sic] that they were induced by Def. to go with him to some out of the way place, that he took their clothing all off and then cut them with a knife and beat them."

The report then continued by adding the earlier complaints from the boys in Chelsea: "Another complaint was made at the same time by Mr. Drury, City Marshal of Chelsea, against the Def. alleging assaults of similar character on two small boys (Hayden and Belch) in Chelsea in the months of Feb. and July last. Johnny Belch (about nine years old), one of the boys assaulted in Chelsea, stated that in July last, he met the Def. in the street and was induced by Def.'s offering a small sum of money to go with him to a locality in Chelsea known as Powder Horn Hill. When they arrived there, Def. stripped all the clothing from the Belch boy, tied him to a post by the hands, and beat him with a rope. All the boys were much younger and smaller than the Def."

The officers were aware of Jesse's crimes, but they did not see him as especially malignant, sending him to work braiding chairs. It was tedious and quiet work, and it kept the other boys from noticing him. But soon enough they learned why Jesse had been imprisoned and began to mock him for it. Prior to being arrested and sent to reform school, he had been belittled and humiliated only for his white eye, but now his desire for little boys made him a pariah.

Mornings in the school began at 5 A.M., and the officers, who slept nearby, rang a bell and watched as the boys attended to their personal ministrations. It was not a pleasant sight. Although each dormitory was meant to hold nearly one hundred boys, it was not uncommon for the school to add another fifty or more to each of the wings by adding berths to the floor or "bunking" children together. Arising all at the same time and holding their night pots in hand as they marched in formation to wash up, the boys often bumped into one another, whether intentionally or unintentionally, spilling urine from the previous night on the floor or, more often, on themselves and others. This in turn led to various brawls and vicious fights that the guards seemed to take their own time breaking up.

The boys' day consisted mostly of work and "moral training," with the fewer number of hours allotted to study. An even smaller amount of time was given to personal diversions. For many years the boys were made to work in the facility's shoe department, as well as the sewing branch, where they stitched all manner of scarves and socks. As the shoemaking business dwindled, a more profitable business arose with the making of chairs. Thousands of boys underwent the tedious task of making the frames and braiding the seats for sixty to eighty chairs during each shift, which consisted of six to seven hours each day. Guards watched from a distance because the boys were required to work in complete silence. As noted, Jesse was assigned to the chair shop.

It did not take long for him to grow tired of his braiding job. A few months after working in the chair shop, he began to complain of pains in his eyes and head. Officials agreed the work was ruining his eyesight, and so, given the stellar attitude he had displayed in the short time he had been incarcerated, they moved him. He was then assigned to supervise the much younger boys, becoming a sort of guardian on the ward, which he fully indulged in.

Officials freely handed out corporal punishment, most especially to the younger children. Although the school had initially been built upon the principle of kindness, it was ruled with the lash. Guards had a full arsenal of torture at their disposal, starting with their hands, which they used often, even if a child did nothing more than drop a spoon on the floor. The whip came in handy. Children were also plucked out of their seats or workspaces and made to get down on the gravel on nothing but naked knees for hours on end. If the boys fought back, they would be brought to the "lodge" and kept there for hours or days without food and water—basically, solitary confinement. Space was so tight at the school that some of the boys looked forward to this punishment because it gave them a small measure of solitude and privacy they never had in the dormitories.

In 1875, a colonel by the name of Shepherd was brought in to supervise the school's daily operations. He quickly saw that that the lodge was not having the desired effect and brought to the reformatory school a device so devious and harmful that the U.S. Navy had outlawed its use nearly ten years before. "I have caused a wooden box to be erected in the attic as a substitute for the straight-jacket I believe will prove to be more effective and healthier than detention in the lodge," Shepherd said. "It is intended for serious offenders and boys who didn't want to be punished by the strap. It is injudicious to use the strap on large boys as they are inclined to be pugnacious, and they want to have a fight; and I didn't want to see an officer mark a boy. When boys were put into a straight-jacket, they were sometimes noisy and were not so likely to receive attention or answers to their calls as they would be in the box."

The box was kept in an isolated location, most often in the attic, where the temperature rose, making it quite hot inside. Most of the children became sick and fainted. Unable to move or breathe, they had trouble screaming and no one heard them.

But Jesse found these tortures to be the only bright spots in the entire institution. He began to admire the whips and instruments of flagellation the officers used; he admired the scars and the red welts that arose on the children's skin, much like a painter admiring a masterpiece. Aroused by the children's tortured, bloodied bodies as they returned to their ward and took their places on the cots, he bribed them into recounting the painful ordeals they had undergone: Had their whipping hurt? Precisely, where had they been hit? How much blood had oozed out? Why had they been punished to begin with? What was the box like? How did it feel being cooped up in there? Listening to the children's stories of torture was physically gratifying to Jesse Harding Pomeroy.

With Jesse locked away in Westborough, Boston's newspapers came to believe that the Boy Torturer's grip on the city's children had ended. Youngsters in Chelsea, Charlestown, South Boston, and the surrounding areas could now go back to doing what they were meant to be doing: being children. As it was still warm outside, there was a sense that perhaps summer could now be extended, that those fanciful days prior to the attacks could be recuperated. Women sat on their stoops and in their square backyards and recalled the World Peace Jubilee of a few months earlier.

Several reporters couldn't help but wonder if Pomeroy had ventured near the Coliseum, if he had heard the Johann Strauss concerts or viewed President Ulysses Grant's speech, if he had stood by listening to the bands from Paris, Rome, and Berlin, but most of all, if he had haunted the grounds for his prey, had moved among the many vendors without being noticed, this "malformed" boy just one amid the many watching the "monster balloon" going up. People shivered at the thought that they, and their children, might have crossed paths with this beast.

But no matter, everyone eventually concluded. This depraved boy had now been disposed of, at least temporarily, his malignity suppressed. Life could return to normal. No one could imagine that Jesse, while incarcerated in Westborough, was focused not on reformation at all, but rather on going aboard a ship, of pirating the high seas of the Pacific and mingling with the cannibals, of listening to the call of the mariners as they patched their netting, all the while just waiting to return to South Boston.

CHAPTER 4

THE BOUNDLESS SEA

Sigh no more, ladies, sigh no more,

Men were deceivers ever,

One foot in sea and one on shore,

To one thing constant never.

—WILLIAM SHAKESPEARE,
MUCH ADO ABOUT NOTHING,
ACT 2, SCENE 3

Jesse Pomeroy spent his time behind the walls of the State Reform School at Westborough wishing that his parents had allowed him to sail on a ship. Had he done so, he believed, his life would have turned out differently.

Coming from a boy without prospects for a better future, his was not a far-fetched desire, nor was it an original one, for that matter. Many young men had been dreaming of the sea for decades, particularly those who lived in Massachusetts, where so many men were actually able to tell real stories about whalers and mariners. Aside from offering decent financial opportunities, the open waters also afforded men other opportunities. For one thing, those sailing the high seas were seen as more virile, and women were assured they made the best husbands and lovers. But more than that, the waters provided the best chance a young man could have for adventures in faraway lands, of meeting pirates and monstrous creatures of the deep, of mystery. At least, that's what the spoken tales and printed stories had one believe.

Such adventures were often described in texts published by mariners themselves, who, having left the waters behind, embarked instead on literature. They were also printed in the penny dreadful and dime novels, which Jesse Pomeroy and boys like him indulged themselves in. But the one text that sparked the imagination about the sea more than any other was Herman Melville's *Typee*, published in 1846. That it was based on the author's own experiences in the Marquesas Islands—so he proclaimed—inflamed the minds of many, as did the advertisements released prior to its publication. "A book with the curious title, by Herman Melville . . . Typee, the name of the tribe of the Marquesas, among whom—the naked, tattooed, beautiful, manly and womanly cannibals—the author was domesticated," read one.

An additional note, and one even more glorious than the earlier one, chimed in: "A new work of novel and romantic interest. It abounds with personal adventure, cannibal banquets, groves of coco nuts, coral reefs, tattooed chiefs and bamboo temples, sunny valleys, savage wood lands guarded by horrible idols, *heathen rush rites and human sacrifices.*"

There was also a dash of vigorous sexual innuendo scattered throughout these reviews, which of course made the book even more appealing to men who dreamed of adventure and sexual mischief in the Pacific islands. But Herman Melville had not begun his journey with lust in mind. He had done so out of need.

Melville was born in 1819, in New York, a city that by then held more than one hundred thousand inhabitants scuttling along the cobblestoned streets lit by iron oil lamps. He was one of eight children born to Allan and Maria Melvill (the *e* was added to the surname in the late 1830s). When Allan married Maria, he displayed modest hopes for their future and the family they were going to have. In a letter to his father, Major Thomas Melvill of Boston, he wrote, "I am neither amorous of riches or distinction, they are both insufficient to ensure happiness or purchase health, a man may do very well in private life with a mere competency, & if I can only provide for the rational wants of my beloved Wife and children, I shall be content with my lot & bless the hand from which all favors come."

Sadly, the modesty he had spoken of in his previous letters was nowhere to be found in his actions. Allan began to desire larger and better homes where his family could live and grow, moving from Pearl Street to Cortlandt Street, until a more fashionable one was found on Bleecker Street; from there, Maria said, she could see the "elegant white Marble houses on Bond Street—& also on Broadway." Allan even sent his children to schools that were too pricey. To keep up with this lifestyle, he started borrowing heavily from family and friends, and his own business as an importer of French goods soon floundered. The family also had to deal with Maria's recurrence of "low spirits," which relatives said were due to a new child being born or the family's financial difficulties "making" her nervous.

One man who often and reliably came to Allan's aid was his old friend Lemuel Shaw, also of Boston, whom he had befriended during a time in Amherst, New Hampshire, where Shaw had been working as a lawyer. The two young men had struck up a friendship, but for Shaw it provided him with something infinitely more rewarding: the opportunity to meet Allan's sister, Nancy, with whom he fell in love. The feeling turned out to be mutual, and marriage was discussed, only to be blunted by Nancy's death in 1813. Though a blow to both young men, their friendship remained strong, and it included the lending of money, mostly from Shaw's end.

Allan and Maria decided the way to ease their financial burdens was to move from New York City to Albany. Linked to New York by the Hudson River, Albany had prospered, particularly in the late eighteenth century and early nineteenth century. When the Erie Canal was finished in 1825, it opened up even greater opportunities for those traveling through Albany toward the Great Lakes. But the advent of this transportation marvel did nothing to ease the Melvilles' burden.

In the late fall of 1831, Allan took what he described as a business trip to New York City, but in reality he went seeking more money from his relations, who this time turned him down. Following an arduous journey across a frozen river, he returned home and promptly became ill. He died in January 1832. At the time his son Herman was twelve years old.

In the days leading to his death, Allan experienced a quick mental decline and raved loudly. His sickbed was on the top floor of their two-story home, but family members could still hear him. The children were not allowed to enter his room, though a later description in Melville's novel *Pierre* hinted that perhaps Herman did so when no one was looking, for a particular line read, "his father had died of a fever . . . toward the end, he at intervals loudly wondered in his mind."

The so-called spectacle of Allan losing his mind and dying remained with Herman for the rest of his life. But Allan's passing not only created an emotional hole in the family, it also put it in a dire financial situation. Herman and his brother Gansevoort had to leave school and find work; Herman took a job at the New York State Bank, where his uncle Peter was the director. Maria had always been prone to chronic headaches and depressions, and she succumbed to them even more now that she was a single mother caring for a large brood of children. That year also brought the Asiatic cholera epidemic, which would kill 136 people just in the month of July. Fearing it would strike her children, Maria took them to the family's farm in Pittsfield, Massachusetts, though Herman soon returned to the city and his job.

Over the next few years, Herman tried his hand at various other jobs, including teaching, but nothing more secure came of it. He also believed his terrible handwriting contributed to his inability to find meaningful employment. That was when, after all else had failed, Herman Melville heeded the call of the sea.

As nineteen-year-old Herman Melville readied to travel as a cabin boy aboard the *St. Lawrence* in 1839, bound for Liverpool, he saw an article published by Lewis Gaylord Clark in his *Knickerbocker* magazine. Clark was very interested in whaling and whaling stories; in 1834 he had published a text titled *The Mutiny*, by Jack Garnett, which became quite famous.

The article that caught Melville's attention was written by Jeremiah N. Reynolds, an ex-naval officer who had conducted several expeditions to Antarctica. In "Mocha Dick; or the White Whale of the Pacific," Reynolds was obsessive and lurid in detailing his meeting with a whaleboat from New York captained by a young man of thirty-five. Reynolds was enthralled by the news about a whale the men had named Mocha, living off the coast of Chile. After failing several times, the whalers had finally captured what Reynolds told his readers was a bull whale, great in size and strength, but more than anything else, "a freak of nature, as exhibited in the case of the Ethiopian Albino, a singular consequence had resulted—he was as white as wool!"

And there was something in that very hue that was malignant, Reynolds and the mariners agreed; something abhorrent about it. When it was seen from a distance some of the sailors assumed the mirage in front of them was a cloud, only to realize too late that it was a white whale rushing toward them.

They believed the whale was aggressive, because when taunted by the mariners, it struck out with unusual and mortal vengeance, splintering their boats. No one knew why this mutation, "a freak of nature," as Reynolds stated, had occurred, only that it made it unusual.

Mocha had often been spotted near the warm coast of Chile. Many boats had fought it, only to be shattered by its tail and crushed by its powerful jaws. Three English whale ships had tried their luck by banding together, then, after several unsuccessful efforts to capture Mocha, they had lost the battle and retreated in dishonor.

The captain described in great detail the lancets that protruded from its flesh as the whale neared the boat, all symbols of the many failed attempts to kill it. "He would sometimes pass quietly round a vessel and occasionally swim lazily and harmlessly," then "armed with full craft, for the destruction of her role," it would circle the boat before attacking it. Possessing a manipulative streak only seen in humans, Mocha appeared to know how the mariners were going to react to it. "His foes would swear they saw a lurking deviltry in the long, carelessly sweep of her flukes," Reynolds wrote.

The captain named the whale "Mocha Dick or the Devil," saying she had become a "ferocious fiend of the deep." He had also come to think of Mocha as "Beelzebub himself," thus forging the link between the supernatural, evil, and the whiteness of its color. But after a long and frightful ordeal, the whale men killed Mocha, "struggling in a whirlpool of bloody foam."

As Herman Melville prepared to sail from the port of New York toward Liverpool, he must have wondered if a similar adventure to Reynolds's might happen to him—whether or not he would meet up with whales like Mocha on his journeys. He did not keep a written record of those months on board, but nearly a decade later he published *Redburn*, a largely autobiographical account.

In it, the protagonist, a young man on his first nautical voyage abroad, seems to echo Melville's feelings when he says, "But I must not think of those delightful days before my father became bankrupt, and died, and we removed from the city; for when I think of those days, something rises up in my throat and almost strangles me. . . . And what made it even more bitter to me, was to think of how well off were my cousins, who were happy and rich, and lived at home with my uncles and aunts, with no thought of going to sea for a living. I tried to think that it was all a dream, that I was not where I was, not on board a ship, but that I was at home again in the city, with my father alive, and my mother happy as she used to be."

The scenes on land, in the streets of Liverpool, were also quite gruesome and visceral, as he described dying bodies in the streets, ignored by passersby and policemen alike. There was madness in the air, and he could not grasp the reasons behind it.

THE NEXT TIME MELVILLE sailed, this time on the *Acushnet*, bound for the Pacific, on January 3, 1841, he would leave from New Bedford, Massachusetts, which had taken on the maritime lead in New England, becoming a larger whaling port than Nantucket. The wealth being generated by the many shipowners could clearly be seen in the magnificent mansions they built set back from the road and ringed by lush gardens and land. New Bedford's connection to the sea, and whaling in particular, could be attributed directly to Joseph Rotch, a man who in 1765 had left Nantucket to try his luck across the bay, bringing with him not only the instruments of his trade but his knowledge as well. This knowledge was further heightened in the early 1800s by Lewis Temple, an African-American blacksmith who owned his shop on the waterfront and had invented the iron toggle tip, which "revolutionized" the kill and increased the hunt for whales.

Nowhere could New Bedford's power and affinity for the waters be more noted than on Front Street, by the waterfront. Here one found blacksmiths, ropemakers, sail repairers, and lumberyards, and all manner of trade associated with whaling was conducted. The homes that had once existed on the waterfront had given way to commercial depots, where tradesmen and craftsmen put their skills to use while inhaling the tangy, salty spray of the Atlantic.

Front Street also offered a good view of the ships docking onshore, the men unloading dozens of barrels of whale oil that eventually illuminated streets and homes across the country. It was there that sails were unfurled to dry and prevent mold from growing on them, their slapping sounds often curiously echoing those of the howling seagulls overhead, and the screeching of vendors advertising the sale of small fresh fishes recently caught.

Not surprisingly, Melville felt an affinity for all this. By the time he made his way to New Bedford, the port was a crowded, loud, bustling place teeming with people, activity, and commerce. Hired as a whale man for the journey, he was the last in line when dealing with a whale. His job required him to get close to the animal, to throw a harpoon toward it, which would in essence pierce its skin, then stab it deeper through its flesh until blood spurted out. But he grew weary of the job almost right away, though an event occurred while on the ship that in retrospect tied to the article he had read two years before about Mocha Dick, and must have stayed with him for a work he would write in the future.

In his memoirs of the time spent on the *Acushnet*, Melville wrote: "When I was on board the ship Acushnet of Fairhaven, on the passage to the Pacific, cruising against, among other matters of forecastle conversation at the time was the story of the *Essex*. It was then that I first became acquainted with the history of her truly astounding fate.

But what then served to speculate my interest at the time was the circumstances that the second mate of our ship, Mr. (John) Hall, an Englishman & Londoner by birth, had for two or three years sailed with Owen Chase. . . . This Hall always spoke of Chase with much interest & sincere regard—but he did not seem to know anything more about him or the *Essex* than any body else."

Then, on July 23, 1841, the memories of Chase continued in Melville's log: "before seeing Chase's ship, we spoke another Nantucket craft (the Lima) & gamed with her. In the forecastle I made the acquaintance of a fine lad of sixteen or thereabouts, a son (William Henry) of Owen Chase! I questioned him concerning his father's adventures, and when I left his ship to return again the next morning (for the two vessels were to sail in company for a few days) he went to his chest & handed me a complete copy . . . of the Narrative (of the *Essex* catastrophe). This was the first printed account of it I had ever seen . . . the reading of this wondrous story upon the landless sea & close to the very latitude of the shipwreck had a surprising effect upon me."

IN OCTOBER 1844, MELVILLE returned to Boston. He brought with him many adventurous tales, though not much in tangible skills. His stories enthralled family and friends, all of whom urged him to set them down on paper. He did so, the result being *Typee*, a novel, he said, based on real events. It was his brother Gansevoort who carried a copy of it during his travels to London, where he presented it to John Murray, the famed English publisher, as a work from a writer who had "never before written either book or pamphlet," nor a magazine article. That statement was not entirely true: Herman Melville had contributed various newspaper articles before, and some of them had even been published.

Whether or not Murray found out, or whether he even cared about it, is unknown; he agreed to publish *Typee*. The agreement caught the eye of the American George Palmer Putman, of Wiley & Putman, who bought the rights for the American edition. On March 17, 1846, *Typee* appeared for the first time in America, becoming one of the most enthralling maritime adventure books readers had come across in some time.

But aside from its unusual setting and the experiences detailed in the book, readers also feared the author might have gone beyond embellishment and altered or fabricated many of the events described as true. This controversy was especially difficult for John Murray, who prided himself on the accurate rendering of events. There was also the notion that the book was so well written, it could not have been composed by a sailor, because readers did not believe such men had vocabularies as illustrative as this writer's.

But the fame Melville garnered from the book was quickly blunted by the death of his brother Gansevoort, who had played such a key role in getting *Typee* published. Smart, original, studious, Gansevoort, and not Herman, was the sibling on whom the family had placed all of its hopes. He excelled in school, and everyone believed he would succeed where his father had failed. Herman, on the other hand, was thought of as "very backward in speech & somewhat slow in comprehension."

But Gansevoort did seem to suffer from the same nervous ailments that plagued both his parents. At the age of twenty, he was visited by a series of calamities that included a loss of his business and a minor fall. The injury was not that severe, but it added to his other woes and pushed him to take comfort in his bed, where he remained for nearly a year. Maria, observing his suffering, agreed that it was much like "her own nervous attacks in the New York years."

While in London in 1846, Gansevoort wrote to Herman and described periods of melancholy when he felt he was "gradually breaking up." The letter detailed the dullness he had been feeling, "a degree of insensibility" that had overcome him sometime earlier and had now taken root in his body and soul. He understood it to be "more akin to death than life." He visited several doctors, and the American ambassador Louis McLane, who met him and believed he was suffering some kind of "nervous derangement." By the time Gansevoort died, on May 2, 1846, he was plagued by several very severe and physical ailments, as an autopsy later revealed. Brain fever was also put forth as one of the possible causes for his demise.

In his brother's death, Herman saw that streak of instability, or twisted mind, as he called it, to which he feared he would eventually succumb as well. But despite his fear, or because of it, his fascination with the phenomenon also grew, though it had probably formed earlier, likely while consulting books on the subject, such as Thomas Upham's *Outlines of Imperfect and Disordered Actions*, as it was possible for him to read these volumes in the New York Society Library, a place he often visited. This book was famous enough to be available on board ships as well, where all the mariners could have access to it, including Melville.

Thomas Upham had been an instructor at Bowdoin College, where one of his pupils had been Nathaniel Hawthorne. It was a very popular book on insanity because it contained in-depth information on what the author called "disordered mental actions."

Another popular text available at the New York Society Library that Melville must have been drawn to was James Prichard's *A Treatise on Insanity and Other Disorders Affecting the Mind*. It contained not only a wealth of information but opinions from other eminent doctors of the time, such as Isaac Ray, who was an authority on insanity. Of particular interest to Ray was mania, which would also be of interest to Melville. In his own writings Melville began to depict the two forms of insanity that were being discussed during his time and fell under the heading of mania: moral insanity and monomania.

One interpretation of monomania, given in the *Cyclopedia*, which Melville was aware of, was as follows: "The term monomania has been proposed by [Jean-Étienne Dominique] Esquirol, and adopted by most writers in mental disorders, to designate those cases of insanity in which the mind is occupied by some illusion or erroneous conviction, the individual still retaining the power of reasoning correctly in matters unconnected with the subject of his delusion."

These writings were highly influenced not only by medical treaties published around the time, but also by newspaper articles that
discussed the issues of insanity, particularly as they referred to trials
and the legalities of insanity. Interestingly enough, there was the 1846
case of Albert J. Tirrell of Boston. Tirrell was accused of murdering a
prostitute, and at trial, he pleaded insanity. But his lawyers deemed his
mental state a by-product of insanity: somnambulism. Tirrell's defense
lawyers argued that he had been under its influence when he committed the crime and was therefore not responsible for the murder. The
argument was so compelling that Judge Dewey (no first name was ever
recorded) agreed, ruling that Tirrell was suffering from a "species of
derangement" and was "not responsible for his act."

This particular crime, trial, and subsequent verdict were reported
in many newspapers, as well as the smaller ones across the country,
such as the *New York Herald* and *Albany Argus*, both available in Lansingburgh, New York, where Melville was at work on a new book.

Melville's knowledge about insanity was also aided by two acquaintances he made in the field: one was the physician Dr. Oliver
Wendell Holmes, who resided on Beacon Street in Boston. The Melvilles had been acquainted with Holmes since the early 1830s, when in
March 1831, Dr. Holmes, then a young Harvard graduate, published
a poem titled "The Last Leaf," the subject being Major Melvill, Herman's grandfather. The poem became famous throughout the state, as
it spoke of the major's contribution during the Boston Tea Party. The
other one of Herman Melville's acquaintances was one of his father's
oldest friends, Lemuel Shaw, who had by now been appointed chief
justice of the Supreme Judicial Court of the Commonwealth of Massachusetts and lived by the State House, on 49 Mount Vernon Street.
Both of these men, together and separately, would boost the young
writer's understanding of mania and moral insanity from a legal and
a medical perspective, allowing Melville to expand his knowledge and
delve deeper into what he feared the most: the twisted mind.

CHAPTER 5

THE GREAT FIRE

*The buildings, like their women, are neat and
handsome, and their streets, like the hearts of their
men, are paved with pebbles.*

—A MR. WARD, ON VISITING NEW ENGLAND IN 1698

On November 9, 1872, a mild Saturday in Boston, a spark from a coal boiler from a hoopskirt factory near Kingston and Summer Street ignited, giving vent to what would become the Great Boston Fire of 1872. The flames destroyed dozens of buildings in their path, and caused millions of dollars in damage. According to Dr. Oliver Wendell Holmes, "The fire looked formidable," though it did not stop gawkers outside of the city from making their way downtown to sneak a peek. (*Boston City Archives*)

As late as 1823, Mount Vernon Street in Boston was also known as Mount Whoredom Street, due to an array of brothels located there, drawing to the area sailors and prostitutes working their trade and giving it a dank reputation. This area was located in what was known as the North Slope, while the South Slope was the home to Boston's high society. Fronting the Boston Common, the South Slope was renowned for its large, opulent mansions in the latest Greek revival style, their windows and front doors laced with elegant ironwork. Many of these homes had small patches of backyards, which were secluded and well maintained and gave the impression of privacy in the midst of a growing city. The residents of these mansions competed with each other with large flowerpots of gardenias and creeping vines, and in the spring there were blooming magnolias.

Mount Whoredom Street was the dividing line that told visitors they had left the South Slope and entered the North. But the smell alone would have been enough: garbage was piled high by the front doors and staircases; angry dogs and cats rummaged through the refuse and bathed in pools of stagnant water; mounds of horse dung were left steaming in the streets like the smallest of volcanoes.

British sailors favored this side of town, where one of them remembered "whole nights spent on drinking and carousing." The main attraction was the companionship of prostitutes and available women in the bordellos, where it was "confidently affirmed and fully believed, there are three hundred females wholly devoid of shame and modesty." For the most part, the two sides of the city did not mingle, until the mid-1820s, when those living on the South Slope began to nudge their way a little more to the north as the area had started to take on a respectable appearance, due in part to the efforts of then mayor Josiah Quincy, who tried to rid the area of the bordellos and prostitutes. The nudging became even more insistent, and soon a race was on to take over this area of town and to build elegant mansions.

Mount Vernon Street was situated within the one square mile that encompassed Beacon Hill, just east of the State House and north of the Boston Common and Public Gardens. The Public Gardens themselves had been designed upon European models, with a pond in the middle referred to as a lagoon, lines of flower beds, a handsome selection of saplings and grass, and many sitting spots spaced appropriately as conduits for reflection. Ralph Waldo Emerson could often be seen there, resting on a bench and taking in the sun, along with his friend the well-known Harvard instructor and physician Dr. Oliver Wendell Holmes.

For most of the year, Holmes resided on Beacon Street. Moving from nearby Charles Street, he purchased two large brownstones overlooking the gardens, one of which served as his home while the other was his study and library. Throughout his years as a doctor, teacher, and writer, he had amassed a large quantity of books and papers that now had to be stored. Not wanting to be too far from them for long, he had bought another house next to the one he already owned and linked the two. He liked this area of Boston. He liked to view the comings and goings of those roaming about the gardens. He enjoyed watching the snow fall on the new saplings and the Bostonians braving the weather in cold New England winters, while children whiled away the hours by sledding down the hills of the Common.

On the evening of November 9, 1872, a Saturday, Dr. Holmes found himself in his library engrossed with some Dutch picture books. His wife was with him, the time being somewhere between 8 and 9 P.M. Suddenly the tolling of bells startled them; fire bells, as he later described them. Curiosity prompted him to set aside his books and walk toward a window facing north, which gave him a wider view of Beacon Street. Overlooking the gardens, he didn't see anything. But tilting his head to the left, toward Tremont Street, he noticed tall flames. "The

Boston fire chief John Damrell was one of the few individuals who had warned the city officials for years prior that the city was on the verge of something catastrophic. Having studied the fire that occurred the years previous in Chicago, Damrell felt that matters were not so different in Boston, where a combination of congested streets, high buildings, and outdated equipment would converge and cause a great fire. He was correct, though officials did not want to admit that. (*Boston City Archives*)

fire looked formidable," he later said. "I went out thinking I would go
to Commonwealth Avenue and get a clear view of it."

Holmes was unaware of it yet, but the Great Boston Fire of 1872
had just begun.

That November evening was a mild one for Boston. The raindrops
of days earlier had ended, and the air had turned unnaturally tepid.
The downtown area was silent at just a hair past 7 P.M., the usual commotion having ended for another week. Gas lamps flickered along the
winding cobblestoned streets and near the empty stores; the daily merchants hawking shoes, boots, hale, bales, boxes, silk, fine hosiery, and
books were nowhere to be found. Theatergoers were preparing for the
evening performances; a large billboard at the museum advertised the
upcoming performance of *Othello*. Others, unable to attend the plays,
were looking for more pleasurable entertainment as they milled about,
as such entertainment was sorely needed.

Three days earlier, on November 6, the body of the merchant
Abijah Ellis had been found in the Charles River, his remains cut up
in pieces and stashed inside two wooden barrels. This grim discovery
had been made by some unsuspecting fishermen. "It seems to be one of
the periods only too familiar to students of the morbid of the human
society," the *Boston Globe* had written. "When one becomes at once more
prevalent and malignant than usual."

At just two minutes after the clock struck 7 P.M., a flicker from a
coal bucket in a boiler room located in a hoop skirt factory near the
corner of Kingston and Summer Streets ignited. The small flame grew
until it reached an elevator shaft, where it soon spread to the upper
floors and outside the building. From there the fire jumped from dwelling to dwelling, and then to the tenement houses that were near the
building. Those who had been walking the area toward a dance hall or
the famed Apollo Club began to hear the tolling of bells; looking in
the direction of the sounds they could see "a sudden lighting up of the
sky, an illumination of spires, a red glare on roofs and windows," the
Globe later reported.

Immediately people began to gather at the site and waited for the men of the fire department to arrive.

Everyone in the crowd assumed that someone else had rung the alarm box, only to discover no one had. Only when Assistant Engineer John Regan, standing in his home on Columbia Street, heard the cries of alarm from nearby did he rush toward the downtown area. By the time he got there, it was nearing 7:15 P.M. He signaled his colleagues in the first department by using the alarm box number 52, which Chief John Damrell later said was one of the most unreliable in the city. At 7:29 P.M., Police Officer Thomas Page gave the second alarm. That was supposed to summon everybody on duty to the site, but by then, nearly a half hour had elapsed since the fire had begun to spread.

When Chief Damrell heard the first alarm, he was in his house on Temple Street, which was not far from the area itself. He immediately rushed out of his house, nearly naked. Pushing through the crowds, he passed Beacon and Park Streets as the second alarm rang out and he reached the fire only when the third alarm was sounding. "I never saw such a sight as what presented itself to me that night," he said. "Within eight minutes from the time the alarm sounded, I was on the ground, and the buildings were literally consumed. . . . It is a phenomenon which I cannot possibly fathom."

Damrell quickly took note of where the fire had begun and was astonished by how widespread it had already become. The wind at that particular moment was coming from the hills and valleys surrounding the Charles River, which wind in his opinion did not seem to surpass "a velocity of seven miles an hour, varying occasionally two to three points of the compass from Northwest to North." His men were already in position, and he instructed them to remain where they were.

Oddly enough, just two weeks before, on Saturday, October 26, a windy and blustery day, the chief and his fifteen assistant engineers had gathered at City Hall to talk about what procedures to use should a fire roar in the city. The Chicago fire was still haunting Damrell, and he had studied it carefully over the months, believing he had taken all necessary measures should Boston face such circumstances. He was also aware of how newspaper accounts had treated Chicago's fire department after the fire ended; Damrell believed the accounts and public opinion of the response had been unjust.

"The fire department of that city was arraigned before the bar of public opinion and put on trial," he said in an address delivered before Boston Veteran Firemen years later, in February 1886. "A careful and discriminating jury rendered a verdict of praise and condemnation for the heroic service performed, including all from the chief down. On the other hand, they were denounced as imbeciles; composed of a class without education, training, principles, or judgment, and performing their duty as the unthinking horse bears the burden to which he is harnessed; that they were demoralized and intoxicated and commanded by a chief who had not the power to grasp nor the ability to organize and bring his force into reasonable discipline." Chief Damrell did not want to be remembered that way.

Around the time of the Boston fire, insurance agents were also examining the city's downtown area and, just like Damrell, understood how vulnerable it was to a fire like the one in Chicago.

Despite the precautions Damrell and his assistants had talked about and taken, they were now faced with several issues they had not anticipated, one of them being that the fire department was practically without any horses because they were suffering from a bout of the epizootic, the equivalent of human influenza. Several weeks before, the disease had made its first appearance in Toronto. Boston had been aware of it, but given the distance between the two cities, it was believed the illness would not cross the border, and Boston's councilmen had been unconcerned about its affecting the city's horses. But horses in other cities to the north of Boston were quickly succumbing to the epizootic, and soon enough the animals in Boston were struck down as well. The epidemic had started simply enough, with a slight loss of appetite in a few of the horses, only to be quickly followed in the rest of them by a severe cough, sneezing, a flow of thick saliva, and "a discharge of yellow mucus."

Two aldermen were immediately sent to surrounding communities in search of healthy horses for the firemen to use, but they were unsuccessful. The disease was affecting more than just the fire department; all over the city animals had been fighting to remain healthy. As such, nearly 90 percent of the horse force was still under quarantine, and all of the streetcar services had been suspended. Also, none of the equipment needed was located in downtown Boston, where the fire raged. Instead it was being housed outside the city's limits.

Of the fire department's 475 men, only 90 were permanent, and they were scattered across the city's districts. The hydrants were old, and only one steamer at a time could be connected to each pipe, rather than several. Damrell had called attention to these issues in all of his annual reports, particularly those published and distributed in 1867, 1868, and 1869. In 1869, he had added to his annual report to the city council a "special communication" to call further attention to what he believed were the city's weaker points.

Another big issue was that their hoses were too short. Water reached only as far as the third or fourth floor, and the buildings were much taller than that, which meant they could do nothing to stop the flames in those upper stories. They perched wooden ladders against the walls and threw water where they could, but most of the windows were closed, so the water could not get inside and tame the flames. Instead, water hit the buildings and turned quickly to steam.

The smaller tongues of flames that seemed to sprout unabated were put out by whichever fireman was nearby and could do so without harming himself. Oddly enough, the only building in the area to escape the flames belonged to the *Post* newspaper, so it was able to continue its business unharmed.

Calls for assistance were quickly sent to firehouses in the nearby communities of Roxbury, South Boston, Chelsea, and East Boston, and as soon as they arrived, they scattered to the various streets nearby to fight the flames sprouting throughout the district.

Onlookers watched in horror as Trinity Church, which had been so carefully constructed from designs made by one of its members, burned and smoldered, sending pigeons nesting under its eaves away in a cloud of ashy white fluff. The church was located at the corner of Summer Street and Bishop's Alley, adjacent to several businesses. Some years before, in 1868, the bishop of Massachusetts had described the area around it and the church itself: "Business has moved up from the harbor; blocks and shops surround the church; dwelling houses had been torn down and gardens desolated. Most of the parishioners had moved . . . the Church and such equipment there were unattractive and inconvenient." He felt, as did many associated with Trinity, that a new location would be most "advantageous." Now he would get his wish.

This wish had also been fostered by the new rector, the thirty-five-year-old Phillips Brooks, who had taken his post in July 1869. Despite his desire for a new church, parishioners had a hard time dragging him away from the smoldering rubble, and he finally left only by force. He had come to Boston after eight years at the Holy Trinity Church in Philadelphia, and from the moment he stepped foot in his new home, he had made it known that he desired a grander building and believed this was an actual need for the city.

Brooks was so persuasive that a vote was taken by the Church Building Committee in December 1870 to purchase some land in the newly filled-in area in the Back Bay, a spot to the east of Copley Square. The cost was $105,000. On March 6, 1872, the eleven members of the Building Committee hired a chairman. It was decided that this was going to be a large church that could seat more than a thousand worshippers. Six architects were invited to submit plans for consideration, and in the end, the commission was awarded to Henry Hobson Richardson of New York City, though the new construction was not set to begin until March 1875.

As the fire continued to rage and people gathered to watch, police cordoned off areas around the perimeter of the downtown. The city was being destroyed, and as Oliver Wendell Holmes later mused, "I saw it (the fire) dissolve the great buildings, which seemed to melt away."

By 8:30 P.M. the fire had engulfed most of the city's downtown area. "Granite fronts were exploding, and walls falling, broke not only by the water-mains and branches, thus allowing the water to flow with freedom, but the gas mains had also succumbed to the shock, and the gas was flowing into cellars and sewers and through drains into buildings," Chief Damrell remembered. "It was a fight for life."

Mayor William Gaston was aware of the gravity of the situation. Even though the area would be empty of merchants and businesspeople, he knew it would be crowded with pleasure seekers strolling the streets near the vaudeville shows and the Apollo theater. He also needed to tame the anger of the citizens who were barging into his office in search of help. He had to put aside his natural timidity and show strength. He quickly made his way to his office in Boston City Hall, on School Street. Prior to being used for official city business, the structure had been the Old State House; it was now overrun with people trying to find their way inside to talk to him. Gaston realized he had to make some powerful decisions, one of which was whether to use gunpowder to blow up the buildings in the path of the fire.

Chief Damrell was against such practice because he knew it had failed in Chicago. But after he was summoned to City Hall and "overpowered" by the mayor and the others in charge, the chief "yielded" to their decision and proceeded "to remove goods and blow up buildings." In theory, this should have worked: with those structures in the path of the fire removed, the flames would have nowhere to go.

Two fire captains, Green and Smith, were given the task of procuring the gunpowder. A boat stocked with powder was also serviced in the harbor. A subordinate of Chief Damrell, Captain Jacobs, was to determine which buildings could be "leveled," then report that to Chief Damrell, who would have final say in the matter. They would search the buildings to ensure that no one was inside, then be at the ready with the kegs of gunpowder. When it was time to set them off, one of the firemen assigned to that particular building would kick the keg with his boot, throw a bunch of smoldering newspaper toward the gunpowder, and then quickly dash out of the building through a window, the structure exploding in a hail of fire and broken glass behind him. This was a harrowing and dangerous ordeal for all these men, but they felt that taking down these buildings would tame the fire and keep it from spreading.

Although Damrell had given permission to Green and Smith, as well as to Captain Jacobs, to perform the job, he soon realized it was not being done in a systematic way and with a "prearranged plan." As a result the buildings did not come down altogether but merely made a great noise, a loud burst of ash and debris, "leaving the floors and stored merchandise fully exposed and in a fit condition for a good bonfire." He regretted the decision right away.

Worst still, during the blowing-up process, several gas pipes were broken and the smell of gas pervaded the area, so that a fear of an even larger disaster overcame the chief and his assistant engineers. In fact, a later report by the Fire Commission said: "The fire . . . was greatly aggravated by the escape of gas from the burning buildings. The fall of heavy warehouses broke the main pipes, and on Monday morning, the escaped gas in the sewers exploded, and caught another fire, which destroyed millions of property and cost two lives."

On November 10, the military also arrived, aided by the city's militia. Residents heard the beats from their drums as they moved from block to block adorned in their long gray coats, trying to frighten away any plunderers who had come for a quick payoff.

ALONG WITH THE BUILDINGS, millions of dollars' worth of hoop skirts, hosiery, fine silks, and mail bags went up in flames and were reduced to ashes. Records belonging to Harvard College were gone. Private papers and antique books, paintings, and adornments became remnants. The newly minted millionaires who made this area their home were returned to their scavenging days. Men saw their livelihoods disappear. Women dragged what remained of their belongings—a broken chair, a roll of blackened fabric, a statue of a Madonna—onto Boston Common, where the merchandise that hadn't burned was being stockpiled.

Over the coming days, the destruction was detailed in the local papers, and eventually the news reached across the country. Readers were struck that barely a year after the Great Chicago Fire, another blaze had destroyed yet another American city. The wrath of God, some said. But people also began to speak about Chief Damrell and his peculiar reaction to the fire and its aftermath.

The *Boston Globe* described the chief as he surveyed the scene of the destruction on the day after the fire and said he appeared to have momentarily lost his ability to talk. Those around him—his colleagues, the reporters, onlookers, even the aldermen—were looking to place blame for the fire. Though police and arson investigators found no proof that anyone living in the nearby dwellings, or anyone passing by, had set the blaze, that did not stop them from wanting to find someone to blame for how the fire had progressed and the resulting damage.

It wasn't long before Chief Damrell became the target. Everyone knew he had studied the fire in Chicago and had anticipated this one in Boston: why was he now so dumbstruck by what had occurred? The public seemed to determine that even if he was not practically guilty, he was morally so. No wonder he could not speak. And there was more. Not two days after the blaze, reporters began to speculate that Damrell had lost his mind. "He had gone crazy," Harold Murdock later wrote in his diary, "and been taken to an insane asylum. All this was pleasant to hear."

Reporters were not the only ones to place blame. Despite the arduous task of preparing for such a fire and all that the chief had done to warn the aldermen and City Hall members, when the report of the commission appointed to investigate the cause of the fire and its management was released, it said of the chief: "The Chief Engineer . . . is described as being cool." Then it went on: "But while seeing this, and while admiring his many good qualities, we cannot fail to see that there was a wont [sic] of preparation for so great an emergency . . . especially a wont of a leader capable of grasping the details of a great plan adopted to the terrible occasion. The fire was attacked piecemeal, as chance occurred. The heroism of individuals was too often wasted, because it was not directed by a master-mind."

But the committee failed to mention the many memos Chief Damrell had drafted in the preceding years, warning that the city of Boston was susceptible to a fire like Chicago's and was not prepared to fight it.

It was also widely suspected that Mayor Gaston had reverted to feeling weakness under pressure, was unable to lead the city, and had delegated his responsibilities to others below him, who had in turn failed. Finger-pointing became a sport everyone indulged in, although a well-known reverend in the city, Dr. Webb, of the Shawmut Church of Boston, seemed to still the wagging tongues and have the last word with one of his orations: "We are under a government which embraces the minutest events," he said. "Some natural law is violated and the

Aside from a lack of coal, old fire hydrants, and few resources from city officials, in November 1872 fire chief John Damrell and his men found themselves fighting one more event that they had not anticipated: an epizootic, a malady akin to the human influenza, that hit the city horses. It caused horses throughout the city to be taken out of service for days, and only a few healthy ones were found for miles around. (*Boston City Archives*)

penalty follows. Has it not been burned into our souls that only men wise in foresight, quick to discern, prompt to act, capable of leading in the hour of danger, should be entrusted with the city's affairs? The penalty for imperfect work or design, as in a ship or safe, is disaster. This calamity is the work of Providence; but he who lets matters rest there without investigation is a fool."

The fire had occurred in a commercial area whose shops were owned by those living on Beacon Street, Beacon Hill, and all along the Boston Common. As such, it became primarily their job to reconstruct what had been lost.

"The good old Boston families," as the *Globe* referred to those inhabitants of the wealthy area, seldom worried about the issues pervading the districts outside their relatively small zone, and in return, those districts like Charlestown, Chelsea, and South Boston didn't care about rebuilding theaters and shops they had nothing to do with.

Besides, these dingy and unsightly districts, as Charlestown, Chelsea, and South Boston were too often referred to, had much more pressing issues to deal with than reconstructing a hosiery factory or a vaudeville theater. A little girl, one of their own, had gone missing in South Boston. At first the police paid attention to her parents' pleas, but they no longer seemed very inclined to try to find her or track down the person who might have been involved in her disappearance.

But her relatives and neighbors had reason to suspect who had harmed her. They said they could see it in his eye.

CHAPTER 6

LOSS OF INNOCENCE

Cruel with guilt and daring with despair, the midnight murderer bursts the faithless air; invades the sacred hours of silent rest and leaves, unseen, a dagger in your breasts.

—SAMUEL JOHNSON, "LONDON, A POEM"

On the brisk morning of March 18, 1873, nearly four months since the deadly fire had devastated downtown Boston, ten-year-old Katie Curran readied for school in her home on 377 South Street, in South Boston, as she did every morning. As she packed her satchel, she recalled that on the day before she had used the very last sheet of paper from her notebook, and she needed a new one to get her started.

A number of specialty shops had grown on both sides of Broadway, tobacconists and small emporiums near and around her neighborhood, and she assured her mother she would be stepping outside for only a moment to find what she needed before classes got started. Katie was a good girl who never strayed too far from home or her mother, so Mrs. Curran felt confident the little girl would be returning momentarily.

But as Mrs. Curran braided Katie's younger sister's hair, she glanced up to look at the clock hanging on her wall and realized that nearly an hour had passed. A gnawing feeling grew in her stomach. By the time the clock struck 9 A.M., she had become so agitated she could not stand being in the house anymore and took to the streets, asking if anyone had seen her daughter.

Mrs. Curran soon learned that Katie had visited Thomas Torbin, who owned a shop at 367 Broadway. She had asked Torbin for a school card, a thin notebook used for classes, but upon learning he didn't have any, Katie had walked out of the premises, moving to the shop next door. Tobin remembered this occurring at around 8:30 A.M. As Mrs. Curran followed the steps her daughter had taken, she soon met a young woman named Emma Lee, who told her that indeed, she had seen Katie. But Emma had quickly left to go to school. Mrs. Curran was relieved someone had seen Katie. But relief did not last for too long. Emma had seen Katie entering the Pomeroys' shop, she told Mrs. Curran. Frantic with worry, Mrs. Curran began hurrying around for help.

Soon enough she came upon Captain Henry T. Dyer and Officer Thomas Adams and, almost in hysterics, told them her daughter was missing. They tried to assure her there was nothing to worry about. After all, Katie was ten years old, not a little child really. They even suggested that Mrs. Curran was exaggerating things. They told her to return home and wait for Katie to show up, which they were certain she would do very soon.

Like other policemen, they were expected to patrol the neighborhood and make certain no unsavory characters roamed about. But there hadn't been any troubles in the area for weeks so they left South Boston and returned downtown, where the burned-out district was still being reconstructed. The fire had wiped the locality bare, leaving behind a clear area on which to rebuild, and now only well-to-do ladies came by every so often to learn when the hat shops and shoe emporiums were due to reopen. Soon, the officers assured the women; very soon.

But twenty-four hours later, after Katie had still not walked through the doors of her home, Mrs. Curran was joined by family and friends who had begun to worry.

DAYS WENT BY, LONG nights spent searching the neighborhood and praying for Katie's return. Although family and friends made every effort to find her, it became apparent that additional help was needed. The Currans were poor and did not have money to set up a reward, but John Curran, Katie's father, approached South Boston's representative, Alderman Powell, for assistance.

Powell also visited Mayor Samuel C. Cobb to plead for help in finding the little lost girl. The mayor heard his pleas, and after days of finagling with City Hall, on April 1, 1874, a poster advertising Katie Curran's disappearance was put up, having being created by the mayor's office: "In accordance with an order of the City Council, a reward of Five Hundred Dollars is hereby offered for the detection and conviction of the person or persons who on the 18th ultimo abducted from Broadway, South Boston, KATIE MARIE CURRAN, aged about 10 years, the daughter of John and Mary Curran, residing in South Boston."

The family took some measure of comfort in the knowledge that now Katie's disappearance was known outside South Boston, and perhaps the sum of money offered for her return would induce someone to come forward with information. They waited, and waited.

ON APRIL 23, 1874, some five weeks after Katie Curran went missing, a man named Edward Harrington was rinsing a bucket of clams he had dug out on the beach, using a little pool of water nearby. The find was not particularly large that day, but as always he had enjoyed the solitary hours roaming along the shores, watching the waves roll in and out, the clouds floating by above his head, the brisk wind against his face.

Although it was still chilly, the scent of spring was in the air, and as he readied to call it a day, at nearly 4 P.M., the faint sun was settling behind some low-hanging clouds. As he swished the clams under the water, he happened to look up and noticed a young boy sprinting toward him. The boy was moving away from the marshes, hurrying toward Edward Harrington while at the same time stealing glances behind him, as if he expected someone to be coming up behind him.

This wasn't the first time Edward had seen a similar thing occur. Earlier in the day, some time between noon and 1 P.M.—he could not recall the precise hour—his brother, Benjamin, who had also spent some hours clamming with him, had pointed out a boy who was also rushing away from the marshlands and heading toward the railroad tracks leading to Crescent Avenue, some three-quarters of a mile from where they were. Benjamin had followed the boy's path, and Edward did the same as the youngster fled from the area, keeping Savin Hill to his left. The boy had been some distance away from them, running and often glancing over his shoulders as if he was fleeing from a pursuer, though the Harringtons never saw anyone else.

The brothers couldn't tell the boy's age, though even from a distance they could see he was tall, probably the same height as Edward. It was also difficult from that vantage point to notice what he had been wearing, though they could tell he had some kind of plush cap on his head. He ran at what Edward said was "a pretty good speed." Finally they lost sight of him once he reached McCay's Wharf. They thought the boy's actions were somewhat curious, but they soon put him out of their minds. At that particular moment the midday sun was warm overhead and it was thoroughly pleasant on the beach, suffused by the tangy smell of the ocean and the fresh breezes.

But now, some three hours later, another boy was running. His name was George Power, eleven years old, and he stumbled as he reached Edward Harrington. He and his thirteen-year-old brother, James, had also come to the shore in search of clams, but they had miscalculated the tide and instead decided to walk the lands around Savin Hill Beach and see what treasures they might find.

When George ran off toward Edward Harrington, James went in the opposite direction and crossed paths with Officer Roswell "Roscoe" M. Lyons, a rookie from Police Station Nine. It was just nearing 5 P.M., and Lyons had been patrolling a quiet area parallel to the shore. He immediately instructed James to calm down, but the boy began gesticulating wildly in the direction from which he'd come. That's when Lyons realized two things: the boy was a deaf-mute and his gestures indicated "that violence had been done to some person."

Using a piece of paper, Lyons wrote the boy a question and asked whether a drowning had occurred on the beach, for such things were not uncommon in the area. But the boy shook his head and wrote back "one murdered." Having wasted enough time already, Lyons followed the boy back toward the beach, where they found George, along with Edward Harrington and three other men, Obed Goodspeed, Patrick Wise, and Elias Ashcroft, who had also been out near the wharf.

Silently, the group waded through the saturated ground and parted the marshes, where, at about "twelve feet from the water line, and close to a small track," the report later stated, they found a pit and within it what seemed like the tossed remnants of a charred wooden doll. Empty clamshells were scattered across the figure, and its legs jutted out as if broken.

As they stared closer, they noticed it was not a doll at all but the remains of a small boy, almost naked and resting on his back. His pants and undergarments had been roughly pulled down to his ankles, and blood had coagulated across his naked thighs, legs, chest, and arms, along with some other sticky substance and muck from the marshes. He must have endured a great deal of pain, his little body moving to and fro, for the heels had sunk into the soft wet sand, "as if he had struggled in dying," Lyons later stated. The child's body was ravaged by stab wounds, slashes crisscrossing his chest and his throat, a wound so deep across his neck that his head had been nearly separated from the rest of his body. One eyeball had been deeply pierced with some kind of sharp object, a knife perhaps, so now liquid oozed out. The little boy had also been nearly castrated and set on fire.

The men didn't notice any weapons nearby, nor did Lyons make any "special examination of the grounds."

"His face was calm," Goodspeed said afterward of the child. "His feet extended, hands were spread at his side, throat cut. There were several wounds on the left hand as if done with some sharp instrument. There was also a mark on the eye."

They all staggered from what they saw. They stood over the murdered child's body for a while, dumbfounded, until other onlookers, on hearing the commotion, began to gather. No one instructed them to tread carefully upon the moist sands, and eventually the crime scene was littered with footsteps nearing and retreating from the marshes. The ground was soft, and the police would later have to contend with these dozens of footprints. Eventually Lyons asked the crowd to disperse, and he carefully picked up the child's body in his arms, leaving the boy's impression in the sand, into which some blood had seeped, and making no special provision to preserve any evidence. He carried the body to the nearby depot, later still to Police Station Nine. From there the little boy's body was taken to the public undertaker's office.

BY NOW IT WAS nearing 6 P.M. On 253 Dorchester Street, in South Boston, Mrs. Lenora Millen, who had allowed her four-year-old Horace to walk down Dorchester Street by himself earlier that morning, had become frantic. Horace had left the house at 10:20 A.M., and she expected him home a few minutes later. It was a five-minute walk to the bakery, where they were frequent customers; five or ten minutes spent picking up a sweet; then five minutes to walk back. The process should not have taken any more than twenty minutes. Perhaps add to that a few more minutes for Horace to stare at the sweet things, and a few more for his indecisiveness. Still, he should have arrived home no later than 11 A.M.

At 11:30 A.M., she became anxious and decided to go out and search for him. Maybe Horace had gotten lost in his new neighborhood, she reasoned. She would scold him, she knew, though not punish him. She was always disinclined to do that to Horace. She was not going to bother her husband, either. After a prolonged period of being out of work, he had started working as a cabinetmaker on Newman Street, so he was not at home.

The Millens had moved into the area only four weeks after Katie Curran had gone missing, on March 18. Of course, they had heard that the girl had disappeared, but they had also become aware that the police suspected a family member of her kidnapping. It was a family matter, they had decided as they settled into their new home. As it happened, they had also moved directly across the street from the Currans, from where occasionally they could see glimpses of John and Mary Curran. Dorchester Street ran parallel to Broadway, an area flanked by rows of dilapidated multitenement houses where the less-well-to-do had come to live during hard times. It had not always been so. In the early 1800s entrepreneurs calling themselves the Mount Vernon Proprietors, and including William Tudor and Harrison Gray Otis, had fought to expand the city of Boston from Beacon Street all the way down to include Broadway and Dorchester Avenue, what was now South Boston.

Great fortunes had been made from these tenements, particularly when the area had been annexed to the city proper in 1804. Speculators on whom luck had shined had gone on to build gracious homes on Beacon Hill, with marble fireplaces, bookcases, and mahogany desks on which they placed the trinkets they purchased on their grand tours of Europe. But as the decades passed South Boston fell into neglect, and those same proprietors sold their homes there and speculated elsewhere. Now this was a place where those suffering financial difficulties could find refuge.

Such financial suffering had hit the John Anderson Millen family most recently. Millen was only in his early thirties, and until a few months ago, he had been working in Charlestown. Now, reduced to destitution, he and his family had had to flee to South Boston, just like others before him, including the Currans and the Pomeroys.

But despite his financial hardship, John Millen believed he was very lucky. He had married a sweet and pretty woman, Lenora, who had given him two small boys, Sydney and Horace; good boys, at that. They were both very handsome, but the younger, Horace, always brought about the most tenderness from both of his parents, as well as from those who came across him. He was a tiny boy, so pale as to resemble marble, with blond hair his mother refused to cut and a soft pink mouth perpetually set in a pout; people often mistook him for a girl.

On the morning of his disappearance, Horace had eaten his breakfast, and not long thereafter, when it was almost 10 A.M., began to whine and beg his mother to let him go to the bakery nearby. His mother had relented and given him permission to go out unaccompanied, giving him precise instructions on what to do and when to return home. It was then 10:20 A.M.

With a few coins in his hands, little Horace had skipped along the streets intent on one of the "drop cakes" his mother had been buying him since moving into the new neighborhood. A woman would later report briefly seeing a little blond boy wearing a velvet cap, a checkered shirt, and knee breeches at around 10:30 A.M., idling near a lamppost on Dorchester Street. He had been in the company of a much older and much larger boy, who had pocketed half of Horace's sweet bun then, taking Horace by the hand, led him away from the spot, veering toward the beach.

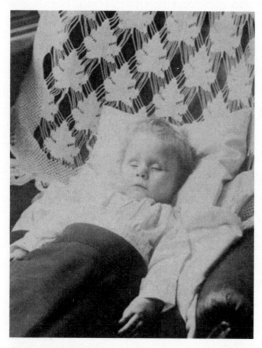

On April 23, 1874, a little boy left his home in a neighborhood of South Boston and was never seen alive again. Horace Millen entered a bakery to buy a sweet, then while leaving the premises met an older boy idling outside, who was later identified as Jesse H. Pomeroy. Pomeroy took Horace by the hand and led him to McCay's wharf. Horace's body was found later that same evening, mutilated and nearly set on fire, a murder for which Jesse Pomeroy was arrested and sentenced to hang, though his sentence was commuted to life in prison in solitary confinement. (*Charlestown Public Library*)

AS SOON AS THE body on the beach was found, Boston chief of police Edward Hartwell Savage received a dispatch from Police Station Nine, which made him aware of the horrid mutilation on Savin Hill. Keenly intelligent and easygoing, Savage had become captain of the North End District only three years after joining the department in 1851.

The Boston Police Department was not formally

organized until 1854, although its roots went back all the way to 1631, its beginnings due to a daring band of night watchmen. These men functioned as a sort of unpaid guards against hooligans, though by 1796 the band's members had finally decided to reorganize themselves and to wear a badge, a hook, and a noise-making rattle they used to call out for help if needed.

By 1838 the night watchmen had also their counterparts in the Day Police, which operated under the city marshal. In 1852 the Office of the City Marshal was abolished and the Office of the Chief of Police established, with the esteemed Francis Tukey as the first official chief. In 1854, the Boston Night Watchmen and the Day Police disbanded and together became the Boston Police Department, with Robert Taylor as its first chief.

In 1861, Savage became chief of the recently named Boston Police Department. He immediately became concerned that there was a gulf between the city's elite and those of lesser means, a gulf that had grown wider since the fire downtown. He had been desperately working to re-store morale and to show people his department cared, but few people believed in his efforts.

By 1872, Savage was less physically robust and his hair had become spotted with gray. It wasn't merely his work that had accentuated his advancing years. His wife's death was a devastating blow, and now he shared a home with an elderly daughter who had never married. This not only saddened but worried him, because he knew he would be leav-ing her alone when he passed. Still, he remained sharp of mind, his wits as keen and cool as they had been in his youth.

He knew immediately upon hearing about the murder on the beach that he needed all of his manpower to solve this particularly gruesome crime. The murder of a small boy took on a whole new dimension for the force, which meant the officers and detectives would have to be reassigned from the downtown area to South Boston. The first thing he did was assign the case to one of his most trusted detectives, the legendary James "Revolver" Wood, an inscrutable beast of a man who

roamed the city in impeccably tailored suits and smoked a pipe per-
fumed with exotic tobacco.

Wood had been born in the small town of Brookfield, Vermont,
but at age fourteen began drifting out west, working the lumber trade
for several years, eventually proceeding to California during the gold
rush before returning east to Boston, shortly before the outbreak of the
Civil War. Like other young men of his age, he enlisted, joining the
Company 3, First Massachusetts Regiment, then Company B, Sixth
U.S. Cavalry. It wasn't long before he was selected as a scout in General Burnside's headquarters, working as an undercover agent delivering
dispatches to President Abraham Lincoln. He was even caught and sent
to the infamous Libby Prison, from which he promptly escaped, later
calling it one of the many "thrilling" experiences of his life.

He returned to Boston in 1866, married Mary E. Collins, from
Gardner, Maine, and during the same year joined the Boston Police
Department, where he served as a patrolman at Station One for five
years. He was quickly promoted to detective and transferred to headquarters, located at City Hall, where he would remain for sixteen years.

Unlike his many colleagues, he became well known for his scrupu-
lous grooming and the silk hats, embodying a keenness that seemed to
have been cut from the personas of his fictional counterparts, though
the several "automatic pistols of enormous size" he wore under his coat
were as real as the crimes he solved. His pipe and a long mustache also
added to the allure he so carefully honed, along with a streak of intro-
spection he indulged in every so often.

Shortly before the case of the boy on the beach came to his attention, Wood had also worked several cases that had further added to
his notoriety. In one he had apprehended the fugitive Dr. David Rozen
Brown, who, according to his files, "had got himself into trouble by
using his surgical skills to procure an abortion on a young woman."
Wood would also be instrumental in the infamous murder perpetrated
by a Mrs. Hull in New York City. Boston and New York detectives
often worked together if a case warranted doing so, and Wood was the

one called upon in such a situation, as in the Hull case. He was very proud of the record of distinction he had thus far collected, admitting to having arrested, or assisted in arresting, 625 perpetrators, who served more than a thousand years in jail.

Savage summoned his men into his office at City Hall and explained the news he'd received from Station Nine. He also told them a set of footprints believed to be the assailant's had been found in the sand. Clouds were threatening rain, and he wished to have the footprints preserved before they were washed away. Wood later reported that during the meeting, Chief Savage first made the connection between the murder and the Pomeroy assaults.

"There is a strange resemblance about this thing to the work of a young scoundrel we've got in the Reformatory," Savage told the group. "He used to have a mania for taking little boys, slashing them about the face with a knife, and then tying them to a railroad track."

"Pomeroy," Detective James Quinn quickly interrupted. "Pomeroy," he said. "But he isn't in the Reformatory. He's left it."

"You're surely mistaken," said Savage.

The chief hurried to the telegraph station box and sent out a message to the district where Jesse Pomeroy's family lived. The answer came right away: Jesse had been released from the Westborough Reformatory on February 6, 1874, and now lived with his mother and his brother at 312 Broadway, in South Boston. His mother and brother ran a small shop across the street, at 327 Broadway.

CHIEF SAVAGE WASN'T THE only one who connected Jesse Pomeroy to the murder on the beach. The *Boston Globe* also quickly made the same assertion. Just hours after Horace's body was found, the paper printed a story that alluded to Jesse's earlier deeds in Chelsea and South Boston: "The similarity of the crimes is so great that it seems almost a logical conclusion that they are the work of one and the same hand." The writer for the paper, which otherwise was a respectable publication, emphasized the last moments of the victim's suffering (of which he had no knowledge); the body's bloodied condition (which he had not seen); and the young killer's morbid and twisted motives (which he did not know).

Although witnesses said they had seen Horace and a tall boy resembling Jesse walking toward the beach, no one could really say if Horace had appeared fearful in the boy's company, nor if they had heard the little boy cry out for his mother or for his sibling. But this did not stop the newspapers from riling up the city by suggesting such details, as well as the older boy's identity.

"He (Jesse) asked the boy if he would like to see the steamer, and the boy said he would," wrote the local *South Boston Gazette*. "When they arrived at the spot where the boy was found, Jesse told the Millen boy to lie down, and the little fellow, not dreaming of the danger, did so. The young fiend immediately sprang upon him, clapping his left hand over the little innocent's mouth to stop his out-cries, and then . . . cut the throat of the little boy that had so implicitly trusted him."

The paper continued: "He cleaned the knife and person as well as he could, and then took a car to Boston proper."

No steamer had been docked in the harbor that day, nor was there reason to believe that Horace had been lured there by the prospect of seeing one. Nor was there any indication that the older boy had asked the little boy to calmly lie down on the sand before smothering him. If anything, the coroner later concluded that a struggle had ensued. But this murky yet sensational storytelling not only emphasized Horace's extreme youth and innocence but overemphasized the killer's morbid fiendishness, assigning to him virtues reserved for monsters and animals.

The newspaper's editors placed the article about Horace's murder next to one about the life of a tiger, describing it as "a fierce and awful beast who lives in Asia and eats food raw." It went on to say, "That wouldn't be so bad if the tiger were particular about his food. But he isn't. He eats deer when he can get them and cattle at all season. But when other food is scarce he eats farmers, travelers, qualified voters and other members of society." The *Gazette* did not mention Jesse in its article about tigers, but the point was made, as it was in another paper, in an article that said he was akin to a dog, more appropriately, a werewolf. "As the poor brute in a frenzied torment with foaming jaws and starting eyes tears victim after victim in his headlong course," began the *Boston Daily Advertiser* on April 28, running along the same vein for several more paragraphs.

Despite there still being nothing that substantially implicated Jesse Pomeroy in the murder, newspapers continued to run their articles, many of them accompanied by an ink sketch of Jesse that put particular attention on the blotchy right eye, that rare white deformity that seemed to hold the answers to all of his malignity. Readers also agreed that his face was the villainous countenance of a killer.

Jesse Pomeroy was born in the Charlestown neighborhood of Bunker Hill, on Lexington Street. His early years were spent roaming Charlestown, as well as crossing the bridge that led into Chelsea, where his earliest victims resided. It was upon the family's move to South Boston, following his return from the Westborough Reformatory School, that his murder spree began. Newspapers wrote endless articles about him and his family, and a sketch appeared during that period that depicted Jesse as a young teenager, sporting a white blotch in his right eye. (*The Charlestown Historical Society*)

Local reporters began to converge on Ruth Ann's front steps, as if they expected her to answer their questions. Instead they received vulgar gestures from behind curtained windows and a litany of profanities.

But what most parents got from those articles was that Jesse Pomeroy was no longer where they thought he was. He was out of the reformatory school and was living among them.

When Pomeroy arrived at the reformatory school at Westborough on September 21,

1872, he was twelve years old, and he was supposed to stay there until he was eighteen. But he was released in February 1874, nearly four and a half years before his sentence was due to expire. All of this had occurred thanks in part to a lovely benefactor who had taken a liking to Ruth Ann.

By the time Jesse had entered the facility, Ruth Ann had become even more embittered and sour than before, as unpopular in South Boston as she had been in Charlestown. She had opened a tiny dress-making shop across the street from their apartment, at 327 Broadway, behind the newsstand her older son, Charles, had opened.

On a frigid morning in January 1874, when Jesse had been at the reformatory school for just over a year, and a gale blew in from the harbor, Ruth Ann and Charles were visited by Gardiner Tufts, a solemn-looking man reminiscent of an undertaker. His bones seemed to shiver when he walked into the even colder shop. But, as it turned out, he worked for the State Board of Charities, and he told Mrs. Pomeroy he was there to conduct a routine visit and would she mind if he took a look around.

Though the shop was shabby, Tufts could see that mother and son worked hard to keep things together. And Mrs. Pomeroy seemed like such a doting mother to both her sons, despite Jesse's failings. Tufts, a bachelor, was touched by such sweet devotion. He left the premises, and as they watched him go, neither Ruth Ann nor Charles expected to hear from him again.

But unbeknownst to them, Tufts reported his findings to the trust-ees at the Board of Charities. He admitted that matters on the home front were not ideal: Mrs. Pomeroy did not have many financial re-sources and finding meaningful work was always a challenge for her. She was divorced from her husband, which meant Jesse lacked a father figure in his life. Even when Thomas Pomeroy lived with his family, the relationship between father and son had been strained, at best; there was evidence Thomas beat Jesse, and the separation between Mr. and Mrs. Pomeroy had occurred precisely after one such beating.

When several neighbors learned that Jesse might be coming home, they had gone to the local police station to complain. But the police, namely Captain Dyer, had promised Tufts they would keep an eye on Jesse, as well as the people who might trouble *him*. Despite these apparent issues, Tufts couldn't help but be supportive of Mrs. Pomeroy's efforts to bring her son home. Tufts agreed that a home environment would be more conducive to Jesse's state of mind than a reformatory school. He also knew Jesse's older brother, Charles, was a hardworking boy who could use Jesse's help, given his line of work. The trustees read the report and in turn, sent Tufts's findings to the Westborough State Reform School, where the officials agreed to hasten Jesse's release.

There was nothing illegal or secretive about what the reform school or the Board of Charities did: they followed proper protocol in the case, and the proper channels were identified and informed. Yet, on the day of Jesse's newfound freedom, his release escaped the notices of newspapermen, who up until then had been so judicious in following him. When the doors of the Westborough facility opened up, Jesse casually stepped right through them "not without some regret," he later said, "for my residence here had been I could say almost all pleasant." His good eye was now set on South Boston.

ON THE EVENING OF the murder, Detective Wood, along with two of his colleagues, Detective Hamm and Detective Dearborn, headed to the murder site, and upon arriving at Savin Hill, along with the rest of the officers dispatched from headquarters, fanned out across the marshes and inched their way through the footprints in the sand. They could hear the swishing of the waters as it neared land, and soon they distinguished two very distinct sets of footprints in the sodden ground, "one set corresponding with the boy's boots," Detective Wood later wrote in his report, "and another set, nearly a man's size but not quite, evidently those of a person leading young Millen." The detectives followed the same path as the victim and perpetrator, eventually concluding that the child had been "decoyed . . . the inference being clear that the child had been lifted over."

"We followed the trail in silence," Wood said. "Sometimes, when the ground grew hard or became grass covered, the footprints were almost obliterated. Then we would come upon them again—always close together . . . the trail led to a place called McCay's Wharf."

Some two hundred feet from the railroad tracks, the detectives lost that trail, though by then they were convinced that one set belonged to Horace and the other to someone older who was leading him on. Not only that. Wood realized that there was such "startling clarity" to them it was possible to make molds of the prints.

"As soon as the plaster was sufficiently dry, we lifted the casts out carefully, then commenced a minute study," he wrote further. "There was a peculiar indentation in the plaster sole impression of one of the larger footprints. For the examination satisfied us that those prints could have been made by only one pair of shoes."

As the detectives canvassed the grounds at the murder site, Officers Lucas and Adams arrived at Mrs. Pomeroy's home just as Jesse was making his way down the stairs. He claimed to have been readying for bed when he was startled by their voices below. But the officers noticed he was still wearing not only his pants, but also a coat and a "plush cap." The officers led him to the parlor and began asking him about his doings on that day. There was no overt fear or anxiety as Jesse spoke to them, his responses flat, calm, even disarming enough that the officers insisted he come with them to Police Station Nine for a conversation. There, among the steel cages and in their own environment, they hoped to unnerve him. Jesse consented, perfectly happy to cooperate with the authorities, he said.

JUST AS DETECTIVES WOOD, Hamm, and Dearborn were returning to Police Station Nine, they saw Jesse being led up a short flight of stairs leading to a wooden door beneath an arched entryway, and as he entered the building, the three mounted the few steps and followed him inside.

Right away Wood noticed the ugly marks and fresh scratches on Jesse's skin. "One scratch about half inch long on the line from the mouth to his left ear; three small abrasions under the left ear; a small red mark on the back of his neck in a line with the bottom of the ear; one scratch in the corner of the neck, on the back part of the left side; two scratches on the back of the left hand, all apparently recently made." Jesse told them the scratches on his face had occurred when he shaved recently.

The officers thoroughly strip-searched him, and on sorting through his clothing, found a dark stain embedded in the fabric of his shirt. His dark gray pants were soaked at the knees, and the detectives assumed he had tried to wash the dirty garments with clean water. His underwear was also wet. They asked him if these were the clothes he had been wearing all day, and he said yes. He didn't own too many articles of clothing to choose from.

They also inspected Jesse's boots, where they found the peculiar indentation that had been visible on the foot molds taken at the murder site. As they removed his boots, they also noticed that his pants were caked with mud, "corresponding with the soil of the marsh." Detective Wood went so far as to taste the mud, which he found quite briny.

They wanted to know where they could find his knife, and Jesse told them it was in the pocket of his vest, located at home. Officers Lucas and Adams returned to Mrs. Pomeroy's apartment, where they found the woman pacing the rooms. She handed them Jesse's vest, a coarse gray thing she had stitched herself. She promised she hadn't removed anything from it. The officers searched the pockets and found the object they had come for, and on returning to the station, they informed Jesse of the discovery.

But Jesse was not rattled by this, nor by anything else. Recounting the day's events in a flat monotone, he confessed that he knew the area they were talking about very well. It was called a cow pasture near the

Old Colony Railroad. He said he went there often, and that explained why his boots were caked in mud. He liked to watch the boats, and the sailing vessels docked at the Boston Yacht Club. Once he had even seen men shooting guns toward some small birds flying in the air. He also knew there was a place where the local men liked to go to and cut firewood for the winter. But for the most part, he said, he liked to walk near and parallel to the railroad tracks, especially when a train whistled by, rather than venturing down by the marshes. The detectives took this in as evidence that Jesse had indulged in a few reconnaissance missions prior to the crimes; he had taken the time to learn the area well.

Dearborn wanted to know where he'd been that afternoon, and Jesse said he had not been anywhere near the beach. Instead, he had walked briskly across the Boston Common, admiring the buildings that were being reconstructed and those that still remained singed by the fire. Dearborn asked him to be more specific. They needed details.

Jesse said he had asked his mother for permission to leave South Boston and go into the city proper, and she had said yes. He had left his usual neighborhood by running down Broadway, over the Federal Street Bridge, along Federal Street, toward the new post office leading to Milk Street, then headed to Washington Street, onto Bromfield Street, and down Beacon Street, which eventually brought him to the Common.

He had stayed there for a while, resting on the benches and watching the strollers, until he went up to Congress Street and into Presbo's Dining Room, a facility patronized by the working class, which in essence had been his ultimate destination. He even recalled the time as being "1 and 3/4 o'clock." He had remained at Presbo's until 2 P.M. without eating, but simply observing the patrons as they swallowed their lunches and endless cups of coffee, or looking at those who were walking and milling about outside the premises. He then left to meet his brother, Charles, who had given him money to buy the newspapers at the Traveller's Office. But instead of running that errand, as he did every day, today he had gone off to Quincy Market to meet his father.

Detective Wood asked if he had met anyone along his path who could corroborate his story. Predictably, no one had seen him, and he had seen no one.

Jesse's account was detailed in all regards: the route he had taken and even the benches he had set upon were clearly outlined; he knew the length of time he had spent at each location as well as how many minutes it had taken him to reach the diner, and how long he had remained there. He even spoke in details of the construction work that was being done on Federal Street and the new water pipes that were being installed near Winter Street, which were to aid the city with the next fire, should one erupt.

Moving away from the details of the landscape, Detective Wood returned to the topic of his clothes, asking Jesse if there was anything unusual about them, particularly his boots. Jesse replied that indeed his boots tipped to the right, the right one had a hole in it, and both of them had low heels. But more than the issue of his boots, Jesse seemed to be concerned about and to miss his knife, which had been found in his vest, a "white-handled knife with two blades, a large one and a small one; the long blade as long as my middle finger," he told them, showing them that finger. "The other a trifle shorter than my little finger."

But when Wood asked him to give more specifics about what he did in the Common—if for instance he had seen a parade or a military exercise, which the detectives knew had taken place earlier in the day in the precise location Jesse was describing—he could not recall anything. Worse still, he was told the detectives had already spoken to his father, who had denied seeing his son at the usual hour, as Jesse claimed. Rather, the visit occurred much later. The detectives had already concluded that Jesse did not meet his father at Quincy Market until after 2 P.M. This meant that Jesse had a window of time—between 11:30 A.M. and 2 P.M.—he could not account for. According to Coroner Allen's estimations, Horace's death occurred in the middle of that time frame. Jesse had no reaction when confronted with this.

Chief of Police Savage was the one who explained to Jesse the charges being formed against him. Savage expected an outburst, but instead noticed how calm Jesse remained.

"We have evidence against you," Savage told Jesse, attempting to coax an admission from the boy, "which will be damaging."

Savage was known for his calm demeanor, even when dealing with the hardest criminals. One of the rules he had set out for himself, and which he eventually wrote down on paper for those who came afterward, specifically stated: "School yourself in all occasions to keep *perfectly* cool; maintain a perfect control of temper, come what will: one that can govern himself can govern others."

But Jesse was not taken in by the chief's affable attitude. He listened closely, then turned to look at Savage and stared at the rest of the group that had collected around the room. He settled his one blue eye on them and quietly replied, "Oh, you can't prove anything."

Jesse's reluctance to speak appeared to Detective Wood as mere bravado. He decided on a different approach.

"Jesse, what made you hurt the little boys?" Detective Wood asked, veering away from the topic on hand. Wood knew Jesse had already spoken of the little boys in Chelsea and South Boston many times before, and that he'd done so without the slightest reluctance.

Jesse told him he didn't know.

"You never saw those little boys until you cut them, did you, Jesse?" Wood continued.

Jesse shook his head. No, he hadn't known them.

"I don't suppose you knew what you were doing?"

"I don't think I did," Jesse finally replied. "I don't know."

"Might you have killed that little boy and not known it?" Wood persisted, as the rest of the officers and detectives looked on.

"I don't know. I might. I guess I did."

Wood later said on the witness stand that he had seen tears in Jesse's eyes at that particular moment. It was also then that someone quietly suggested to Wood that they take Jesse to view Horace's body.

Jesse heard what was being proposed and declined to go. "I don't want to go."

"Why?" Wood asked. "We want you to go and see if you know him."

"I know him."

"If you know him, you killed him, didn't you, Jesse?"

"I guess I did," he said. "If I did, I am sorry, and I don't want my mother to know it." The room was quiet for a time, until Jesse continued. "I suppose you will sketch that in the newspaper as you did before to hurt her feelings." It was obvious he had seen and read the articles written about him during the Boy Torturer's reign.

"No," Wood told him. "We won't put it in the newspaper."

Jesse pointed to a man standing in the rear of the room, half hidden by the light, and said: "There, that's a reporter now."

Wood told him no. The man was not a reporter but an officer from the station.

Jesse said all the police officers wanted to be the first ones to cash in on the reward being offered. Wood was surprised to hear that because there was no reward for Horace's killer, and he told Jesse that.

"There is a reward for the girl," Jesse whispered enigmatically.

That prompted Wood to ask if Jesse knew anything about the whereabouts of Katie Curran, who had not been found yet.

Jesse smiled at him and said no; only what he had read in the newspapers, where notices of a reward had been printed.

Preparations were being made to go to Waterman's undertakers, though Jesse was resistant to the plan. But if he had to go, he said, he wanted to be accompanied only by Detective Wood. The police had no inclination to bargain, and the entourage included not only Wood and Jesse, but Detective Dearborn, Officer Adams, and Captain Hood.

They were greeted by George Waterman, the son of the proprietor, and entered the parlor room, where a tall blaze burned in a woodstove. Wood and Jesse walked to stand next to the flames, as if for warmth.

Waterman then led them down a somber corridor, and Wood asked Jesse to enter a smaller room where he could view the body and perhaps tell them if he recognized the little boy. Once again, Jesse refused to do so. Wood persisted, and Jesse again said no.

The body was laid out on a shelf within a glass case with sliding doors, in a room that could be entered by a right-sided door. Captain Hood walked through it, while George Waterman stood by, watching the exchanges between the officers and the boy.

"I can see him from here, and I know him," Jesse finally said.

Waterman knew that was impossible. From where Jesse stood, he could not see the body fully laid out, but only the outline of it. Even Waterman could tell that if Jesse recognized the body, it was not because he was seeing him now, but because he had known him sometime earlier.

Wood was growing impatient and began grasping Jesse by the right arm and dragging him inside, to where the body rested. He would later state that Jesse trembled like a leaf under his clutch. The dead boy was on the table, covered by a sheet, which Wood removed. He later wrote that Horace was "an extremely fine-looking child," who had been stabbed twenty-one times near the vicinity of the heart. His throat had been cut from ear to ear. This had not been a swift and painless death.

"Take a look at him," Wood instructed. But Jesse refused to do so, directing only an eerily furtive glance with his marbled eye toward the table.

"Jesse, do you know him?" Wood asked.

"Yes."

"Jesse, did you kill him?"

"Yes," he finally whispered.

"Look at him again," Wood said.

"No, I have seen enough."

Wood asked if he had killed Horace with his knife, to which Jesse attested. Dr. Horace Everett of South Boston, who later analyzed the knife, agreed that his examination had revealed spots of blood on the blades, and dirt from the marshes.

Once again Wood took Jesse by the arm and led him outside the room.

"Jesse, did you kill him?" the detective asked again. And again Jesse confirmed it. Wood asked the same questions over and over in the presence of Officer Adams, and Jesse continued to say yes.

Back at Police Station Nine, Jesse was led into a room normally reserved for the safekeeping of suspects, where Captain Hood, Officer Adams, Detective Wood, and others gathered. Wood took hold of Jesse's knife and opened it.

"I suppose you cut his throat with this blade, Jesse, didn't you?" Wood asked, opening the large blade. Jesse became very quiet.

"I suppose you made the stabs with this blade?" Wood now opened the little blade and brought it up to his eyes. He then looked at Jesse and asked: "How did you get the blood off the knife, Jesse? Did you wash it?"

"No, I stuck it in the marsh, in the mud," Jesse admitted.

Wood nodded. "How did you get the blood off from your hands, did you wash them?"

"No, I did not get any on my hands."

Jesse's unflinching statements silenced Wood, though Dearborn still had one question for him: how had he managed to leave the marshes without being seen? Jesse couldn't answer. He told the detective he could not remember that.

Despite some minor gaps in the boy's story, the detectives were satisfied with the evidence on hand. Jesse Harding Pomeroy had also admitted his guilt, so there was no reason to search for another killer or to believe an alternative theory to the crime. As it stood, justice would be had in the murder of Horace Millen. If only anyone in the room had bothered to write down all of Jesse's confession and asked for his signature.

FOLLOWING THAT LENGTHY CONVERSATION, Jesse was taken back to his cell, where the detectives gave specific instructions to the captain on duty not to allow any visitors to speak to the boy, unless the request had been fielded through them first.

On the afternoon of April 24, the day after he was arrested, Jesse was visited by a member of the State Reform School, who would later be identified as Stephen A. Dublois. Dublois told the man on duty he wished to speak to the boy in private. As it happened, he arrived when the detectives had momentarily left the premises to have supper in a nearby diner.

The captain in charge, swayed by the powerful influence Dublois seemed to project, not only allowed the man to enter Jesse's cell but gave him ample time for a private conversation. No one heard what was said, but on the following day, when Jesse was brought before the Coroner's Jury to testify, he recanted his confession and denied his involvement in Horace's murder. Rather, he argued that the detectives had bullied him into making a false statement and confession.

Wood asked Jesse what had been said between him and Dublois.

"He said that there was nothing against me but circumstantial evidence," Jesse told Wood. They were speaking in the back room again, but this time Jesse was showing a measured sense of defiance he'd not had during their previous conversation. The trustee had also told him "to answer no more questions that anyone would ask me," Jesse said.

It was an unusual turn of events. Wood noted that the boy who had shaken like a leaf at the undertaker's had now turned insolent.

"Jesse," Wood said. "Tell me all about the little boys that you cut. You are not afraid to tell about them."

Then Jesse denied knowledge of that as well. He told the detectives he had never seen those little boys and certainly had done nothing to them. He said he had been committed to the reform school because his attorney had not properly defended him; the judge had allowed the young boys to testify against him, he continued, which should not have been so. Defiant, that was Jesse now.

Wood left the room and allowed Dearborn to enter. He asked Jesse if he recalled the conversation they had had on the previous day. Jesse said he did. But when asked about the little boy, Jesse coyly said, "What little boy?" He had never seen Horace until the detectives had brought him to the undertaker's and ushered him into the room, regardless of how much he said no. Now he did not want to discuss the matter anymore.

Why? Dearborn wanted to know.

A member of the State Reform School had spoken to him and advised him to "keep my mouth shut."

Had the man said anything else?

"He said if I had done anything, I ought not to say it," Jesse replied. "There was no evidence to convict me of it."

He also neglected to mention that he had just received a letter from his mother. "Jesse, you know you did not do those things, so why do you not stand up and try to clear yourself of it?" Ruth Ann had asked him. She had also instructed her son not to tell anyone he had done any of those things, if indeed he hadn't done them. To keep quiet. Jesse thought quite a bit about his mother's words. It was not the first time he felt he should deny the charges and now, given the advice from the trustee of the reform school and most especially from his mother, his resolve was solidified.

His attorneys, Joseph H. Cotton and E. G. Walker, were well-known men his mother had persuaded to represent her son. They had agreed to do so based on the limelight the case would shine on them. They were made aware of this change, and during a visit with him, they warned him that his contradictory statements would not be well received by the jury.

They said he was impeding their progress. Jesse admitted that he had told Wood he thought he had killed the little boy, and that if he had done so, he was sorry about it. But he pleaded that he had grown confused. The police were asking so many questions and he didn't know what to say anymore. He had told them what he believed they wanted to hear just to shut them up. As a rule, the attorneys generally tried to keep their personal feelings hidden, but on this occasion Cotton "smirked," Jesse later said, as if he didn't believe him.

The attorneys instructed him to keep his story as clean and as simple as possible. By first saying he did the crime, and then saying he didn't do it, he was creating confusion. Jesse understood that by admitting to it, they would claim insanity, for which he would "only be shut up for a year or two." So once again he admitted to committing the murder.

WHEN JESSE LATER WROTE his autobiography, he said he felt he had been maltreated and the confession taken under duress. This maltreatment had come in particular from Wood.

"They used nasty language to me, called me all sorts of names, and I venture to say that never was a boy my age placed before in such conditions. . . . I did not have hardly an idea of what I was arrested for," Pomeroy wrote, trying to elicit sympathy from his readers. "I was nearly dead with fear, and hardly knew what I was saying . . . our conversation I do not remember, but he [Wood] promised me that, if I told him what I did, he would do all he could for me when I was tried. I told him—for I had heard enough of the officers talk to know who, and what was done to the boy."

When journalists later learned that Jesse had confessed, they could not resist reporting that and it became difficult for them, as well as their readers, to come up with a plausible explanation for why he had committed those deeds.

"The boy Pomeroy seems to be a moral monstrosity," wrote the *Boston Globe*. "He had no provocation and no rational motive for his atrocious conduct. He did not know the little lad Millen at all, but enticed him away and cut and hacked him to death with a penknife nearly for sport." This behavior, the paper felt, fell under the umbrella of what was now considered moral insanity.

IT WAS THOMAS UPHAM'S 1840 medical book, *Outlines of Imperfect and Disordered Mental Actions*, that first popularized the idea of insanity, or of moral insanity. Upham's book applied the disorder to people who "give themselves up to their object for better or worse, not temporarily, as it were, through all time." The book touched upon such subjects as "insanity of the affections," and of the "moral sensibilities." But one term seemed to apply to Jesse even more than the others: *mania*, a form of "general derangement often involving violent behavior." This also included moral insanity and monomania.

Upham's book was not new to many of the reading public. It had been popularized by writers soon after its publication, particularly in the works of Herman Melville, who had studied it deeply and referenced it in his texts, assigning to characters in his novels many of the traits of moral insanity and monomania detailed by Upham. It was from Melville's works that readers and laymen alike had first become familiar with such terms as *moral insanity* and *mania*, words that were now being applied to Jesse Pomeroy.

Many of the physicians who accepted the notion of mania as a disease also believed it shifted patterns with the weather, more common during the extremes of heat and cold. But that was not so with Jesse, because he had committed his deeds at various times throughout the year, regardless of temperature shifts. But one thing working in his favor was age: for the most part, doctors were aware that mania first appeared in youth, progressed in early adulthood, and declined with advancing middle age.

Philippe Pinel had first conducted in-depth studies of moral insanity in France during the early 1800s, and classified it as *"comportment manie sans delire,"* or mania without delirium, though it was another physician, James Prichard, who coined the term *moral insanity*. His definition included "morbid perversion of the feeling, affections, and active powers, without any allusions or erroneous convictions impressed upon the understanding; sometimes coexisting with apparently unimpaired states of the intellectual faculties."

It could also include the feelings of hate, fear, and melancholy, all
of which Jesse was believed to be suffering from. This could very well
expand into *homicidal monomania*, which, if true, explained Jesse's doings.
"These maniacs perceive, compare, and judge correctly," the famed psychiatrist Jean-Étienne Dominique Esquirol had written. "But they are
drawn aside, from the slightest cause, and even without an object, to
the concession of acts of violence . . . they are irresistibly impelled, they
assure us . . . to destroy their fellow beings."

But this definition meant little to those who read that Jesse Pomeroy was thought to be a "moral monstrosity" or suffering from what
was called "moral insanity." What did moral insanity actually consist
of? Was it a defect of the brain, people asked? Did the illness reside in
the bones? Somewhere in the belly? The general public wanted something tangible, not some wishy-washy explanation from a doctor; they
needed something they could point a finger to and elicit an explanation
from. Everybody agreed that Jesse was suffering from something, yet
that something was invisible.

In June 1874, the Supreme Judicial Court of Massachusetts issued
a murder indictment against Jesse Harding Pomeroy, that he "feloni-
ously, willfully and of his malice aforethought, an assault did make."
Jesse pleaded not guilty, and his lawyers began to mount a defense by
reason of insanity.

CHAPTER 7

KATIE

I know indeed what evil I intend to do,
But stronger than all my afterthoughts is my fury,
Fury that brings upon mortals the greatest evils.

—EURIPIDES, *MEDEA*

Boston police had given up on finding Katie Curran, the little girl from Southie. With no new information on the case, interest had quickly waned, and those few who had gone to look for her stopped altogether. Only her mother and some neighbors continued to believe she had not gone that far and remained convinced she would return soon.

On the morning that she disappeared, she had been seen entering the Pomeroys' store, but it was not Charles she had encountered, but Jesse. Charles was off distributing his papers, and Jesse was left opening the shop. Since his return from Westborough, he had been trying hard to assimilate back in the neighborhood, but those in the community had not been pleased to see him return.

Jesse didn't usually run the shop, but instead worked for his brother as a newsboy. He carried nearly all the newspapers being published at the time, dragging them throughout South Boston as well as the downtown area of the city, where he enjoyed visiting what he referred to as "the burnt district." But it wasn't entirely unusual for him to be assigned tedious tasks at the store that were similar to ones he had performed at the reform school: get up early, cross the street, lift the gate, open the shop, sweep the floor, run a rag over the counters for the dust that had collected overnight, count the coins. He did everything in minutes, having learned efficiency at the reformatory school, showing what a good and responsible boy he was. Or so his mother said.

On that windblown day of March 18, some minutes after the shop opened, Jesse was met by William Kohr, a local boy who also worked for Charles. The two talked for a few minutes while Jesse counted some coins, until a little girl of no more than ten walked into the shop inquiring about some note cards, Kohr later remembered. Jesse said he believed he had one remaining in the basement that he could sell her for three cents, but before he opened the door to go downstairs, he asked Kohr for a favor: would he mind going out for some "cut-up meat"? His mother had told him to do so, but he had forgotten. William Kohr would later tell the police, Mrs. Curran, and anyone who asked that he had agreed and left the premises. The reporters latched on to this detail about the "cut-up meat" and wrote about it as they filed their stories. Kohr also told police that when Kohr returned from the errand, about ten minutes later, Jesse was still at the counter counting his coins, and the little girl was no longer in the store.

The police asked Kohr if he believed Jesse could have harmed Katie right there and then, but the boy said he didn't think so because the back of the store opened into Silver Street and there was a window that looked into that street. Anyone passing by could easily see inside. The police took this from Kohr as a suggestion that Jesse had somehow lured the little girl downstairs, but when they searched the basement of the shop, they found nothing to suggest that anything criminal had taken place.

DESPITE ALL THE EVIDENCE brought against Jesse, his mother continued to be his one and most fervent supporter. And she supported him loudly and spoke of his benevolence to neighbors and those who frequented her shop, which often included friends and relatives of the Millens and Currans. Around this time, there also emerged a rumor on the streets of South Boston that Ruth Ann had been "intimate" with Captain Dyer, the man who had claimed that little Katie had simply run away or perhaps drowned when playing near the harbor. Dyer also happened to be a friend of Gardiner Tufts, from the State Board of Charities, and both of them had played a role in Jesse's release from the reform school.

Captain Dyer was not discreet about his feelings about or connection to the Pomeroy woman, a matter neighbors of hers attributed to desperation: Mrs. Pomeroy was not a pleasant woman—nor was she an especially pretty one. It was unlikely that she would arouse lust in many a man. Neighbors scornfully glanced her way, looks Ruth Ann took full-on without bowing down or even averting her eyes for a second. After a while her own stares became so forceful and pointed that those same neighbors had to look away, aware that Ruth Ann feared no one and was ashamed of nothing. Only later would those same people understand Mrs. Pomeroy's own reasons for her entanglement with Captain Dyer.

The neighborhood's dislike for Ruth Ann increased as time passed, and not surprisingly her business suffered. People abandoned her altogether, and soon enough she could not even keep up with the rent and had to give up the store. On Sunday afternoon, March 31, neighbors watched as Ruth Ann and Charles dragged rolls of fabric, colorful spools of thread, and collections of sharp needles across the street to their apartment, from where she tried, without much success, to eke out a living.

One person watching was John Nash. He felt sorry for this joyless, chronically bitter creature, but he also realized an opportunity had opened up. He owned a little grocery store at 342 Broadway, not far from Ruth Ann's store, and for some time he had wanted to expand. As soon as Ruth Ann vacated the premises, Nash struck a deal with the owner, and for a low price bought the entire building next to his in June 1874. The whole structure had undergone renovations sometime before, but Nash decided to further improve it in order to allow for the larger space he had envisioned in his mind.

The cellar was the only spot that had stayed the same throughout the years. Just like others in the area, it was a rotten, fetid place that stretched beneath the entire building. It reeked with the stench from a little privy in the corner, and there were also two meters that occasionally let out a whiff of gas. If one dared to venture in the cellar he would be greeted by the drip . . . drip . . . drip . . . of a rusty faucet that leaked day and night. One dark corner held old wood and coal as well as a large mound of refuse.

When Nash purchased the store, the tenants living above began complaining to him about a "bad smell" they said had been coming from the basement since the end of May. John P. Margerson, who resided just above it, first noticed the stench when he went to get some wood and coal. For the most part, he did not know any of the tenants, including the Pomeroys, and did not associate with them, though once, while collecting firewood, Jesse had come down. The boy had stood a moment by the doorway looking at him, Margerson later said, and Jesse "did not get away till after I did." Margerson told Nash about the peculiarities of the cellar.

Margerson's wife, Nellie, also noticed the smell around June, and she had tried to find out where it was coming from. She had gone to the basement several times and made a handful of cursory searches, though she had never found anything unusual nor did she meet anyone there on those visits. But as the days progressed the odor increased, especially as the temperature grew warmer.

Some of the tenants thought an animal had crawled within a broken crevice and died there, the smell being its carcass decomposing. Others believed the culprit was the building's age, its foundation rotted, though it was not an unusually old building. Nash searched the cellar but did not find a source of the foul odor other than some papers that had been burned near the water closet. Still, to pacify his tenants, he hired two local workmen, Charles McGinnis and Patrick O'Connell, to empty out the cellar and sort through what had been left behind.

The hearty scent of mildew reached the two workmen as soon as they opened the cellar door, but as they stepped inside the stench became more visceral, like the sour smell of rotting meat. As they descended the staircase, the odor everybody had been complaining about became stronger, but they kept going because they were being paid good money to do this job. They placed handkerchiefs over their mouths and moved toward the heap of garbage, working quickly and methodically as the mound became smaller and smaller. On their second day of work, they made a gruesome discovery: preserved beneath the ashes, a forearm now jutted out, darkened by bits of decomposing flesh, the fabric that clothed it decaying and sticking to the remains.

THERE WASN'T MUCH LEFT of Katie Curran. Beneath the heap of coal and ash, her remains were in an advanced state of decomposition, the fabric of her clothing decayed. Those who saw her body were disturbed by what they soon learned: her skull had been detached from the rest of her body. During his examination, Coroner P. P. Ingalls was not able to determine if that had occurred because the murderer slit her throat so deeply he decapitated her, or if the two men working in the cellar had inadvertently struck her remains with a shovel. The two workers denied this, McGinnis being adamant that the body had come apart on its own and he "did not separate it." As the officers stared at the little girl's remains, they noticed that, except in a few spots, the flesh had been rotted away and mixed with the damp ashes and cement of the cellar.

Although the clothing was frayed, the officers could tell she had been wearing garments meant to keep her warm: a gray "shaggy" sack of sorts, adorned with black beaver trimming, white buttons, and a black silk braid. Under it she had tied a splotchy apron and a black little dress tucked at the waist, a blue flannel petticoat, white cotton underwear and chemise, and a pair of white cotton stockings. Katie had gone out wearing mittens, and they were still on her hands when she was found.

The coroner found it extremely difficult to examine her and removed each article of clothing delicately and carefully. But following a thorough examination, there were several things Ingalls and the police were able to ascertain: Katie's clothes had either been ripped or cut down the front of her body; it looked to Ingalls as if the front seams had been torn apart without any attempt to undo the buttons or unbuckle the waistband. A portion of her petticoat had also been cut away around the middle. The chemise had rotted away, so this could not tell them anything.

Although her thighs and abdomen were already putrefying, the coroner was able to determine that several wounds had been inflicted with a sharp instrument, possibly a knife. Near her groin he also found a stab wound, one that bloomed all the way to her genitals; this had commenced at her abdomen, although in that spot the flesh was now decayed, and he could not tell precisely the point where the knife had entered.

Katie also had a cut near the side of her abdomen, nearly five inches long. The upper portion of her body was entirely degraded, so it was impossible to tell if any wounds had been inflicted on her chest and upper torso. She had suffered several broken bones throughout her body, and a large fracture to her skull. The coroner concluded the blow to the head had been strong enough not only to subdue her but might actually have killed her. It seemed very plain that Katie's clothing had been pulled apart, or ripped, before the stab wounds were inflicted because the fabrics that remained did not show any cuts through them. Shockingly, the white stockings were still on her legs, held in place by tight rubber bands.

Ingalls determined that there was nothing skillful in the way the stab wounds had been inflicted, the implication being that the murder had been committed by someone who was either relatively new at it, in a frenzy, or frightened by the experience.

Detective Wood was also brought into the Katie Curran case, and he too agreed with the coroner's explanation of the events. He believed Katie had been drawn down to the cellar perhaps with the notion of seeing some newborn kittens, a ruse that often worked on the young ones. The girl had walked ahead of Jesse, Wood surmised, whereupon "half-way down he seized her by her hair, and pulling her hair back-ward, cut her throat. He then dug a hole in the cellar and buried her," which he then covered up with a heap of garbage.

Although this made sense, the whole ordeal must have commenced and ended in the span of ten minutes, because Jesse was back upstairs by the time Kohr returned from his errand. This gave Wood some pause because a young boy who most likely didn't have experience mur-dering and hiding people would have needed vastly more than ten min-utes to commit the crime. It was also unusual that there was no trace of blood on the floor and walls. All in all, with the Katie Curran murder and the Horace Millen murder, the detectives had nothing more than a lot of circumstantial evidence. But Wood didn't mind this at all. He preferred this to eyewitness testimony, which he said was often extremely unreliable.

When the detectives arrived at Katie's home, it was apparent that Mrs. Curran and her husband had been expecting them. She was wear-ing a swath of black garments, and the detectives saw instantly that she had aged since they had last seen her. She wailed upon hearing that her daughter's body had been found and what condition it was in. The detectives unfurled a tiny bundle for her to scrutinize. It was a tattered patch of fabric from the shawl Katie had been wearing the morning she went out for a few minutes to buy a school notebook.

AS WORD GOT OUT that Katie's body had been found, crowds began to push their way onto the street and toward the house on Broadway, lunging forward toward the basement for a better view of the place, as if anything at all of Katie still remained.

On July 19, 1874, the *Boston Globe* immediately echoed the feel-ings surging throughout the neighborhood—the belief that Jesse was responsible for this crime as well: "There must be something wrong in the regulations under which an inmate of the Reform School, sentenced for his minority, can be pardoned out on probation and turned loose on the community without regard to the crimes that he had committed or the propensity which he had displayed."

In addition to the extreme anger felt toward Mrs. Pomeroy, some explanation was demanded from Captain Dyer. He had shown considerable "laxity" in his search for Katie, and many felt this was in part due to his feelings for Mrs. Pomeroy, which the whole neighborhood was aware of. They shouted defiantly for him to appear and explain himself, but he would not. No one in the crowd knew that when Dyer learned Katie's body had been found, he had gone home, eager for a nap.

As it stood, the stories that were printed proved to be harsh toward not only Jesse Pomeroy, but the police department as well, who had failed so miserably in the search for Katie Curran. An article printed in the *New York Times* on July 21 showed that the story had not only reached the outskirts of Boston, but had traveled well beyond the confines of Massachusetts and was now being followed closely everywhere with the same fervor Bostonians were displaying. The *Times* said in part: "[I]t may be said that Boston is not to be congratulated in the skills of its detective Police." These were the same detectives who were often called down to New York when help was needed. Now they were being rebuffed. The *Times* continued: "A four months' search for a missing child failed to discern anything, though the remains were thinly buried in an ash heap in the cellar of the home in which a boy charged with the murder lived when the child disappeared."

On the very same day the article appeared in the *New York Times*, Mayor Samuel C. Cobb asked to speak to Captain Dyer, urging an emergency meeting at Boston City Hall. He had just received a visit from J. J. Flynn, a representative from the South Boston community, where Katie lived, explaining the reasons that the neighborhood felt Dyer had been so unconcerned in his search for the little girl. Flynn had included the belief that the amorous feelings Dyer possessed for Mrs. Pomeroy had clouded his judgment.

Cobb was the only man who had not known of Dyer's friendship with Mrs. Pomeroy, and on July 21 insisted on speaking to the captain to air out their grievances. Sitting in a somewhat uncomfortable position, Dyer denied all the accusations being flung against him. He had searched the store for Katie, he told Mayor Cobb, but had found nothing. He had initially monitored Jesse, he explained; he had watched his doings, his walking paths, his habits, but eventually, Dyer said, Jesse had proved to be of no trouble to anyone so the vigilance was relaxed. Dyer did not divulge anything about his relationship with Ruth Ann, nor did he say anything about his friendship with Gardiner Tufts. Mayor Cobb listened but was adamant that Captain Dyer needed to resign.

Also in late July a reporter from the *Boston Globe* visited Gardiner Tufts with the intention of asking about his instrumental role in Jesse's release from the reform school. The reporter wanted to know how he felt now about the boy, now that two children were dead and Jesse was standing trial for murder. Colonel Tufts fumbled with an explanation and said he would express himself only in writing. He was allowed to do so and released a statement to the reporter, which was published on July 23, 1874.

Tufts said that Jesse had been given a thorough medical examination upon arriving at the reform school and had been pronounced completely sane. He had also shown model conduct, making him a prime candidate for rehabilitation. After sixteen months family situations were examined and deemed not only suitable, but also comfortable enough for his return. Jesse was to go to work with his mother in the store and perform the required tasks that would keep him busy.

Everyone seemed on board with letting Jesse go, everyone that is, other than a handful of officers in South Boston, who told the Board of Charities that several local families had indicated their displeasure with Jesse's return. Those same officers also feared that Jesse would be harmed by those very same families. "The families are very indignant," the officers told the Board of Charities.

All the paperwork had been given to the superintendent of the reform school. In turn, the superintendent had asked for Captain Dyer's opinion. Dyer felt kindly toward Jesse and knew there would be no issue with him returning home, most especially if Jesse minded his own business. Dyer also assured everybody that if someone still bothered Jesse, he would offer him protection. Dyer concluded it was just to "give him a chance to redeem himself," because "it wasn't best to be down on a boy too hard for too long." This had been only his personal opinion, but it was effective because Jesse had been released on February 6.

When Katie's remains were discovered, Chief Savage, accompanied by Chief of Detectives James W. Twombly, visited Jesse at the Suffolk County Jail to tell him and hopefully to get him to confess to the crime. Jesse received the news as he did everything else, quietly perched atop his bunk, seemingly bothered only by having been roused from sleep. They then told him his mother and brother had also been arrested and charged with conspiracy. They did not say it was actually "supposed complicity," and that the arrest really meant nothing. They knew that neither Ruth Ann nor Charles had done anything; but rather, they had been escorted to the police station for their own safety. A large crowd had gathered outside their apart-

Ten-year-old Katie Curran was the first known murder victim of Jesse Pomeroy, though her remains were not found until well after the murder of Horace Millen. On March 18, 1874, she disappeared from her South Street home, in South Boston, while on her way to a tobacconist to buy a school essential. The last known place that she was seen alive was a shop owned by the Pomeroys. Although several searches were conducted by the police, including in the Pomeroys' shop itself, these were done halfheartedly, and her remains were not found until late June of 1874, some three months after her disappearance. (*Charlestown Public Library*)

ment, and it was growing ferocious, a pulsating entity with a natural bent toward revenge.

Jesse said he didn't think his mother had done anything nor that she knew anything about it. In his later autobiography, Jesse wrote that he felt bad for his mother and became determined to save her, as if out of a sense of obligation. "I felt bad that they were arrested, and resolved to do all I could to get them out, so I kept in my mind the proverb, 'One may as well be hanged for stealing a sheep as for stealing a lamb,' altering it to suit my case, 'One may as well be hanged for killing one as two, etc.'" he wrote. "So in the morning I had resolved to say I did it, but if I confessed to one I must the other, I said to myself, but, however, as I said it, I kept in my mind the proverb, and as I knew well enough of the facts, I set to work to think out how I could give testimony of killing the girl."

AVIDLY SEARCHING FOR LINKS of a familial predisposition for blood, crime, and mental defects, in July 1874 the *Boston Globe* ran a particularly vile article that spun a tale of gore and blood in which Mrs. Pomeroy became the main protagonist, and on which Jesse's behavior could be blamed. Although the article implied she had consented to the interview, Ruth Ann always denied that she had.

"Among other things," the article said, "she said that her husband was a butcher, and that during the period of her pregnancy she went daily to the slaughterhouse to witness the killing of the animals, and that somehow she took a particular delight in seeing her husband butcher the sheep, the calves, and the cattle, and not infrequently she assisted him in this bloody work." The article went on to claim that she said "that after Jesse was born and became old enough to hold a knife in his hands, he was all the time, when opportunity afforded, jabbing a knife into pieces of meat, and when still older and about his father's market, he did the same thing. . . . He was simply *marked* by his mother, as other children had been, only in a different way."

When Thomas Pomeroy read the articles about his son and his ex-wife, he also took to the papers. Pomeroy said that the whole idea of his butchering animals having something to do with Jesse's attitude was utterly ludicrous. Pomeroy also quickly pointed out that he had never really killed any animals at all and his job had simply involved moving pieces of meat from one market to another.

"I never saw animals of any kind being slaughtered," he told the paper. He also thought the idea of Jesse's being marked rather silly. "I do not believe in the theory of persons being marked. . . . The only gentleman of science that questioned me on the subject of Jesse was a phrenologist, and he did not seem able to understand Jesse's mania at all."

Pomeroy went on to say that Jesse had never struck any animals, nor had he stuck a knife into dead meat at any point. "I think his vaccination had more of an effect on him than anything else," he said, echoing Jesse's belief that the smallpox vaccine had made him ill. "He was vaccinated when he was four years old and shortly after, his face broke out and had the appearance of raw flesh, and some fluid issued from the wounds that burned my own [skin] when it dropped on it, from which I judged the fluid to be poison."

Some readers latched on to that statement, immediately feeling that Jesse's whole being had been poisoned. "That lasted until he was six months old," his father went on, "when his whole body was covered with large abscesses, one of which was over the eye, and caused the cast or fallen appearance that it wears now."

Thomas Pomeroy was not the only one who did not believe in the idea of being marked by a person's job, or by blood, as the papers were implying. Well-known doctors such as P. P. Ingalls, the physician and coroner from South Boston who had examined Katie's remains, agreed that the whole so-called theory seemed preposterous. He had never heard of such a case nor had he witnessed one in his practice or received information from his colleagues, which would have made the theory valid. Still, some persisted. Dr. Ingalls said no, but when pestered further agreed that perhaps just because he hadn't heard of a case didn't mean that none existed. And that was enough. But Ingalls went on, declaring the boy needed to be studied for further evaluation.

But in one editorial that had appeared earlier in the *Globe*, on April 24, 1874, a sentence pointed to Jesse's apparent defect, one that many adhered to in explaining Jesse's crimes and had nothing to do with his mother's delight for blood nor his father's butchering ways: Jesse suffered from what was called "Moral Depravity." He was a monomaniac.

A FIERCE DEBATE ABOUT what to do with Jesse Pomeroy had been going on since little Horace Millen's body was found near the marshes. It revolved around an age-old question: how does one go about discriminating between what is legally right and morally right? Despite his age— Jesse was now fourteen—some people expected nothing less than an execution. Others wondered how responsible Jesse was for his behavior and actions. Did he know the difference between right and wrong?

"We sent him to a reform school, and some meddlesome interloper forthwith stepped in, snapped his fingers at the law and Jesse was pardoned out," an unnamed author editorialized in the *Boston Globe* in July 1874. "If we send him to the penitentiary for life, he is sure as statistics to be pardoned out at the end of six years, by which time he will be a man; and if a youngster kills two and tortures twenty before he is sixteen, who can tell what feats of homicide he may perform at twenty-one? If he is put into a lunatic asylum, the chances are that he will be sane enough to escape, or to lull his keepers into a belief of sanity."

What was to be done with him? For many, the only likely place to hold him was the Bastille, Boston's infamous prison. They believed that what Jesse actually needed was long-term imprisonment to cure him of his immorality and murderous tendencies.

SUCH A STINT IN the state prison would have brought Jesse back to his old neighborhood of Charlestown, which he had left in August

1872. Like those who lived in Charlestown, the prison was familiar to him and his family, as were the noises that escaped from the building on a daily basis. But Charlestown had not been the first site declared for the prison.

Governor John Winthrop was the first to order that Castle Island, in Boston Harbor, be used as one of the earliest prison fortifications in Massachusetts. He did so in the summer of 1634. In 1776 the British blew it up, though troops under the command of Lieutenant Paul Revere were immediately sent to restore it. On March 14, 1785, the General Court of Massachusetts passed a provision "providing that the island within the Harbor of Boston, commonly called Castle Island, shall be a place for the reception and secure confinement of all such persons as shall be sentenced to confinement and hard labor for the term of their natural lives, or for any shorter space of time." Eventually it was renamed Fort Independence, although it continued to be known as Castle Island.

One of the most famous enlisted men to serve on the island was named "Edgar A. Perry," the alias used by American author Edgar Allan Poe. Poe served eight months in 1827 on Fort Independence while a member of Company H in the First U.S. Artillery. While there, he became aware of the legend surrounding the Christmas Day duel in 1817 between Lieutenant Robert F. Massie and Lieutenant Gustavus Drane. The two young men, while drunk, had engaged in a fight that quickly escalated into a duel which ended in Massie's death.

Although several servicemen witnessed the duel, and while Drane had not been well liked by any of them, none of those servicemen agreed to testify against him, which resulted in Drane being transferred rather than court-martialed. This was the official story given, but the legend told of the same witnesses later delivering their own version of justice toward Drane. Poe must have liked the story because it formed the basis for "The Cask of Amontillado," which was published in *Godey's Lady's Book* in 1846.

The idea of having a prison on Castle Island had originally seemed ideal, as it was only a short distance from the mainland of Boston. But that very distance proved its undoing. During the summer, when the waters were at their warmest, inmates would escape by swimming all the way to shore. And in winter, when the water was iced over, it provided escapees a direct, albeit slick road to liberty.

In 1803 the Massachusetts Senate passed a bill to begin building that year a new state prison onshore. The nearly five acres of land in Charlestown, near Lynde's Pond, a green and calm spot just outside Boston proper, had been chosen not only for its apparent beauty, but also to bely the penitentiary's true intentions.

The prison was located inside a quadrangle, which encompassed a large and separate kitchen, along with a small church. Built entirely of granite, the structure was nearly 250 feet long and 40 feet wide. Its four floors held 304 cells, each one measuring a little more than 7 feet by 3½ feet wide, their short height only adding to the place's already claustrophobic feel. The doors were made of iron, and each cell contained an iron grating located on its highest position to allow faint light to stream in.

William Crawford, an Englishman who visited the prison, wrote of his experiences in a book called *Penitentiaries*, which he published in 1834, and in which he provided a detailed description: "The walls . . . which are 18 feet high, enclose a quadrangular space, about 500 feet in length and 240 feet in width, and are bounded on the northern and western sides by a creek and river. Approaching the prison on the south side is a commodious wharf. The buildings of the old prison . . . consist of two wings, with the warden's apartments and guardrooms in the center," he said. "In the rear of the buildings is a garden and a warehouse next to the wharf. Along the top of the prison walls is a platform on which several watch-boxes for sentinels are placed at convenient distances. On the west side a basin has been constructed for admitting canal boats, by which stone, wood, & C are conveyed to the prison through an opening, which is secured by strong gates. Near the dock is a large shed, 130 feet long and 60 feet wide, open to the roof, in which convicts are employed cutting and working stone. There are also workshops occupied by cabinet makers, tailors, shoe makers, brush-makers, coppers, and blacksmiths."

The first two convicts arrived at the prison on December 12, 1805, and by the end of the month, the population had risen to thirty-four. For the prisoners' uniforms, the board decided on a humiliating combination of half-red and half-blue fabric. But more important, the officers guarding the prison were given a gun and a box containing at least twelve cartridges, along with a bayonet to be used as the prison's regulations decreed, giving the officers a certain measure of protection.

Most prisoners were young, brought up in "an unstable home, lacking any formal education or apprenticeship," which allowed the youngsters to fall "at the bottom of the economic ladder . . . [and] given his desperate economic condition, he [the typical inmate] fell [into] bad company," one of its earliest chaplains, Rev. Jared Curtis, surmised. Most inmates were being imprisoned for crimes against property, and only a few were committed for murder.

A large majority of them were from foreign countries, and a disproportionate number, oddly enough, had worked as mariners and captains at sea. Curtis thought there was nothing odd about this. Lack of funds often prompted young men to try their luck on the open waters, and there they would be brought "in contact with some whose depravity was notorious and seemingly infectious."

One inmate told Curtis his companions aboard a whaleboat had been "a very wicked set of fellows," who had instructed him to "swear, drink, gamble & everything else that was bad." He blamed his experience on the boat for his subsequent life of crime and mental decline.

On February 24, 1806, the prison suffered its first escape: an inmate managed to unshackle himself and scale the walls of the prison. Despite its reputation, an attempt had not only been made but in fact brought to fruition. The man was never found. By 1807 the prison was swelling with inmates. Rev. Curtis wrote in his diary that the prison was populated with "the most incorrigible and God-forsaken men that I ever found. Malicious, impudent, sourly, denying God & man."

The guards were subjected to a devious and unruly crowd, and despite the prison's strict laws, escape attempts occurred frequently. On one occasion an officer shot an inmate in the hand while he attempted to jump over a wall. The question of whether an officer had the right to shoot an inmate continued to be discussed and took on a greater significance when another inmate was shot and killed during a failed try for freedom. But the guards remained armed, and in the late 1860s, Warden Gideon Haynes, a former state senator, pointed out that officers were given loaded pistols as part of their uniforms, which seemed to "imply the right to use them should occasion require."

As the prison became even more crowded and methods of control failed, other regulatory methods became customary, including the use of mental degradation and solitary confinement, which had been implemented in the 1830s.

Solitary confinement had originated at the Eastern State Penitentiary, which was built in Philadelphia in 1829. The method was inspired by Quaker philosophy. The initial intention was that if the offenders could be kept isolated for a time, they could find their way to a higher self, to a higher power, to God. This would eventually reform them. Inmates were placed alone in their cells with only an open view of the sky visible from a hole in the ceiling, called at various times the Eye of God or the Dead Eye.

Looking skyward was supposed to lead to spiritual enlightenment, but the dreary light coming in on dismal days did not inspire repentance or prayer, and the results of the experiment became apparent soon enough: instead of the inmates finding God or nirvana, they went crazy. Some withdrew into themselves; others who hadn't been outwardly violent when they came in became even more so; and still many more lost their mental faculties altogether. An inmate at the Eastern State Penitentiary named Harry Hauser went on to call his experience in isolation "a living tomb." But despite this, solitary confinement was still implemented in many other prisons, including Massachusetts State Prison.

At Charlestown, prisoners were actually not allowed to talk to one another once they were locked inside their cells. Guards were posted at spots where they could allegedly "hear a whisper from the most distant cell." Even such a whisper would be severely punished. The punishment followed a strict gradation system: initially, solitary confinement would be enforced for a few days, meaning that the inmate wouldn't even be able to take his meals with his fellow prisoners anymore. Usually this was terrifying enough that after a few days, the person reformed.

Sometimes the warden was forced to take away more of the few privileges the inmates had been granted. Instead of solitary confinement while looking skyward, it would now be in total darkness. If this didn't work, what followed was the removal of food, and if this wasn't enough, the prisoner's cot would be revoked. Thus the inmate was left alone, settled in darkness, hungry, and made to sleep on the cold cement floor.

Still, to many these punishments were mild compared to the ones inmates underwent at Sing Sing Prison, in Ossining, New York, where corporal punishment was added. When asked about it once, Elam Lynds, one of its famed wardens, who served from 1825 until 1830, admitted that he didn't find the use of the lash particularly brutal: "It was necessary to begin with curbing the spark of the prisoner, and convincing him of his weakness," he said.

By this time prisons, much like asylums, had become popular tourist attractions. The Massachusetts State Prison was not the only one to receive an influx of daily visitors; Cherry Hill in Philadelphia and Sing Sing in New York were two of the most popular in the country. In the winter of 1827, Rev. Jared Curtis, in a letter to his son, wrote that "probably the number who will have visited the prison . . . during the last and mid-present months will not fall short of three thousand."

In 1831 Alexis de Tocqueville, a French magistrate, visited the United States and its prisons. Like many other Europeans involved in the legal system, he had heard about the "success" American prisons were having with their prisoners. He was determined to know why. Upon arriving and visiting several of the institutions, he immediately understood the reasons behind it: solitary confinement. It was the silence that made prisons so successful. While, taken at face value, this seemed like the advent of a new reform policy, in actuality it frightened him, as he mentioned while visiting the prison at Auburn, New York, where "the silence within these vast walls . . . [is] that of death," he wrote. "There were a thousand living beings living in there . . . and yet it was a desert solitude."

But it wasn't just solitary confinement that kept convicts in check. In 1849 a new method of punishment being used at other prisons, called the shower bath, was instituted at the Massachusetts State Prison. As described by Warden Gideon Haynes: "the convict, after being divested of his clothing, was seated in a small closet, his legs, arms, and neck closely confined in wooden stacks, rendering it impossible for him to move or change position in the slightest degree; the water, which fell six or eight feet, could be let on in small or large quantities on the will of the operator, usually varying from half a barrel to four barrels. This mode of punishment . . . has been unquestionable proven to be injurious in many cases, and sometimes fatal. It is, perhaps, the most inhuman form of punishment inflicted in modern times."

One of the convicts most often subjected to the shower baths was Abner Rogers Jr. Rogers, who was serving a five-year sentence for larceny, was very disruptive and had already spent a great deal of time in solitary confinement. On June 14, 1843, he was heard making a ruckus while in isolation, so much so that he was removed from that cell and subjected to several stints in the shower baths, after which he was sent to work. The punishment didn't settle him and seemed to bring on even more outbursts. Warden Charles Lincoln Jr. noticed this as he passed by the shop some minutes after 5 P.M. with a visitor, and made note of it to the man walking with him. Shortly after Lincoln mentioned these outbursts, Rogers sprung from his chair and dug a knife into the warden's neck, killing him instantly. Rogers was immediately taken to his cell.

Sometime later, Rogers was taken into the prison yard, where the warden's body was laid out. He didn't cry out at the sight, but trembled violently and asked: "It is the warden. Oh dear! Have I killed him? Can it be?"

After that, shower baths were no longer used as a form of punishment. Rogers was tried and acquitted on the grounds of insanity, then sent to the insane asylum in Worcester, where he committed suicide a few months later by jumping out of a window.

The next warden was not surprised by Rogers's murderous act, nor by the ones other convicts committed: "Is it strange that, driven to desperation by the lash and shower-bath, with intellect and reason often clouded, they should sometimes turn upon their tormentors and, taking vengeance into their own hands, astonish and electrify the community with the atrociousness of the crimes they were capable of committing?"

Prisoners were meant to obey and be degraded or, as Lynds put it, "convicts ought to be brought to the situation of clay in the hands of the potter, subject to be molded to whatever form the government of the person may think necessary to secure the cooperation."

BY 1874, MANY BOSTONIANS felt that Jesse Harding Pomeroy, a fourteen-year-old boy possibly suffering from some form of mental illness, deserved a stint in the state prison, to be molded precisely like the clay spoken of, to keep company with many of its hardened criminals because he had become no better than any of them. But for others the prison and the punishments it inflicted were far too mild. What Pomeroy truly deserved was a noose around his neck.

Although he had not been found guilty yet, most people believed he would be and that death was the only fitting end for him. The *Worcester Gazette* echoed the public sentiment and its support of a quick hanging and wrote: "To us it seems only rational to consider him something less than a human being—to a certain extent, an animal, dangerous and cunning. It will then be a duty—to put him out of the world, and we are not sure but this course would be quite as much a kindness to him as a matter of justice to the country."

Jesse was an anomaly in a society that sought out order and justice, and in trying to reconcile with the idea of justice and evil as they figured in the form of a fourteen-year-old boy, the death penalty became but a kindness bestowed onto him from the loving people of Massachusetts.

CHAPTER 8

THE WOLF AND THE LAMB

Silent and still, near Bunker Hill

A prison stands high and frowningly

Its walls, though old, Have a touch of gold

As the morning sun comes crowningly

Tis a lonely home, Under the gray dome

That looms in the air so boldly.

The world outside, A changing tide,

Ever will turn from it coldly.

—POEM FROM AN UNKNOWN CONVICT IN THE
MASSACHUSETTS STATE PRISON

As December 8 neared, doctors continued to interview Jesse Pomeroy. The state had also hired a well-known Boston psychiatrist named John E. Tyler as a consultant to talk to Jesse in order to conclude whether the boy was insane. Jesse's lawyers always agreed to these interviews, and Jesse appeared more than willing to speak to as many doctors as would come his way. His lawyers and the doctors did not deny he was a killer; but they wanted to make the case that he had been overcome by a sudden impulse that caused him to strike against the victims.

But if that were true, critics rebutted, how did Jesse's lawyers explain that even for his crimes against the children in Chelsea and South Boston, he had waited until he was alone, then walked across the bridges and carefully selected each child, brought along a knife and rope, and made sure no one saw him lure the child away? And more important, he had taken precautions to avoid being seen when he was finished with the crime. He had employed a similar method in the murder of Horace Millen, and a pattern of wickedness had been evidenced with Katie Curran. Someone operating on impulse would not make such moves, which represented clear-cut premeditation.

Dr. Tyler met Jesse at the Suffolk County Jail (also known as the Charles Street Jail) while he was awaiting trial. They met first on September 16, 1874, and on several occasions afterward, as December 8 approached. Tyler noticed that aside from his albino eye, Jesse seemed in good health and displayed very good eating and sleeping habits. Jesse sat quietly and studiously in his cell, and appeared "rested." But Tyler was there to evaluate his moral capabilities, not his physical stamina.

Jesse said he felt no pity for the children he had abused, nor for the ones who died at his hands. Tyler was of the initial impression that the boy recalled the events only vaguely and did not understand why he had done what he did. "He refers to a peculiar sensation, commencing in the lower part of the left side of his head, and passing over the crown to the other side, as having always proceeded those acts of violence."

Jesse told the doctor he could feel vibrating noises in his head, a roaring in his ears as if from an approaching thunderstorm. Tyler wondered if a case of "mania, melancholy, and dementia" was the culprit.

Tyler asked Jesse to explain further those feelings he experienced in the head. In his later autobiography, Jesse detailed what he had said to the doctor and why. "As I had been subject to head aches I told him of the pain, so in reality it was nothing but the literal truths only applied to a subject which might do our case good," he wrote. "I told him (Tyler) that at the time of doing it and just before, a sudden pain would start near my ear (just under it), and go from one side to the other; that the feeling which accompanied it as that I must do something, which something I did not know; but just at that time other feelings would come, telling me to whip or kill the boy or girl, as the case was, and that it seemed to me that I could not help doing it. That was the explanation I gave of the pain in all the cases."

What Tyler didn't realize—or preferred not to acknowledge—was that Jesse Pomeroy was toying with him. Jesse further admitted in his autobiography that he thought the doctor was very amusing, a "nice little gentleman" and someone to whom he could easily tell a "story." He tried very hard to convince Tyler he had not meant to hurt the children, that he yearned for "mere companionship," though he was then overcome by strange feelings and "he could not help doing" what he did.

No one believed him, of course, and on April 24 the *Boston Globe* had editorialized, "The plea of criminals, whether juveniles or adults, that they cannot help it, is a dangerous one. It may be that they are driven on by an impulse to evil that seems to them uncontrollable, but we are inclined to think that means might be found to check this indulgence in evil propensities."

Jesse lied throughout his interviews and in his autobiography even acknowledged that he'd done so. "I resolved to make it appear that I did not remember all the circumstances attending the crimes," he wrote, "and I also knew my counsel would have to make a plea of insanity for my doing it."

It became apparent that Jesse had read the articles written about insanity and moral insanity in regards to his trial. Aware of the famous cases involving mental derangements, including ones presided over the past by Justice Lemuel Shaw, he went about molding himself into the character he believed had the best chance of getting away with murder.

Dr. Tyler and Jesse met several times, and in his final report, the doctor wrote: "None of his statements respecting the homicides were clear; on the contrary, they were dreamy and confused . . . when asked why, his reply is always, 'I had to . . .' None of the usual incentives to crime appear in his case: no offence had been taken, no grudges, no envy felt, no type of gain or advantage appear . . . if no reasonable and satisfactory *external* motive for these extraordinary acts exist [sic], or can be found, then we are compelled to look internally." Tyler proposed several organic diseases, including epilepsy, but somehow none of the symptoms associated with the illness seemed to fit Jesse. Then Tyler arrived at a possible conclusion and solution over what to do with the boy: "It is evident that such a boy as this should be *carefully* restrained of his *liberty that others may not be endangered*" (emphasis in original). He also wrote: "The disposal of the boy must certainly be such as will secure the safety of others. . . . It is my belief he is *insane*."

WHEN THE TRIAL BEGAN, Jesse's behavior in the courtroom did not help his case. He smirked at the evidence, twirled his fingers, and even let it be known he was bored during the testimony of those who spoke on his behalf, most especially when his mother gracelessly took to the witness box. She stared at the jury and the spectators, her face pinched so tight she appeared to be in pain. Jesse's attorneys, Joseph H. Cotton and E. G. Walker, as well as Charles W. Robinson Jr., who joined the team two days later, had advised her not to look so scornful and to soften her features; she was to refrain herself from blaming the victims and their families, and, most of all, to keep her sneering to a minimum. Her job was to elicit sympathy for her son.

Ruth Ann wrung a handkerchief in her hands and occasionally passed it across her eyes. Those nearest to the witness box later remarked that it must have been for show because her eyes remained dry throughout her testimony. She vehemently disputed the evidence against her son and instead described a beloved little boy who had suffered from various illnesses, most especially one he had as a toddler, which doctors said was "brain fever" and made him delirious and shivery for three days.

She said he couldn't sleep a full night and during the daytime was assaulted by vicious and relentless headaches. He also suffered from dizziness he could not rid himself of, and was pursued by nightmares that trickled into his daytime hours. He was never the same again, she said. It was also as a small child that his malformed eye had come into being. She described in full details Jesse's beatings at the hands of his father, Thomas Pomeroy, the double-folded belt over his naked backside and legs, his running away to the river, only to have Thomas follow him and drag him back to their house.

Ruth Ann also told about the shop she had rented on Broadway, beneath which Katie Curran's body had been found. She hadn't seen any blood in the cellar, nor did she notice any bad smells while she was still in possession of the space. Even Charles, who had often frequented the cellar, hadn't mentioned seeing anything strange, not even around the water closet, where Katie's remains were found. Furthermore, she added, Charles and Jesse had shared a bed—wouldn't Charles have noticed if his brother's clothes had been stained with blood?

When Charles took the stand, he also said he had not seen anything unusual in the cellar or in his brother's demeanor. He had been present when a search of the basement was conducted the previous April, he said, even accompanying and helping Officer Adams and Officer Griggs from Police Station Six. Charles hadn't noticed any ashes around the water closet and was sure all the stones spoken of had been there since his family moved in.

Griggs admitted that they spent no longer than an hour looking through the space, particularly near the water closet, where they probed "the dirt and ashes" with a cane, as they had neglected to bring a shovel to help them with the ordeal. They looked through the stones, which to him seemed to have been there untouched for a long time. The floors and wall showed no evidence that a child had been murdered and, in his opinion, "we should have found the body if it had been there at that time." This statement startled those in attendance, and gave credence to Mrs. Pomeroy's theory that Katie's body was placed in the cellar by someone else who had killed her elsewhere.

Griggs also said Katie's murder did not fit Jesse's pattern. It did not resemble Horace's murder in the least. The girl's murder was a crime of opportunity. It seemed to have occurred at the spur of the moment, when the girl showed up to buy a note card. In Horace's case, the murder had been planned, the boy chosen, decoyed, then murdered on the beach. The evidence in Katie's murder could indicate that Jesse hadn't done it at all.

These observations should have caused people in the community to doubt the charges against Jesse and to have granted Ruth Ann some sympathy. But they didn't; Officer Griggs's assertions were quickly forgotten.

A neighbor of Ruth Ann's also testified, and maybe unintentionally helped her. A Mrs. Margaret said she occasionally took in the Pomeroys' laundry and did so on the days around March 18. She had not noticed blood staining any of Jesse's garments, as she certainly would have. Blood was distinctive on clothing and difficult to get rid of.

A young woman named Minnie Chapman, who worked for Mrs.

Pomeroy, also took the stand and spoke of Mrs. Pomeroy and what she knew of her sons. Minnie was just seventeen years old and had been acquainted with Ruth Ann from her days in Charlestown. The young woman still lived in Charlestown, though on occasion she stayed with Ruth Ann when the weather was tough or when she did not want to travel. She never opened the shop herself but rather started her workday around noon, and she knew both Pomeroy brothers well.

Charles, the one closer to her in age, she said, appeared more dependable and industrious and helped his mother; lately he had also taken on a newspaper delivery route, even hiring several of the younger neighborhood children to work for him. Minnie admired these traits in Charles, though when it came to Jesse, she could not say very much, or preferred not to.

The crowd noticed that she was not very fond of him, reporters later said, that she did not find him as helpful around the store as Charles was, saying that he always bickered with his brother and his mother. On the day of the little girl's disappearance, she had gone to the store around noon, her usual time, and found Jesse there. No, she hadn't seen anything strange about him, she testified. No more than the usual.

As people spoke for and against him, Jesse folded his hands behind his neck and stared intensely at the ceiling as if a painting had been forming there; he was even heard chuckling under his breath. He seemed to be making a mockery of the judicial proceedings, which those in attendance did not appreciate. Prior to the trial, he had told some of the jail guards that no jury would send a boy his age to the gallows. His lawyers, Jesse said, had been arguing insanity, and he believed he would spend at most a year or two in one of the state's finest mental facilities. But against the theory of insanity was Dr. Theodore W. Fisher, who, along with some colleagues, felt that Jesse's violence was driven by jealousy.

Fisher was among the experts who believed that Jesse's hatred of the children was spurred by resentment and enviousness, particularly toward Horace, who, unlike Jesse, was a handsome boy much loved by his family. Did it surprise anyone that one of the wounds he had inflicted on the child had been a stab in the right eye, precisely in the same spot where Jesse's own albino eye had grown? These experts thought Jesse's hatred and antipathy ran so deep it was impossible for him to ignore.

Fisher also said this hatred and grudge was made worse by the hobbies Jesse indulged in: the "twin evils" of masturbation and dime novels.

ONE PHYSICIAN WHO HAD agreed with this notion of masturbation and dime novels leading to insanity was Isaac Ray, a particularly friendly and communicative man who enjoyed sharing his knowledge with others. He was one of the foremost experts in legal insanity, and in 1838 he wrote a book titled *A Treatise on the Medical Jurisprudence of Insanity*, where he detailed the relationship between mental illness and the law.

One of his other famous books, published in 1863, was *Mental Hygiene*, and in both texts Ray reiterated the idea that books like dime novels, and the more scandalous publications such as the penny dreadfuls, played an important role in the formation of mental illness: "Murder, suicide, and other crimes, need only to be brought before the attention, in the shape of some actual example, especially if marked by striking incidents, in order to be repeated by many in whom, by reason of objective training, or morbid tendencies, whether congenital or acquired, or both combined, such narratives always touch some congenital chord," he wrote.

"The truth is, they often excite the very class of emotion in which those examples originated; and thus is accomplished the first steps towards a repetition of similar acts. The results produced are in two ways: either directly, by touching some congenial spring in a mind prepared for it by morbid proclivities; or indirectly, by familiarizing the mind with the aspects of vice, and thus blunting the original keenness of the moral perceptions."

Had dime novels corrupted Jesse's moral standards? Had these novels made him familiar with the brutality of knife wounds? With the savagery of stabbing? Had he been educating himself for the crimes he was about to commit? Had he been lured in by their explicit sexuality?

CHARLES ROBINSON, JESSE'S SENIOR counsel, outlined some of the mitigating circumstances in the boy's life in an attempt to explain his behavior. He cited the beatings Jesse had been subjected to by his father, the taunting and cruelty inflicted by the other schoolchildren, the fevers and convulsions, his sickness. He pointed out how pained and sensitive a boy he was. He asked the jury whether they truly believed such a boy could have "without any notice or provocation, deliberately and with premeditated malice aforethought, cut, mangle and murder him [Horace] in cold blood."

But the jury could see Jesse doing all of those things and more. With premeditated aforethought, he had cut, mangled, and hurt several children in Chelsea and South Boston, violating them in the most intimate and brutal manner. Was it so difficult to imagine he had graduated to murder?

Robinson knew the jury saw the boy as a murderer and was prepared to make an insanity plea. Jesse's mind was diseased, Robinson told them, and that was what had allowed him to commit those acts. "The boy was not a monster born with barbarous influences," Robinson cried out to the jury. "He was a product of *Massachusetts*—an outgrow of her civilization for the last fifteen years; a pupil of her school, a son of her citizens." Robinson was implying, not so subtly, that the state had failed Jesse Harding Pomeroy, and was therefore partly responsible for his actions and should now take care of its wounded son. The boy was "the victim of a mental and moral . . . and congenital weakness," he said, and the commonwealth now aimed to inflict further injury. Wouldn't they show some "kindly" sentiments toward him?

THE INSANITY PLEA HAD been in use in various forms since the twelfth century. In 1723 British judge Robert Tracy wrote "The Wild Beast Test," in which he set out his criteria for someone to be accused of murder: "It must be a man that is totally deprived of his understanding and memory, and doth not know what is doing, no more than an infant, than a brute, or a wilde beast—such as one is never the object of punishment."

But not until 1843 did the insanity plea truly came into being, when the trial of Daniel M'Naughten took place in England. M'Naughten was acquitted of murdering Edward Drummond, a man he believed was actually Sir Robert Peel. All the evidence supported the case that M'Naughten was delusional when he believed that Drummond was about to injure him or had already done so. In response, M'Naughten felt he had to defend himself. His lawyers brought forth evidence that M'Naughten had no control over his actions and could not tell right from wrong.

Lord Chief Justice Nicholas Tindal instructed the jury to decide whether Daniel M'Naughten "had or had not the use of his understanding, so as to know whether he was doing a wrong or wicked act." He also said that if the jurors were "of the opinion that the prisoner was not sensible at the time he committed it, that he was violating the laws of both God and man, then he would be sentenced to a verdict in his favor." M'Naughten was acquitted, but the chief justice was faced with such a great furor of protest that Queen Victoria had to request legislation to come up with a better set of regulation for future jurors. These eventually became known as the M'Naughten rules. These rules would in time cross the Atlantic and influence the American legal system as well.

Not everybody agreed with Jesse's lawyers' assumption that he was insane. Even reporters began to think the boy was of sound mind, and an article in the *Boston Herald* suggested: "He does not look like a youth actuated by the spirit of a fiend, and with the exception of a peculiarity about the eyes, he has no marked expression in his face from which one might read the spirit within. The idea that he is insane is not supported, except by the extraordinary character of his conduct." Attorney General Charles R. Train agreed.

WHEN THE DEFENSE RESTED, Attorney General Train presented the case for the commonwealth. His first witness was Eleanor Fosdick, who had seen Jesse and Horace together by the bakery. She corroborated the testimony of another neighbor who had also seen Jesse and Horace on the street. Fosdick lived in an apartment across the street from the bakery, and she said that on the morning of April 22, she parted her curtains to allow sunlight to stream in, as she did every day. On this morning she saw a boy skulking against a doorway opposite hers, as if waiting for someone. She remembered thinking the boy was shifty because he looked each way several times in a manner that made her suspicious.

When asked by Train if she recognized that boy in the courtroom, she pointed at Jesse and said, yes, yes, that was him. She said she had stood by the window for several minutes, watching the boy until moments later a cute little blond boy holding a sweet bun joined him in the doorway. When they headed toward the beach, she lost sight of them. Fosdick's testimony was compelling, but it did little to implicate Jesse.

Next up was Elias Ashcroft, one of the men who had gathered around the pit when Horace's body was found in the marshes. He now testified that earlier he had seen Horace walking by the railroad tracks in the company of an older and bigger boy, who was tightly holding the child's hand. Ashcroft hadn't really noticed the older boy's face; instead he had watched the little boy because he had reminded him of his own son, who was about Horace's age. His wife also dressed their boy in those silly frocks more adept for a little girl than a boy, and Horace's outfit had made him smile. Ashcroft said he hadn't paid too much attention to the older boy and hadn't noticed any distinguishing features.

Ashcroft was followed by Robert C. Benson, who was only fifteen years old. On the day of the murder, at 11:15 A.M., Robert left his house, located on Eighth Street, and headed toward the beach to spend the day watching the clam diggers. He had followed the path parallel to the railroad tracks, toward McCay's Wharf, and soon came across a ditch, which he easily jumped over to the other side. From there he had seen the bridge near the boathouse, though he had not walked as far as that.

From where he stood, he could clearly see Edward Harrington and his brother, Benjamin, digging into the moist sand, as well as Elias Ashcroft waddling nearby. He stood there for a few minutes then walked toward a boat near McCay's Wharf.

At just that moment he saw an older boy, whom he later recognized as Jesse Pomeroy, walking along the beach with a little boy. The two had just made their way across the ditch Robert had crossed and were now heading toward a smaller one. Robert estimated the pair were some "twenty-five yards" away from the boathouse.

Jesse and the little boy kept on walking, until Robert crossed paths with them. They didn't react strangely to being seen, and Jesse asked Robert about the gun blasts coming from the direction of the men on the beach. Robert told him the men were trying to shoot some ducks that were flying by. They didn't say anything else and went their separate ways. But Robert kept on looking back toward Jesse, he said, because he noticed that "he took the baby up with his arms and put him down" on the other side of the ditch. Robert then went home and didn't give any more thought to Jesse and the little boy, though he had recognized the little boy as one he often saw playing in the streets of South Boston with his slightly older brother.

Robert was asked if he was certain the boy he encountered on the beach was Jesse Pomeroy. Robert said he was. He had noticed that Jesse "had something about his right eye," although he couldn't tell what it was. Robert saw Jesse again at the police station. And yes, he also recalled the time of their encounter on the beach. The bell had just struck noon when they crossed paths on the sands of South Boston.

BEFORE THE TRIAL, AND also during it, newspapers in Boston and New York—as well as many across the country—were not entirely objective in their reporting about Pomeroy's doings, and as soon as Horace was found murdered, clear dividing lines went up, and these sides were strengthened when Katie was discovered. The doctors who had talked to Jesse before the trial were not given gag orders by the court, and several of them, eager for publicity, spoke to the papers. As expected, their words were twisted and reshaped with each retelling, further adding to Jesse's infamy.

The jurors, as everyone else did, read the papers voraciously, and had already formed their opinions long before they came face-to-face with Jesse. And it's unlikely that his disturbing and disquieting disposition did anything to change their minds.

Many agreed that simply looking into his eyes was indicative enough of his guilt. Soon after the trial got started, a reporter for the *Boston Globe* declared that "a single glance at the boy's countenance" was enough to "see how it was possible for him to perpetrate the outrages for which he was taken into custody." Sure of himself, the reporter continued in even more flamboyant detail: "they are wicked eyes, sullenly, brutishly wicked eyes, and as in moments of wondering thought the boy looks out of them, he seems one who could delight in the writhing of his helpless victims beneath the stabs of the knife . . . the prick of the pen, as he was so often delighted in . . . it is altogether unsympathetic, merciless. But worse than all the rest is the sensuality that hangs like lead about those sunken eyes, and that marks every feature in his face.

The pallor of his complexion, the lifeless, flabby look that pertains to his cheeks, compounds with his view."

THE SADISM JESSE DISPLAYED in real life had the same overtones people were already accustomed to reading about in the countless crime stories published in magazines and newspapers, as well as the countless crime pamphlets that were so popular in those years. The popularization of crime reporting in newspapers had occurred as early as the 1830s. The year 1833 saw the premiere of Horatio Sheppard's New York *Morning Post* and Benjamin H. Day's New York *Sun*, papers geared toward the working classes that featured stories of the sensational and wondrous, the disturbing and lascivious. The headlines often screamed out: "A Double Murder!" "A Secret Tryst!" "Bloody Accident!"

On May 6, 1835, James Gordon Bennett's *New York Herald* first appeared and declared its contents were "for the great masses of the community—the merchant, mechanic, working people—the private family as well as the public school—the journey-man and his employer, the clerk and his principal."

Bennett's paper got great attention in 1841 with its cover of Mary Rogers, a young woman who disappeared from a boardinghouse where she lived with her mother. Mary was a popular girl who worked at the counter of John Anderson's Tobacco Emporium. Rumors circulated at first that perhaps she had run off with a young lover, someone she might have met at the store. But three days later her body was found on the New Jersey side of the Hudson River.

Dead bodies were often found floating along New York's and New Jersey's waterways; suicide rates were high during that era, not to mention accidental drownings, especially while intoxicated. But it was obvious right away Mary had been killed. The coroner's report said: "From marks and bruises, there were evident signs of the body having been violated, and that the bruises about the head and the face . . . was [sic] sufficient to cause death . . . by person or persons unknown."

Immediately the *New York Herald*, as well as other papers, including those in Boston, latched on to the story. "A young and beautiful girl had been seduced and murdered within hail of this populous place," the *Herald* wrote. "The horrible murder of Mary Rogers excites daily a deeper and wider interest in our city." People flocked to the place where she was found to gaze at the murder scene; reporters wrote of the "horrid marks of violation and violence on her person" and speculated that perhaps she had "been murdered by a lone assassin either known to her or not."

The story oozed with sexuality and eroticism, and soon enough it led to the serialized crime story. Readers waited each day for the new installments in the Mary Rogers saga, as if they were unfolding chapters in a novel. Mary evolved into one of those characters found in a detective novel, a character caught within the wild urban landscape of New York, ripe with the smell of horse dung, the hustle and bustle of commuters, the noise, the depravity and the violence; the muck washing out from the rivers; and the inept police department and the detectives, who always seemed to be a step behind the murderer stalking the city streets for his next victim. It was foul, terrifying, degrading, and humiliating, and yet people loved it all.

Bennett's *Herald* gave readers the first glimpses of Mary's actual form when he wrote: "When we saw her, she was lying on the bank, on her back, with a rope tied around her, and a large stone attached to it, flung in the water. The first look we had of her was most ghastly. Her forehead and face appeared to have been battered and butchered. . . . Her features were scarcely visible, so much violence had been done to her. On her head she wore a bonnet. Her dress was torn in various portions— her shoes were on her feet—and altogether she presented the most horrible spectacle the eye could see. It almost made our heart sick, and we hurried from the scene, while a rude youth was rousing her leg, which hung in the water, and making unfeeling remarks on her dress."

Three weeks later the *Herald* reported on the autopsy, which was presented by the mayor and the coroner, Dr. Archibald Archer. The police officers spoke freely about the violations done to Mary, and in turn reporters embellished the details. Even Edgar Allan Poe couldn't help himself and was swept away by the tale, publishing "The Mystery of Marie Roget" in 1842.

When Charles Dickens visited the United States in 1842, he took notice of these papers. He often scoured the tabloids in his own country and even used them for his stories, particularly those published in the *Newgate Calendar,* a log of criminal deeds and trials in England. However, the American press startled him. The editors and writers, he claimed, enjoyed "pimping and pandering for all degrees of vice or taste . . . and imparting to every man in public life the coarsest and vilest natures."

He even immortalized the New York press in his novel *Martin Chuzzlewit,* describing the din of the paperboys and the papers themselves as such: "Here's the morning New York *Sewer!* Here's the morning New York *Stabber!* Here's the New York *Family Spy!* Here's the New York *Private Listener!* Here's the New York *Peeper!* Here's the New York *Plunderer!* Here's the New York *Keyhole Reporter!* Here's the New York *Rowdy Journal!* Here's the New York Papers!"

Boston's papers were not any better than the ones in New York. Taking a cue from them, Boston's newspapers began to saturate the pages with their own crimes, particularly when in 1849 their own salacious story took center stage, what would be known across the country as the Webster-Parkman Trial.

Early in 1842, Dr. John White Webster's financial situation had become so dire his very survival was dependent on a loan he received from Dr. George Parkman. As the years progressed, he managed to repay Dr. Parkman in full. But Webster's woes did not end, and soon he found himself in trouble again and agreed to another loan. As collateral, Webster put up all of his belongings, including a set of rare minerals Parkman had always coveted. But this time Webster was unable to repay the loan, and by 1849 he still owed the majority of the sum.

Parkman was not an easy man to discuss business with, and he began to pressure Webster for the money, which caused Webster to seek another loan, this time from one of Parkman's own brothers-in-law. As collateral for this loan, he gave up what was left of his property as well as the set of minerals he had already promised to Parkman. When Parkman found out about this, he was so irked he asked Webster to repay the loan in full or else he would bring in the police.

On November 22, 1849, Webster invited Parkman to his office at Harvard Medical College to discuss the situation. The appointment was made for 1:30 P.M. on the next day. He promised Parkman he would repay the loan in full.

Friday, November 23, 1849, turned out to be a typical fall day in Boston, with its typical classes in session at Harvard Medical College. Several witnesses later recalled seeing Parkman walking into the institution and making his way to his classroom, not far from where Oliver Wendell Holmes was lecturing to his own students. Webster's class, on the floor below, was about to end, and his students remembered nothing unusual in the lecture or Webster's demeanor. The only out-of-the-ordinary event many would later recall was that while Parkman was seen going into the building at around 1 P.M., no one had noticed him coming out of the institution, nor walking the grounds nearby. It was as if the institution had swallowed him whole.

Word soon trickled into the Harvard's corridors and throughout the city that Dr. Parkman had disappeared. Dr. Webster couldn't deny that the two had met on that Friday for Webster to repay a loan, but the police were satisfied with the explanations he gave for that day.

Parkman, a very wealthy man, had loaned out quite a bit of money, and he was very shrewd in his attempts to collect on his debts. The police believed a meeting could have occurred with someone outside of Harvard, and there had been foul play. A large reward was set up, and many people eager to cash in arrived with stories about the doctor's whereabouts: one suggested that he had been kidnapped and taken aboard a whaleboat. Someone else hinted that he had been killed in a nearby town, and his body was in a morgue there; another said the doctor was pushed off a bridge and his body had floated to the ocean.

Letters arrived daily at the city marshal's office, all of them with fantastic stories about Parkman, which the police immediately realized were meant to steer them away from the Harvard community. The marshal stashed the letters away in a folder and a week passed with no sign of the missing Dr. Parkman.

Even though Webster was the last person to have seen Parkman, suspicion never really fell on him—at least until people actually started to pay attention to his movements. Many in the college soon noticed an alteration in Webster's attitude. He visited his laboratory during "unaccustomed" hours and locked the doors behind him. This was unusual because he always kept the doors open, allowing colleagues and students to enter when they wanted. Now, when someone knocked, he did not open right away, but instead stalled. Waiting outside, many could hear a great rushing of water inside, and when they finally walked within, they were startled by the unusually tall flames leaping in the hearths; students were accustomed to the fires, but never before had they burned so vibrantly, with such intensity, displaying such ferocity.

Everyone wondered what Webster was doing, but a school janitor who took care of the laboratories was especially concerned. One day his curiosity got the better of him and he investigated Webster's private working quarters. When the doctor was out, the janitor posted his wife outside the door while he went inside and discovered body parts, portions of which were "suspended from above by a grapple made of fishhooks," he later reported to the marshal.

Police searched the rest of the laboratory and found additional body parts, which were all from Parkman. They also poked around in the furnace and found bone fragments and a set of false teeth, which Parkman's dentist said belonged to his patient. More than that, the towels used to soak up the blood under the hanging body parts were monogrammed with a *W,* and the officers also found the clothes Webster had apparently been wearing during the murder. They were smeared with blood. The city marshal also concluded that Webster's handwriting was similar to the handwriting on the letters he had received.

Webster was arrested right away.

On March 19, 1850, he appeared for his trial at the Old Courthouse in Boston. The city, as well as the rest of the country, was riveted by the stories and gossip relating to the trial, Webster's apparent ghastliness, and the blood that seemed to ooze out of the very tongues of those who spoke about it. Reporters, of course, enjoyed this story, especially because it increased circulation at most of the papers by significant numbers. Details, real and not so, were doled out in abundance, including Webster's attempt to kill himself by ingesting a large quantity of poison. He was rescued in time, which highly disappointed Webster.

Judge Lemuel Shaw presided over the trial. He had taken great care with the preparations and allowed only people who had a ticket to enter the courtroom, one of them being his son, Lemuel Shaw Jr. So many people wanted to attend the trial that two groups were set up: a morning group and one for the afternoon. This went on for eleven days, the trial often running from 9 A.M. until 7 P.M. There was always a crowd outside on the street and it seemed to become larger with each day.

Many people testified but the most riveting was Dr. Oliver Wendell Holmes, who knew both Webster and Parkman. At the time, Holmes held the title of Parkman Professor of Anatomy and Physiology, an appointment established in honor of Dr. Parkman.

When the parade of witnesses was finished, Shaw explained to the jury the laws they had to follow, and the matters to take under consideration. Yet when the jury returned a verdict of guilty, critics argued that Shaw had given the jury such flawed instructions they had no choice but to deliver a guilty verdict.

Many across New England and the country came to believe that Webster would have been acquitted if not for Shaw's instructions. The animosity was directed not only toward the jury but to the judge. There had been room for reasonable doubt, some argued, but the verdict did not reflect that. A paper in Philadelphia printed an article titled "Judicial Murder," while one in New York declared that "prejudice, or something worse, had swerved him [the Chief Justice] from the path of judicial integrity."

A larger pamphlet was also published in New York titled "A Statement of reason showing the illegality of that verdict upon which sentence of death has been pronounced against John W. Webster for the alleged murder of George Parkman." Shaw received dozens of letters denouncing the verdict, and some even threatened his life. But despite these criticisms, Shaw handed down a sentence of death, following the law.

Webster appealed for a pardon, which was denied. He and his lawyers also argued insanity, but Shaw did not even consider it a possibility. Because of this case, Shaw had to make his notions on insanity known, as they applied to this case and as they would apply to others that followed. "In order to constitute a crime a person must have intelligence and capacity enough to have a criminal intent and purpose," he wrote. "And if his reason and mental powers are either so deficient that he is not well, not conscious in controlling his mental powers, or if, through overwhelming violence of mental disease, has intellectual power as for the time obliterated, he is not a responsible moral agent, and is not punishable for criminal acts."

Shaw felt that Webster was fully within in "intellectual powers" when he killed Parkman, and therefore he did not fit within the bounds of the insanity rules he had set up. Webster was executed on August 30, 1850. But Shaw had established an argument on insanity that would be spoken of years later, particularly in Jesse Pomeroy's case.

WHEN THE VERDICT IN the Pomeroy trial came back, it was Judge Horace Gray who read the jury's decision: Jesse was found guilty of first-degree murder, which carried a mandatory sentence of hanging. He would be sent to the gallows, Gray said, so that he "would serve as an example to all others who might thereafter be disposed to gratify a morbid love of cruelty." On hearing Justice Gray's words, the smirk Jesse had possessed throughout the proceeding days disappeared from his face. But the jurors must have felt some sympathy for the boy despite the brutality of the crimes, because they advised the court to allow for some discretionary mercy when handing down its sentence.

In the Commonwealth of Massachusetts, the governor decided when a sentence of hanging was to be carried out. Governor William Gaston, the former Boston mayor, was by now fifty-five years old. Although he had seen much during his tenure in office, he was stunned by Jesse's deeds. Still, he was in a very awkward position: he was not keen on the state executing a minor, but his personal views seemed to be the opposite of what his constituents desired. Some called for the execution to take place right away, while others begged for leniency.

Gaston's lieutenant governor, Horatio G. Knight, who favored the death penalty, showed the governor letters and articles calling for Jesse's hanging. Knight hoped that reading about the antipathy toward the boy would compel Gaston to sign the warrant of execution on his desk. But instead Gaston did what he did best: he stalled.

"When will the Governor and Council act upon this case?" the *Boston Journal* wrote on May 2, 1875. "Is procrastination to prevail until the patience of the country is exhausted? Do men in such positions lose the power of reaching definite conclusions which characterizes them in private life?"

Such an avalanche of petitions asking that the boy be killed arrived on Gaston's desk that he didn't have the time to read them all. Many came from Chelsea and South Boston, and a number were signed by mothers of very young children. A woman wrote in an editorial, published on May 28, 1875, in the *Boston Globe*, that she was "one of those 'blood-thirsty women'" who begged the executives to forever disgrace the noble name of Massachusetts by placing her gaunt hands around the delicate, slender neck of Jesse Pomeroy and twisting it off." It didn't seem to matter to these people that Jesse was only fourteen years old. They all wanted to watch him dangle from a noose.

IN HIS ESSAY "REFLECTIONS on the Guillotine," Albert Camus wrote about his own father's desire to view an execution. Prior to World War I, in a town in Algiers a man committed a brutal murder for which he was sentenced to death. It seemed as if death by guillotine was warranted because the man had slaughtered an entire family consisting of farmers and their children, and he had also robbed them of their few belongings.

The press had publicized the trial with great abandon, giving vent to the readers who believed, in Camus's words, that "decapitation was altogether too mild a punishment for such a monster." Camus's father, Lucien Auguste Camus, was a relatively mild man, but he too had been shocked by the violence of the crime and allowed himself to be swept away by the rush to see the man hung. Though he had never attended an execution before, like most of the town's population he decided to make a day of it.

The guillotine was set up at the other end of the city, so Camus's father got up while it was still dark outside and made his way there, joining the rest of the populace. But when he returned, he didn't speak to anyone of the experience. "My mother could only report that he rushed wildly into the house," Camus later wrote in his essay, "refused to speak, threw himself on the bed, and suddenly began to vomit . . . instead of thinking of the murdered children, he could recall only the trembling body he had seen thrown on a board to have its head chopped off."

The people in Massachusetts didn't see hanging a boy of fourteen as an act of revenge, nor did they see it only as part of the law. To them, hanging Jesse Pomeroy was an act of God's will. The whole procedure had a deeply religious connotation to it, which made the hanging that much more bearable. It was God's way of handling the unfit, and to a certain extent, it showed his love.

When Jesse learned of the petitions signed against his commutation, he failed to understand why so many people wanted him dead, particularly women. He did not understand that mothers feared for their own children, and their children's children. The only way to prevent harm from coming to any of them, these women felt, was to rid themselves of Jesse Pomeroy.

Many at City Hall believed that Governor Gaston was overcome by a lack of necessary aggressiveness. They muttered that he was taking too long to decide what to do with Pomeroy, and yet he kept thinking about it. While Gaston pondered what to do, Jesse sat in the Suffolk County Jail and waited.

AS JESSE WAITED TO see if he would be executed, people across the country took a further interest in him and his case, especially in the life he had led prior to being arrested. Doctors who hadn't even met him proposed that he suffered from a congenital disease, while psychiatrists who hadn't studied him at all adhered to the idea of moral insanity and monomania, ideas put forth by their colleagues involved in the case. Others felt he was merely a jealous and hateful boy, simply a bad seed. And many were in agreement that the novels he had read throughout his childhood had predisposed him to evil acts.

Even the newspapers were beginning to agree that perhaps his reading material, coupled with a lack of parental guidance, had been at the heart of Jesse's issues. Days after his trial ended, in December 1874, the *Boston Daily Globe* published an editorial that echoed those feelings. "Can there be any question that instead of allowing him to gloat over the recital of fiendish atrocities, which stimulated the worst tendencies of his nature, the best parental care would have ascertained and corrected those blood thirsty characteristics?" the paper asked. "Jesse Pomeroy would probably have never developed a high moral character, but had he passed the period of youth under inscrutable discipline, his sense of the danger of indulging his cruel propensities would have saved his victims and society from atrocity."

One man who wondered if reading had indeed caused evil in Jesse Pomeroy was James Thomas Fields.

Fields was born in Portsmouth, New Hampshire, in 1817. His father, a sea captain, died when he was only three years old, and he was raised by his mother and her family. In 1839 Fields joined the publishing and bookselling firm of William Ticknor, located on School Street in Boston, where he became a junior partner. He rose so swiftly he became a full partner in 1846, and the firm took on the name of Ticknor & Fields, becoming one of the most recognized publishing houses in the country.

Fields was especially well liked and published some of the best literature written at the time. But he also brought to the States books by contemporary British authors who soon became his closest friends, among them Charles Dickens. In 1854 Fields married Annie Adams, a pretty young woman with dark hair parted in the middle that she gathered at the nape of her neck in a loose bun. Together they fostered intimacies with the likes of Ralph Waldo Emerson, Henry James, and Dr. Oliver Wendell Holmes. A man of habits, Fields kept his whiskers curled at the sides and wore patent-leather shoes for what he considered important meetings. April 6, 1875, was such a day.

Although he was a congenial man, he was truly irritated by the country's new passion for dime novels. He had lately noticed readers turning away from serious literature toward "criminal and exciting cheap books," watching as boys and young men gathered at bookstalls, pennies in hand, eager for the next edition of these terrible publications, which he felt were lowering the standards of morality in America.

When Fields heard about Jesse Pomeroy's own penchant for these books, he knew he had been proven correct. He wanted to talk to the boy to see if his theory held some truth to it: that Jesse's reading had instigated his murderous sprees. "I suspected that Jesse Pomeroy, who had murdered two children and mutilated several others," he wrote, "had been warmed up to his nefarious deeds by a steady perusal of bad books, and I resolved to have a talk with him if possible."

Jesse had first entered the confines of Suffolk County Jail in April 1874, and there he remained during his trial and soon thereafter. Upon stepping foot within its enclosures Jesse was immediately assigned a number—16721—that just like his white eye would forever mark him, identify him, and distinguish him as one of the jail's inmates. He was only fourteen years old when he passed through the doors. There were many other young men already occupying the institution, most of them pickpockets, forgers, counterfeiters, assailants, or sexual deviants. But at fourteen Jesse had the distinction of being the youngest one held there on account of murder charges, and eventually the youngest one convicted of murder and awaiting execution.

From the moment the guilty verdict was handed down, the judge was besieged with requests to speak to Jesse prior to his planned execution. Reporters were anxious to have an exclusive interview, which they could perhaps expand into a book, which would then catapult them into the limelight.

Justice Gray had denied all such inquiries until he received one from James Thomas Fields. Fields emphasized that he had no interest in writing an article, nor a book about Jesse. His was a learning expedition. The "interview," as he nonetheless called it, would be recorded in his own private diary among notes detailing trips to Paris and other European capitals, visits to museums and pastry shops, and notes about the private life of Charles Dickens. To Judge Gray, this understated the interview's significance, but Fields's talk with Jesse Pomeroy turned out to yield one of the most accurate portraits of the young killer ever published.

Having finally been granted permission to visit Jesse, on April 6, 1875, Fields set out from his large brownstone at 37 Charles Street, in Beacon Hill. Charles Street was home to many who shared Fields's interests. For a time Dr. Oliver Wendell Holmes had been a neighbor, first at number 21, then at 164, until he moved closer to the Common.

By now nearly two and a half years had gone by since the Great Boston Fire, and the city was undergoing that "wonderful transformation," as the *Boston Morning Journal* had recently detailed in one of its many articles. Soon after the blaze, trade had been moved elsewhere and shops opened in the suburbs, where commercialists were conducting their business. Now in the rebuilding stages, architects were implementing many of the new building codes that had not been there prior to the fire, changes Fire Chief John Damrell had advocated when he returned from inspecting the fire damage in Chicago.

Of particular interest were those lumberyard mansard roofs that had aggravated the chief; they were now being replaced by flat roofs that were not only pleasing to the eye but fire retardant. Most of all, the downtown streets were being widened, creating more space everywhere.

Although Fields admired this new construction, he was pleased that the fire had not touched Charles Street or any of the homes in that area, and that the old charm still existed. Henry James, one of the Fieldses' dear friends, described their home in his *American Scenes* as being like "the little ark of the modern deluge, here still the long drawing-room that looks over the water and towards the sunset, with a seat for every visiting shade." James also wrote that the Fieldses were "addicted to every hospitality and every benevolence, addicted to the cultivation of talk and wit."

At the time of the interview with Jesse, Fields was fifty-seven years old and had retired from publishing. He was still young, but he felt his strength was waning due to some health issues plaguing him. He also felt he had seen much of life: his travels and marriage had brought him pleasure; his jobs and subsequent friendships satisfaction. He also had suffered a great deal of pain, including the early loss of his first wife, in 1850; as it happened, she had been a cousin of his current wife. Nothing people did anymore could surprise him.

As he neared the jail, Fields remembered a note he once received from his friend, the poet and writer James Russell Lowell. At the time

Fields was in the process of publishing the reminiscences of his friend Nathaniel Hawthorne, and Lowell's note had come at an auspicious moment. It said: "Be sure and don't leave anything out because it seems trifling, for it is out of these trifles only that it is possible to reconstruct character sometimes, if not always." Fields had taken the advice, not only for the Hawthorne project, but others as well. He recalled these words again as he made his way to meet Jesse.

As he entered the old edifice of the Suffolk County Jail (or Charles Street Jail), he expected to gain some information that would cement those views on dime novels he had already formed in years past, then leave the premises and return to his comfortable home. That was the point of his visit. Stubborn, as he was often called, he wanted to be proven right that the particular brand of literature that readers were now indulging in could spawn a murderer, making it more dangerous than readers could imagine.

He was immediately assaulted by the prison's sounds and noises, the clang of steel bars opening and closing, the wailing of harmonicas. Standing on the guardroom floor, he had a wide view of those cells, all 228 of them, each one eight by ten feet long. Designed in 1851 by Gridley J. F. Bryant, a prominent Boston architect, the structure was a large and imposing combination of steel and granite.

One of the guards gave Fields the option of meeting Jesse in the tiny and windowless cell he occupied or in a slightly larger one adjacent to it. Fields chose the larger one so he wouldn't be entirely cooped up with the boy. Two chairs were set up barely "four or five feet apart," facing one another. Jesse was brought in, and Fields noticed right away that his hands seemed "enormously large and powerful."

"I also noticed a striking blemish in one of his eyes. Looking as if he had received an injury to it," according to Fields's notes. He was later told that Jesse had suffered smallpox as a boy, and the blemish was a vestige of the illness.

"If the eye had not been disfigured," Fields wrote, "I would say the face had an intelligence in it; the forehead was narrow rather than wide, and the size of the head was the usual one for the boys of his age, which he told me was fifteen."

This description of Jesse contradicted newspaper accounts, which said he was tall with a heavy jaw and a massive head, almost unnaturally so.

Fields asked Jesse if he had been told the reason for the visit.

"From a morbid curiosity," Jesse replied. A hint of a smile played on his lips as he said this, his voice low and calm—so much so that Fields had to strain to hear it.

Fields asked Jesse if he liked to read.

"I read everything I can get," the boy told him flatly.

"When did you first begin to be fond of reading?" Fields asked.

"I guess about nine years of age."

"What kind of books did you first begin to read?"

"Oh, blood and thunder stories."

"Were the books the only ones?"

"Yes, mostly Beadle's dime novels."

"How many Beadle's dime novels do you think you read from nine years afterwards?"

"Well, I can't remember exactly, but I should think sixty," Jesse replied.

"Do you remember the titles of most of them?"

"No, sir. But Buffalo Bill was one of the best of them."

"What were the books about?"

"Killing and scalping Indians and so forth, and running away with women. A good many of the stories were out on the plains," Jesse said, awfully calm again.

"Did your parents know you were reading those books all through those years?"

"No, I kept them away from them." That was not true. Mrs. Pomeroy was aware of her son's reading habits and had been told often by the staff at the primary school and the reform school.

"Do you think you read more books than any of the boys?"

"Yes, sir. A great many more. I had a kind of passion for them."

Jesse was very forthcoming and appeared almost proud of his answers, something Fields had not anticipated.

"Do you think those books were an injury to you, and excited you to commit the acts you have done?"

"Yes, sir. I have thought it all over, and it seems to me now they did. I can't say with certainty of course, but perhaps if I should think it over again, I should say it was something else," Jesse replied enigmatically.

"What else?"

"Well, sir. Really. I can't say."

"As you sit here now, do you feel perfectly well in your head?"

"Yes. Perfectly. I have no desire to be a criminal. I wish to be like other people."

"Do you feel sure that if you were again in the world with other people that your conduct would be the opposite of what it has been?"

It was the question many wanted to ask.

"When I think it all over, the past four or five years seem like a dream. I feel perfectly sane . . . if I could always be as I am now, in the same state of mind I am sitting with you, that I should be all right; but I could not tell you what I might do in half an hour from now. I might do just the same things over again."

"Then," Fields interjected, "you do not feel sane?"

Jesse thought a moment and then replied, "No, sir. I do not."

Fields realized that Jesse displayed more than simple "reading intelligence." In discussing dime novels, he told Fields they had "inflamed his mind" and "excited his passions."

Jesse expressed himself in a way that was unusual for a fifteen-year-old. Fields later wrote that "the language he used was perfectly grammatical. Rather above his years. His sentences were constructed with great cleverness and he never hesitated for a word." Jesse said he had been a student in the local public school for years, but when Fields asked if he had attended Sunday school, Jesse merely "smiled as if he recognized the incongruity between that kind of institution and the acts he had committed."

Fields asked Jesse if he had felt anything at all after he had committed the deeds. "Not at all," Jesse told him.

More than a century later, in September 1999, the renowned forensic psychologist Robert D. Hare detailed some of the most common traits found in psychopathic killers in his book *Without Conscience: The Disturbing World of the Psychopaths Among Us*. He pointed out that "a strong lack of conscience" is one of the hallmarks of these individuals. "Their game is self-gratification at the other person's expense," Hare said. "Psychopathic killers, however, are not mad, according to accepted legal and psychiatric standards. The acts result not from a deranged mind but from a cold, calculating rationality combined with a chilly inability to treat others as thinking, feeling humans."

Pomeroy exhibited a wide range of the symptoms Hare described.

As Fields continued to question him, Jesse noticed that a guard was entering his small adjoining cell. He disliked people going into his private area, so he got up, walked toward the attendant, and asked if something had been brought for him. Fields took this moment to end the interview, collected his belongings, and made his way to the corridor.

But before he left, Fields looked back toward Jesse, and saw that he had been returned to his cell and was staring at him from behind the iron bars. Jesse then smiled at him with a "courteous expression," bowed his head as if onstage, and said to Fields, "You have a good day, sir. I am much obliged to you."

The gesture possessed a formality Fields did not understand. He had no clue why Jesse felt obliged to him; it was he who should have thanked the boy for the interview.

As he stepped outside onto the street and into the cold spring air, Fields was overcome with a peculiar sense of unease. "The whole impression left upon my mind after this interview is hardly to be described," he wrote in his diary. "I had seen a boy committed of extraordinary crimes, the likes of which the jailor and the sheriff said they had never heard of before." Jesse was about to be executed, yet to Fields he seemed "more thoroughly self-possessed than any innocent boy."

At that time there was no word in the English language to describe a psychopath. That term would not be used until the mid-1880s. The phrase "soul suffering" was the only thing available to describe what men and women like Jesse were believed to be undergoing. These words were a direct translation from the Greek *psyche* (soul) and *pathos* (suffering).

Fields stuffed the diary into his coat pocket and made his way toward the Public Garden, where some semblance of normalcy reigned. He had been given permission to speak to Jesse only once, so he would not see the boy again. And he did not want to.

Yet questions remained. Although Fields had determined from his interview that Jesse had read and perhaps been influenced to some extent by dime novels, Jesse had also hinted that there was more to his deeds than his vices, and Fields had recognized that as well, though he had not been able to point his finger at just what *it* was. Jesse had also been smart enough to recognize that if he had been allowed to go free, despite his desire to lead a normal life, his impulses would not allow him to do so. So, what was that elusive *something* that prompted Jesse to kill, the same something Fields had just glimpsed?

MONTHS PASSED AND JESSE still remained in jail. There was no news about when, or if, his execution would take place. In late 1875 Governor William Gaston lost his bid for reelection. Alexander R. Rice, the governor-elect, said he was willing to hear Jesse's appeal as a first order of business. He agreed that the "Pomeroy question" had not yet been resolved.

Rice was born in the Lower Falls village of Newton, Massachusetts, on August 30, 1818, to a very affluent family. His father had been part of the paper manufacturing business, which provided Rice with the funds for an extended and refined education at Union College in Schenectady, New York. Active in both business and politics, he became well known and well liked throughout the Boston community, due mostly to his calm yet steely determination, traits not found in his predecessor, Gaston.

By the time Rice took office and focused on the Pomeroy case, two years had gone by and the rage against the boy had abated somewhat. After hearing evidence from both sides of the debate—whether to execute or not—the new governor decided to commute Jesse's sentence. "I do thereby grant him . . . a commutation of the punishment he is liable to endure by the aforesaid sentence and here-fore commuted to that of imprisonment in our State Prison for life."

But that was not the end of it. Jesse would not only be kept in prison for the remainder of his days; he would be locked up in solitary confinement forever. He could now look forward to a seven-by-nine granite coffin with two portholes drilled up high, which would give him a little bit of air and light. He would bake in that room during the summer and freeze in the winter.

If those holes had been low enough, he would have been able to look out from them and glimpse the Charlestown apartment he had shared with his family before they moved to South Boston. He could have seen the old Chelsea and Charlestown bridges, and the road he had taken during his jaunts to Chelsea in search of small boys. He could have noticed the riverbanks where he had stood after his father had beaten him, and from where from time to time he had launched a line hoping to bait a fish. He could have seen the tiny canoes anchored near the banks of the river, bobbing and lulling as the water rushed toward the sea.

But instead he could see and hear nothing and would have no one to talk to. Many prisoners faced with solitary confinement, even if for only a short span of time, found the anticipation of it so daunting that they committed suicide.

On September 7, 1876, nearly three months before Jesse turned seventeen, he entered the gray walls of the Massachusetts State Prison—the Bastille, as it was known—to begin his new life. It was a gray, drizzly, depressing morning, a somewhat befitting day for the occasion that seemed to foretell the direction of the upcoming months, years, and decades.

Gideon Haynes, one of the prison's wardens, wrote a description of solitary confinement in 1869 that summarized what greeted Jesse: "The walls of these detached cells are of granite, four feet thick, with no opening but for the door, which is made of iron, weighing nearly twenty-five hundred pounds, secured by heavy bolts, and fastened with massive padlocks, the object being to guard against the convicts getting out and not against parties getting in. These cells are so isolated from the main building that no sound can pass from one to the other. The entrance to them is through the store-room, the door of which is on the west of the building; on the sides of this room are small windows, which, in the warm season of the year, are left open for ventilation."

Jesse's new landscape was made of gray steel and cement, tightening all around him.

As the heavy door locked behind him and sealed him inside, Jesse did not cry, nor did he try to make a run and grab the door handle, as others before him had done. He stayed strangely quiet and oddly seemed at peace as he adjusted to the confined space and deafening silence of the musty room. What should have deeply troubled him, officials noticed, made him almost drowsy. He was alone, isolated, without anyone, not unlike his life in the outside world, surrounded by people but where he had always been ostracized.

But he later revealed that despite his outwardly adaptive nature, he had already made up his mind that he was not going to spend any more time in that hole than was necessary, and that fight for freedom was to begin at that very moment.

CHAPTER 9

THE TWISTED MIND

*Oh the nerves, the nerves; the mysteries of this machine
called Man! Oh the little that hinges it: poor creatures
that we are!*

—CHARLES DICKENS, *THE CHIMES*

As the newsboys unleashed their thunderous screams of "Extra! Extra!" announcing the latest news about the change in Jesse's prison sentence, Bostonians were surprised. Two years had passed since the trial, and though Jesse had not been forgotten, new crimes and scandals had taken over people's attention. No one expected the new governor to make Jesse's petition his first order of business, but he had.

Two years earlier few had questioned if it was inhumane to send a fourteen-year-old boy to the gallows, and now even fewer were asking if it was inhumane to place a sixteen-year-old boy (who would soon turn seventeen) in solitary confinement for the rest of his life. He had been spared his life, critics argued; an olive branch had been extended toward him. But there were still some who questioned whether sending a boy who suffered from a mental illness to solitary confinement in prison would help him in any way. They were also skeptical that his sentence would deter others suffering from the same condition from committing similar crimes.

One such critic was Dr. Oliver Wendell Holmes. As he sat in his brownstone overlooking the Common browsing the latest reports about the case, he became aware that public sentiment ran high in this case; he knew the boy needed to be dealt with; but he also believed those sentiments had arisen not only from a wave of panic but also from one of misunderstanding.

Holmes had been against hanging Pomeroy from the start, and had even joined those who wished to have his sentence commuted, though he realized Jesse needed to be committed to some kind of a mental facility for treatment and for study. He had drafted letters to Governor Gaston expressing his sentiments, but those letters had gone unanswered. Then Holmes did the next-best thing. He took to the papers. In April 1875, an article appeared in the *Atlantic* titled "Crime and Automatism," which spread Holmes's reputation even further, as it outlined in very detailed points the reasons he believed Jesse Pomeroy should not go to the gallows.

From the very beginning, Holmes did not deny that Pomeroy's crimes were of "singular atrocity and wanton cruelty," but he argued that it was precisely the ugliness of those deeds that had allowed "many thinking persons" to wonder about the state of the boy's mind, the conditions under which he had labored when he had killed Katie and Horace, and even prior to that, when he had abused the boys in Chelsea and South Boston.

Holmes argued that because Jesse seemed indifferent to the pain he had caused, it stood to reason that he "must have a moral nature very unlike that of ordinary human beings," and nothing was "more difficult than to study such a being fairly. Instinct, Law, and theology have all taken up their position with reference to him," he said, pointing a finger toward those who called for a hanging, even from the pulpit, not only because it was the legal thing to do, they felt, but because they found in the act a form of divine retribution.

Holmes was also aware that Pomeroy was often associated with evil, seen as a boy akin to the devil, no longer human but imbued with some kind of power only seen in supernatural beings. "It has transferred the whole subject of moral transgression from the region of the natural to that of the supernatural. It lent the devil to the lawyers to help out their indictments," Holmes said. Instead, he believed Jesse should be studied "calmly, exhaustively, and independently of all inherited prejudices. The idols of the market, of the bench, and of the pulpit must be treated as so many . . . stones by the naturalist who comes to study men. . . . Savage instincts, barbarous visages, ancient beliefs, will all find themselves confronted with a new order of facts which has not been studied, and with new interpretations of facts which have never been hazarded."

One of the arguments that had come up at the trial was the notion of free will: the state had argued that Jesse was under the command of free will when committing his crimes and was not, as his lawyers wanted the jury to believe, suffering from any delusions. But Holmes disagreed: "The will, like the wind, is anything but free; it is largely governed by organic conditions and surrounding circumstances . . . and all provisions are made for its anticipated decisions." This echoed Charles Robinson Jr.'s words that Jesse's environment and upbringing had contributed to his killing spree.

"Now, the observation of certain exceptional natures," which Holmes believed Jesse Pomeroy possessed, "tends to show that a very large portion of their apparent self-determinations or voluntary ac- tions, such as we consider that we should hold ourselves responsible for, are in reality nothing more or less than reflex movements, automatic consequences of practically, irresistible causes existing in the inherited organization and conditions."

In the article he quoted a French doctor of medicine named Prosper Despine, who in 1868 had also done a study of the criminal mind. In applying Despine's theories to Pomeroy, Holmes wrote: "Crime will be like our ordinary every-day acts, without moral character and without moral responsibility. A careful study of criminals shows that in a large proportion of cases they are devoid of the ordinary moral instinct; that they have no struggle beforehand except of purely selfish principles, that they have no true remorse for their guilt, and that their apparent repentance is nothing but fear of the future suffering with which they are threatened."

Worst still, the reason people hated and disliked criminals so much was not only the acts they had perpetrated, but also the fact that they saw themselves reflected in those persons. "Our impressions about their mental conditions," Holmes wrote, "are mostly mere reflections of what we would think would be our own feelings."

Holmes believed there was no reason to hang Pomeroy, or anyone else, for that matter, because "hanging is not the best use to which the criminal can be put." His argument against the death penalty was "on the ground that it was unjust as applied to moral idiots, immoral considered as revenge, useless as a means of intimidation, and dangerous to society by cheapening the value of life."

He was aware that it was "instinct" that made people respond to someone like Pomeroy, rather than the thoughtful examination of the facts. "Our most widely accepted theologians owe their dogmas to a few majority votes passed by men who would have hanged our grandmothers as witches and burned our ministers as heretics," he said. "Insanity was possession in times well remembered. Malformed births, monsters." He was pointing out that times hadn't changed all that much after all.

There should be the "deepest pity and tenderness," Holmes wrote, knowing well that his words would not be taken to heart.

His essay was printed all over the country and widely talked about as it decidedly took a view against hanging Pomeroy; it was also blasted by those who could not wait to see Jesse dangle from the noose. It was not revenge they wanted, argued those who read Holmes's article. It was simply a measure of justice.

HOLMES'S ACQUAINTANCES WERE NOT surprised that he'd become interested in such a popular case. It was not the first time. There was the Webster-Parkman trial back in 1850, after all, in which he had testified and become involuntarily involved.

Born on August 29, 1809, in Cambridge, Massachusetts, Holmes had earned his education first from the Phillips Academy in Andover, Massachusetts, and then at Harvard College. Upon graduation, in 1829, he had spent a short time studying law before turning to medicine. Along the way he had also dabbled in literature, particularly poetry, for which he seemed to have a particular affinity.

Like others before him, his medical studies and career were supplemented by various stays at the medical colleges and institutions of Europe, where he not only learned the latest theories for practical medicine but also visited many insane asylums, particularly in France, to see how the mentally ill were being treated. In 1836, he graduated from Harvard Medical School and officially began his medical career; not only that, he also began teaching, soon thereafter taking a post at Dartmouth Medical College before being hired, in 1847, by his alma mater to serve as the Parkman Professor of Anatomy and Physiology. There he served as a dean until 1853 and taught until 1882.

It was soon after he got tenure that his colleagues Dr. Webster and Dr. Parkman became embroiled in that tale of deceit, mayhem, and murder, culminating with a hanging. Webster's deeds were regarded as being so treacherous they were spoken of throughout the commonwealth and the nation at large in lurid detail, and years later the Pomeroy case would remind Holmes and others of the same salaciousness. It was even more appalling to Holmes that the incidents took place just a few steps away from his classroom.

HAVING KNOWN BOTH WEBSTER and Parkman, Holmes had felt the cloud of that trial over him as it progressed and ended with the hanging. Harvard College was also marred by the ordeal, so when the term came to a close, all were ready for a respite away from the premises. For Holmes and his family that meant locking up the brownstone on Beacon Hill and moving to the seclusion of the Berkshires, in the village of Pittsfield, where the family had built a farm named Coral Meadows on a parcel of land they owned. Aside from rest from his duties there, Holmes looked forward to spending time with his friend Herman Melville.

Holmes and Melville had met prior to becoming neighbors in Pittsfield, at several literary events and parties in Boston. One such occasion was in July 1849, at a soiree given by Melville's father-in-law,

Judge Lemuel Shaw, at his home on Mount Vernon Street. Shaw and Holmes had, throughout the course of past years, discussed law, literature, and even insanity during meetings and parties they attended.

Holmes and Melville saw each other not even a week after Shaw's party, at another social gathering given by the writer Richard Henry Dana Jr. There the two men talked further, with Melville sharing stories of the South Seas and Holmes describing trips taken throughout the Massachusetts countryside. They were presented with many other opportunities to strengthen their friendship, not the least of which was the proximity of Judge Shaw's home and Dr. Holmes's, both on Beacon Hill. It was only a short distance between the brownstones.

At the time of those meetings, Melville was writing his novel *White-Jacket*, which would be published later in 1850. A maritime tale taking place aboard the fictional *Neversink*, one of its main protagonists was the Surgeon Cadwallader Cuticle, M.D. Although Surgeon Cuticle was a fictional character, upon reading *White-Jacket* and particularly those sections describing Cuticle, those familiar with Holmes could tell he had inspired the young author.

In addition to being a friend, Melville was also one of Holmes's patients, and lately Melville's family had been deeply concerned about him. He was only in his mid-thirties then, and though he had been in good health until that point, he was now suffering from back spasms and sciatica, complaints Holmes tried to address, along with the ones Melville's relatives pointed to that involved the author's mental state. But Holmes never found anything unusual or defective in Melville's overall thinking. He diagnosed the issues as mere quirks that were the result of financial strains and familial circumstances, as well as the literary profession itself. He explained this to the Melvilles, but the author's mother, Maria, was adamant about seeking additional help for her son's mental state, as was Herman's wife of only a few years, Elizabeth Shaw, the daughter of the judge.

The Melvilles and the Shaws had known each other for years, and the judge had been supporting the family since Allan Melvill's death in 1830. This was not only financial, but also emotional, providing a shoulder on which to lean when the need came up. For many years prior to the meeting, Elizabeth had been friendly with Herman's sisters, making many visits to their home in Lansingburgh, New York.

Given the families' friendship, it seemed that Herman and Elizabeth must have known each other since their youth, but there is no evidence of that. The two grew up in different states and under very different circumstances, which did not allow for face-to-face meetings. Elizabeth often traveled to New York to meet the Melville girls, and in turn they visited her in Boston. Maria Melville wholly approved of this friendship between the girls because she knew this connection to the judge could be beneficial to her family.

Elizabeth Shaw was born on June 13, 1822, in Boston. Her mother, Elizabeth Knapp Shaw, suffered severe complications from the birth and died shortly thereafter. The judge's mother, Susanna Shaw, assisted in the newborn's care, along with the help from a nurse the judge immediately hired. The judge already had a two-year-old son, John Oakes Shaw, whom he also placed under the care of Susanna Shaw. On August 29, 1827, Lemuel Shaw married a woman named Hope Savage, who eventually gave birth to two sons, Lemuel Jr. and Samuel Savage Shaw. In 1831 the new family left the home they had been living in on Kneeland Street and moved closer to the State House, on Mount Vernon Street.

Shaw believed that a thorough education was important and that his children should take advantage of the opportunities he could provide them. When Elizabeth was only three years old, he hired a private tutor for her, the lessons continuing until she was almost twenty. One of the instructors was Mary Lamb, who also taught Elizabeth's brother John.

By 1836 Elizabeth was also enrolled in a school for "young ladies," which she left in 1841 with a prominent education that could have led her to college, though by then the family had decided she had received enough formal schooling. Another part of her education was in religion. She was raised in a deeply religious family that counted her grandfather and great-grandfather as ministers.

Like other young ladies of her class, Elizabeth loved social gatherings and parties. Her letters showed that her primary concerns were lovely fabrics and dance parties, though when her family wanted her to partake in more formal social affairs she did so. On December 23, Elizabeth made her social debut. She was naturally shy, and that occasion, although exciting, was marred her own lack of self-confidence.

In May 1845 Elizabeth traveled to New York to visit the Melville girls, and this time Herman was there, having just returned from one of his trips abroad. They saw each other again the following March, when Melville accompanied his sister Helen to Boston. On that trip, Melville presented Shaw with a copy of *Typee*, which he had dedicated to the judge. It was not entirely clear when Herman and Elizabeth decided to marry, but in June 1847 the announcement of their engagement was printed, and two months later, on August 4, they became husband and wife. The news came as a surprise to many proper Bostonians.

No one doubted that Elizabeth was a proper young lady brought up with the utmost refinement. But few saw her as a great beauty and her intelligence was not particularly impressive, though her studies showed she had above-average capabilities. As the daughter of Judge Shaw, she possessed an enviable dowry and was certain to inherit a large sum upon her father's death.

Her choice of husband was also questioned. Though Melville was known for having written *Typee* and *Omoo*, those books were full of unabashed sex, naked natives, and cannibalistic rituals, which gave him a salacious reputation. The two didn't seem to match in any fashion.

Melville's somewhat lurid, sexy, scandalous depiction of the lovely Fayaday in *Typee* seemed to suggest that great physical beauty was a high priority for him. Elizabeth didn't have that and so the gossips of the day decided the marriage was a financial deal. Herman never acknowledged that money played a role in his choice of Elizabeth, but if money and finances didn't matter to him, they certainly did to his mother.

People loudly criticized her for not only facilitating but actually pushing her son's marriage to the girl.

Following the wedding the two honeymooned in New England and Canada. The trip was a relaxing and restful ordeal, perhaps in preparation for what awaited Elizabeth. When they returned, they moved to New York City, at 103 Fourth Avenue, where they lived with Herman's brother Allan and his new wife, as well as Maria and Herman's four unmarried sisters. Judge Shaw had enabled the purchase of the large home by giving the couple two thousand dollars as a loan.

The situation was not easy. Herman was at work on a new book, and Elizabeth felt constricted; she had never shared a home with so many people. She did her best to appear cheerful, and in a letter to her stepmother on December 23, 1847, she described her new life: "We breakfast at 8 o'clock, then Herman goes to walk, and I fly up to put his room to right, so that he can sit down at his desk immediately on his return. Then I bid him goodbye with many charges to be an industrious boy and not upset the inkstand, and then flourish the duster, make the bed, etc in my own room . . . then Herman insists on taking a walk every day an hour's length. So unless I can have rain or snow for an excuse, I usually sally out and make a pedestrian tour a mile or two down Broadway. By the time I come home it is two o'clock and after, and then I must make myself look as bewitchingly as possible to meet Herman at dinner. . . . Excepting call, I have scarcely visited at all. Herman is not fond of parties, and I don't care anything about them."

With the publication of his third book, *Mardi*, a shift began to occur in Melville's writing. *Typee* and *Omoo* dealt with the more popular subjects of cannibalism, overt sexuality, and South Seas adventures, but the tone changed with *Mardi*. A contributing factor was probably the books he was now reading, including one he had borrowed in mid-January 1848 from the New York Society Library. *Observation of Man* by David Hartley detailed the author's interest in the theory of vibrations as a way to understand the mind and the soul. It was no coincidence that *Mardi*'s main protagonist echoed Hartley's words in proclaiming he felt a sort of "involuntary interior humming," and saying his head was "full of reverberations."

Years later Jesse Pomeroy would suspiciously use similar-sounding excuses when trying to explain the reasons for his crimes. Also in *Mardi* Melville used the term *monomania* for the first time, reflecting a new-found interest in and passion for the topic of mental illness, and helping bring it to the forefront of the general public.

That Melville was disturbed and fascinated by madness had by now become obvious to all. In a letter dated April 5, 1849, he wrote to his friend the publisher Evert A. Duyckinck, and described another friend: "Poor Hoffman—I remember the shock I had when I first saw the mention of his madness—but he was just the man to go mad—Imaginative, voluptuously inclined, poor, unemployed, in the race of life distanced by his inferiors, unmarried—without a port or heaven in the universe to make . . . this going mad of a friend or acquaintance comes straight to every man who feels his soul in him—which but few men do."

The more Melville delved into the insane mind the more havoc it played on his own. To placate his worried family, in October 1849 he traveled to England aboard the British ship *Southampton*. The trip had been suggested as a sort of mental respite and was financed by his father-in-law, Judge Shaw. Aboard the *Southampton* he met and bonded with a passenger named George Adler, who was then a professor of German at New York University. Adler was born in Leipzig, Germany in 1821, and immigrated to America with his parents in 1833. He grew up in New York City and studied at New York University, where he remained as a teacher, earning the distinction of a full professorship in 1846. He also wrote and edited many textbooks, some in English and others in his native German. Many assumed that Adler's first meeting with Melville occurred aboard the *Southampton*, but the two had actually met earlier at a party hosted by their mutual friend, Evert Duyckinck.

At the time, Adler, like Melville, had recently completed a writing project that had sapped all of his energy, in his case *The Dictionary of the German and English Languages*, an enormous volume of 1,371 pages printed in tiny type and to which he had devoted many months. That he had published the volume when just twenty-eight years old further underscored the magnitude of his accomplishment. He had also concluded that a sea voyage might rejuvenate him physically as well as mentally. As he later revealed to Melville, the project had been so trying he had found himself "almost crazy . . . for a time."

But the trip proved to be useless for Adler. He returned to America and continued to suffer from delusions and hallucinations, which eventually prompted those closest to him to commit him into the Bloomingdale Asylum in New York City.

While in Europe, Melville explored Paris, searching out the places that had been recently recommended to him by Dr. Augustus Kinsley Gardner, a friend who would eventually become the family's physician in New York. The two had become friendly some years before due mostly to their common interest in insanity. Despite Gardner's knowledge of the subject, his specialty was obstetrics and whatever else women and infants suffered from. He refined his psychiatric knowledge by training at the Poor House Lunatic Asylum in Boston, which eventually led to him being in charge of the Bloomingdale Asylum in New York, where Adler was confined and where eventually Melville's own niece, Lucy, would end her days. In addition to friendship, Melville could count on Gardner as a reliable and readily available font of information. Whether Gardner also allowed Melville to visit the Bloomingdale Asylum and walk through its corridors remains unknown, though it is possible.

HERMAN MELVILLE COULD HAVE visited the Bloomingdale Asylum, or any other in the area, on his own, without permission or approval from anyone because such places, like most of the country's prisons, had become major tourist attractions during the 1800s. Visitors entered the thresholds as much as to catch a glimpse of the residents as for the buildings' architectural importance.

Another of New York State's famous asylums was Utica Asylum, which was built in 1843 to resemble a large educational edifice or a courthouse. It was meant to evoke "grandeur" to those who passed beneath the arched doorways and "trust" to its patients and their families. The green lawns and hearty smells from the blooming and well-maintained flower beds gave the impression of a "cheerful and quiet retreat." But its many windows were kept securely locked, the tall wooden fences possessed the general air of being impenetrable, and a plaque above the entrance door read: "Who enters here must leave all hope behind," a not-so-subtle reference from Dante's *Inferno*.

Hiram Chase, one of Utica's famed superintendents, despised the idea of visitors, though under the state's regulations he could not prevent them from entering. He felt that in their eyes the patients became only "a gazing stock for the multitude of visitors who daily flock to the asylum, take a walk through the first hall, gaze in at the patients as they would look upon wild animals in a menagerie, and then depart."

In May 1850 Herman Melville was at work on a new project, and in a reply to a letter written to him by a friend, Richard Henry Dana Jr., inquiring about the "whaling voyage" book, Melville wrote, "I am only half way in the work. . . . It will be a strange sort of book, tho', I fear; blubber is blubber, you know; though you might get oil out of it, the poetry runs as hard as soup from a frozen maple tree."

In July 1850 he bought a copy of *The Natural History of the Sperm Whale, to Which Is Added a Sketch of a South Sea Whaling Voyage*, by Thomas Beale, a surgeon. It had been published in London in 1839. Melville read the book voraciously, marking several passages, as he did in all of his reference books, noting sentences that would find their way into his new work. Beale described whales as naturally quiet mammals, though when instigated, they were capable of uttering the most terrifying groans, so loud they could be heard from great distances. Beale also detailed the physical characteristics of whales, paying particular attention to the head. It was so large, he wrote, it almost seemed disproportionate. And certain people who read Beale's book believed the head was where the whales' malignity and cunning disposition resided. This notion of a large head holding malignity within it would later extend to humans. An unusually shaped cranium gave credence to the idea that those whose skull was oversized suffered from criminal tendencies, such as occurred in the case of Jesse Pomeroy.

The History of Nantucket, by Obed Macy and William C. Macy, also gave Melville detailed information about the island, and in particular revealed the history of the doomed whaling ship *Essex,* which Melville already knew about. But despite these additional aids, the writing was proving difficult. It was not the text but the circumstances under which he was forced to create.

His son Malcolm was born in Boston in 1849, and his little niece Maria was born just two days later. It was a loud, crowded, and overwhelmingly hot house. In mid-July 1850, the Melvilles decided to move for the summer from New York to Pittsfield. Herman's cousin Robert owned a home there, and short on money, had decided to rent it. By the time the Melvilles arrived the place was already full. In addition to Melville, Elizabeth, and baby Malcolm, there was also Herman's brother, his wife, and child, along with Robert and his family, plus several tenants, a widow, and a couple intent on buying the farm. The place was very crowded but Herman liked it enough that with his father-in-law's assistance he decided to buy the property. He renamed the place Arrowhead.

Some seven miles from Pittsfield, in the village of Lenox, Nathaniel Hawthorne had taken up residence with his family in a small, red-shingled cottage. Melville was only in his thirties when he met the forty-six-year-old Hawthorne in 1850. *The Scarlet Letter* had just been published, making Hawthorne one of the country's most well-known novelists. There was something very striking in Hawthorne—he was handsome, blue-eyed, and mysterious, possessing an allure that seemed to hold some secret to be discovered, or so Melville came to think.

In addition to their residences in the Berkshires, the authors had something else in common: Hawthorne too was "a self-confessed lover of all sorts of good and good-for-nothing books." Some of his acquaintances were struck by this penchant for the unusual, for the ghoulish, so much so that his publisher, James Thomas Fields, recorded in his diary certain bits of a conversation they had once had: "Hearing him (Hawthorne) say once that the old English State Trials were entertaining reading and knowing that he did not possess a copy of those heavy folios, I picked up a set one day in a book shop and sent them to him. He often told me that he spent many hours over them and got more delectation out of them than tongue could tell, and he said, if five lives were vouchsafed to him, he could employ them all in writing stories out of those books. He had stitched, in his mind, several romances founded on the remarkable trials reported in the ancient volumes; and one day, I remember, he made my blood tingle by relating some of the situations he intended, if his life was spared, to weave into future romances."

Hawthorne was utterly fascinated with the nature of evil, which he believed indiscriminately resided within everyone and could be brought to the surface when unusual circumstances were visited upon a person. This fascination linked him to Melville, who had already experimented with these themes in many of his books, most recently in *The Confidence-Man*, published in 1849. He had used that book to explore evil in a general sense but had tapped into the Americans' enthrallment with evil characters by opening the novel with the murderous sprees of the Harpe Brothers, real-life frontier bandits and killers who had captured the public's imagination with their despicable deeds.

The Harpe Brothers, who were actually not brothers at all but cousins, were also believed to be the first American serial killers, their deeds so abhorrent that sightings of them were related in newspapers with chilling details and language that made readers fear them, yet yearn to read the next installment in their saga.

During this time in the Berkshires, both authors' interest in insanity and lurid tales, as well as Dr. Holmes's, was further sparked by the stories that were published in the local papers, particularly the *Pittsfield Sun*, describing what went on in the asylum nearby, the almshouses built across the area, gruesome stories of suicides and bloody murderous tales of homicidal sprees. Melville had also continued his subscription to Bennett's *New York Herald*, further compounding his curiosity and knowledge of the subject.

Melville visited Hawthorne often, perhaps as a way of finding peace and quiet that didn't exist at Arrowhead, which was loud with women's talk and babies' crying. He either sought refuge at the Hawthornes' or upstairs, in a room he had designated as his own. There he had a desk that had once belonged to his uncle, one that had been stored in a granary for more than a decade. Melville found that pigeons had smeared it with excrement and that eggs had hatched within its drawers. Nonetheless, he had restored it to its original purpose.

He often arrived at the Hawthornes' in the company of a large dog and wearing a farmer's hat, his hulking body seemingly abuzz with talks of eternal salvation or damnation, depending on his mood. Hawthorne listened more than he talked, as did his wife, Sophia, who was struck by his visits.

On September 4, 1850, Sophia wrote a letter to her mother expressing her feelings toward Melville, who had by now become such a visible figure in her household. "Mr. Melville is . . . a man with a true warm heart & soul & intellect— . . . I am not sure that he is not a very great man—He has very keen perceptive powers," she went on, zeroing in on Melville's eyes. "He seems to see everything very accurately, & how he can do so with his small eyes, I cannot tell. His nose is straight & rather handsome, his mouth expressive of sensibility & emotion—He is tall & erect with an air free, brave, & manly. When conversing, he is full of gestures & forces, & loses himself in his subject—there is no grace nor polish—once in a while, his emotion gives place to a singularity of wild expression out of those eyes, to which I have objected—or indrawn, but which at the same time makes you feel—that he is at that instant taking deepest note of what is before him—It is a strange, lazy glance, but with a power in it quite unique . . . it does not seem to penetrate through you, but to take you into himself."

Despite the friendships he was forging in the Berkshires, the time he spent there was not pleasant, because he was tortured in his writing of what was known then as *The Whale*, which his wife, Elizabeth, said was done "under unfavorable circumstances." She detailed how he would "sit at his desk all day not eating anything till four or five o'clock—then ride to the village after dark—would be up early and out walking before breakfast—sometimes splitting wood for exercise."

In August of that same year, Evert Duyckinck and a friend, a writer named Cornelius Matthews, arrived from New York for a two-week visit. They would be added to the already expanding crowd: the Morewoods, who had become fast friends of the Melvilles; the Hawthornes, who lived nearby; Oliver Wendell Holmes and his family, also residing nearby; and James Thomas Fields, the Boston publisher, along with his wife.

Summer dimmed, fall retreated, and the silent days of winter began to roll by slowly, the desolation of Pittsfield trying to both the body and the soul. And even in the Berkshires, the sea was never far from Melville's mind. Months of heavy snow had covered the hills and valleys in a sea of white, and, burrowing in the cloistered arms of his study, Melville often thought, while peering from a small window, that it was as if he were peeking from the porthole of a ship. The lands were as white and as bleak as the ocean upon which he had sailed as a youth.

"I have a sort of sea-feeling in the country, now that the ground is covered with snow," he wrote Duyckinck in December 1850. "I look out of my window in the morning when I rise as I would out of a port-hole of a ship in the Atlantic. My room seems a ship's cabin; & at night when I wake up & hear the wind & rolling, I almost fancy there is too much sail in the house, & I had better go on the roof & rig in the chimney."

He was not well and permitted himself and others only a few in-
terruptions to even dine with them, working on the book at a feverish
pace, even as the children shouted in the rooms below. The routine
continued until Christmas, when they were invited to a holiday dinner
at the home of neighbor and friend Sarah Morewood. The tension
Morewood felt within the family was palpable, especially coming from
Melville. "I laughed at him and told him he was slightly insane," she
later wrote. "He responded that long ago he came to the same conclusion himself."

By April 1851 the snow had melted and the ground had thawed
and small buds had sprouted on the apple trees. Melville was still im-
mersed in *The Whale*, and that month received a gift from his father-in-
law, Lemuel Shaw. Undoing the string from the package, he found a
new copy of Owen Chase's narrative describing the *Essex* catastrophe,
as well as another book that would be detrimental to finishing his
own: *A Narrative of the Mutiny on Board the Ship Globe, of Nantucket, in the Pacific
Ocean, Jan. 1824*, by Thomas Marly. Aside from tidbits on marine life
and whales, it also described the ship being rammed by a whale and the
mariners' desperate attempts to survive the attack.

As nature awakened from a long sleep, so did his family, who
seemed to resurrect after the long hibernation. Melville did not appreciate this. Strained by financial woes, as much as by lack of time
to write, he yearned for peace and quiet. "I am so pulled hither and
tither by circumstances," he wrote to Hawthorne that June. "The calm,
the coolness, the silent grass-growing mood in which a man ought to
always compose—that, I fear, can seldom be mine. Dollars damn me;
and the malicious Devil is forever gaining in upon me, holding the
door ajar."

The next month, another letter to Hawthorne revealed that *The
Whale* was about done, or as he put it, "The tail is not yet cooked." By
then Elizabeth was pregnant with their second son, and her stepmother
and father arrived for the season to assist. In September he officially
changed the book's title to *Moby-Dick*, and by October it was published

in London. The baby was also born that month, but the happiness these new events brought was tempered by Hawthorne's departure from Lenox to West Newton. Melville took the news hard, as he had come to rely on Hawthorne for conversation as much as for respite and drink away from Arrowhead.

Reviews quickly came in, many of them hostile toward the characters that littered the pages of *Moby-Dick*. Though Melville's desire had been to move away from writing the sensational stories that he had created earlier in his career and that were now littering the country, it was precisely to such literature that *Moby-Dick* was relegated. "So much trash belonging to the worst school of bedlam literature," the *Athenaeum* wrote. Others, like the *Courier and Enquirer*, believed the text "the gusto of true genius," and George Ripley, in the December 1851 issue of *Harper's*, did find it "a poignant allegory intended to illustrate the mystery of human life." But even the ones that praised it could not compete with those that loathed it. The *Boston Post* thought it a work full of "oddities and artificialities." The character of Ahab in particular was not well liked, his words and tendencies being maniacal. The long passages describing the whaling business also proved irksome.

But more than anything, readers could not comprehend the demonic yet human characteristics assigned to the whale, Moby Dick. "Not was it his unwanted magnitude, nor his remarkable hue, nor yet his deformed lower jaw, that, so much invested the whale with natural terror," chapter 41 read, "as that unexampled, intelligent malignity which, according to specific accounts, he had over and over evinced in his assaults. More than all, his treacherous retreats struck more dismay than perhaps aught else."

Mariners feared not only the whale's malignity, but its color as well. "It was the whiteness of the whale that above all things appalled," for "it strikes more of panic to the soul than the redness . . . in blood."

Moby-Dick tells the story of a monomaniac captain whose vengeful quest against a white whale in the end spells his doom. The white whale had, on a previous journey, dashed Ahab's spirits to pieces and ripped his leg apart. In so doing, the whale had also shattered the captain's spirit and mind. The book follows Ahab's journey to hunt and kill Moby Dick, who has by now become the representation of all the evil in the world. Nature is barbaric, Ahab has come to realize, and in return he is going to show it his own brand of barbarism.

In chapter 41, Melville actually used the word *monomaniac* to describe the captain and his quest. "It is not probable that this monomania in him took its instant at the precise time of his bodily dismemberment," he wrote. "Then, in darting at the monster, knife in hand, he had been given loose to a sudden, passionate corporal animosity; and when he received the stroke that tore him, he probably but felt the agonizing bodily laceration, but nothing more. . . . Then it was, that his torn body and gushed soul bled into one another; and so interfusing, made him mad. That it was only then, on the homeward voyage, after the encounter, that the final monomania seized him, seems all but certain from the fact that, at intervals during the passage, he was a raving lunatic."

There is no doubt that Ahab is mad, nor is there any question that he is aware of his own madness. At one point he says of himself: "Why think me mad—Starbuck does; but I'm demoniac, I am madness maddened!" He had "cherished a wild vindictiveness against the whale, all the more full for that in his frantic morbidness at last came to identify with him, not only all his bodily woes, but all his intellectual and spiritual exasperations."

The book was saturated with madness. Ahab was not the only one who suffered such mental imbalances—to some extent so did all the characters on the *Pequod.* They were all victims of some kind of mental alienation. The whale was described as a "monomaniacal incarnation of all the malicious agencies" in the world, and words such as *lunacy, madness,* and *monomania* jumped across the pages.

In 1851, soon after the book was published, a whale rammed the ship *Ann Alexander* near the same spot where the *Essex* had sunk. This whale was also especially brutal, smashing the boat with extreme ferocity and returning for a second, final blow. The crew was forced to leave the *Ann Alexander* and find refuge in the smaller canoes bobbing nearby. An acquaintance eventually told Melville what happened, to which he replied, "I wonder if my evil art has raised this monster."

Of course, he had not done any of those things. What he had done with *Moby-Dick* was forge a link between madness, evil, the lure of the hunt, and, inexplicably, the color white, which until then had symbolized purity. Now the color had the power to alienate as well as allow it to stand out. White had been tainted forever.

CHAPTER 10

PATIENCE PERSONIFIED POMEROY

Beware of the fury of a patient man.

—JOHN DRYDEN, *ABSALOM AND ARCHITOPHEL*

On a balmy and humid Sunday in July 1875—even before Jesse was shut off in solitary confinement at the Massachusetts State Prison—inhabitants of the commonwealth awoke to the sound of newsboys excitedly hawking the latest issue of the *Boston Sunday Times*, which they proudly announced held "The Autobiography of Jesse H. Pomeroy," a long pair of articles published over the course of two Sundays. These articles were also reprinted in the *New York Times*, allowing readers outside Boston to catch a glimpse of the fiendish Pomeroy. The city was startled not just that a fifteen-year-old boy convicted of a cruel crime had written this by himself, but that he was so adept at using legal jargon in the writing.

Pomeroy quickly recounted the place and time of his birth; the names of the Charlestown and South Boston streets where he had lived with his family; the time he had spent fishing with his brother and visiting his father at the Navy Yard. Then, beginning with the Katie Curran story, he gave his version of the events for which he had been sent to prison.

He wrote that on the day after Katie disappeared, he was working in his brother's shop when a neighbor named McNeil entered and looked around.

"It is very strange, isn't it, about the disappearance of that girl," McNeil told him, as he idled by the door.

"What girl?" Jesse was unaware of what had occurred in his neighborhood, or so he said. McNeil asked if he hadn't heard that a little neighborhood girl, Katie Curran, had disappeared.

No, Jesse said. He hadn't heard anything. McNeil went on say that she had disappeared the day before and had perhaps been kidnapped. In his newspaper account Jesse wrote: "The man told me the little girl had been seen crying, and it was generally thought her father had sent her to a convent." Rumor had it that the girl's father was opposed to her religious upbringing and had a friend of his snatch her up while she was on her way to school, then smuggle her into a convent of his choosing, somewhere in the western part of the state. Jesse wrote that this was when he first learned about Katie's disappearance, and after he was already in jail, the chief of police told him her body had been found.

But Jesse's primary purpose in writing the autobiography was "to show that the verdict was unjust, and instigated by a spirit of prejudice" toward him, "that the evidence was not sufficient to warrant that verdict."

He pointed out that police never found any blood belonging to Katie on his person, nor had anyone noticed a rancid stench of decomposition coming from the basement. "If that body was there from the 18th of March to the 18th of July, why didn't someone notice the smell?" His mother had asked this as well, suggesting that the body had been placed there after they had left the premises. Jesse knew the residents of the building often visited the basement and they would have notified the police had they noticed something foul.

He was also aware that his neighbors had not seen anything peculiar in his movements when Katie disappeared, because if they had seen anything unusual, they would not have hesitated to point him out to the police. If he had killed the girl, wouldn't his movements and attitude have been indicative of that? But his arguments were rehashed from the trial and provided nothing new to clear his name. Doctors who studied him had testified that it was precisely the calmness he exhibited after the murder that indicated a callous mind.

In addition, he tried to help his case regarding Horace Millen by introducing an argument that was even more confusing and uncon-

vincing than his previous one in the matter of Katie Curran. He insisted that the court had failed to prove that he killed Horace Millen.
According to Jesse, the prosecutors presented a case for a premeditated act, which meant it was conducted by someone with a sane mind.
But Jesse felt the evidence showed the murder was done by someone
insane, who "could not help doing it." He reasoned that only an insane
person could commit such atrocities. He said that allowing beachgo-
ers to notice him clearly pointed to his insanity. "I would have taken
some pains to keep myself from being seen when I did it or was going
to do it," he argued. He would have tried to get rid of all the evidence
as well, such as the mud from his boots and the pocketknife. That he
hadn't done so pointed to his unstable mind, and those who had been
witnesses at the trial supported his theories.

He did not deny being with Horace by the bakery on the day the
boy was murdered. He also admitted to swallowing half of the little
boy's drop cake, which Horace had offered; Jesse also said he walked
Horace toward the beach. But that meant nothing, he argued. The
foot molds the detectives had taken on the beach suggested only that
he had walked the area at some point, and he had admitted doing
so many times before. Had anyone witnessed the deeds that occurred
on the sands of Savin Hill Beach? Had anyone seen him play with a
knife before plunging it into the little boy's body? Could anyone point
toward him with certainty?

He knew people found him cold, but that was not his nature. "I
know the crime that has been committed, but I do not feel its awful-
ness," he wrote. "I do not realize that which I am charged. Nature has
given me a mind, that when anything wrong comes, or when bad news
comes, I do not manifest any feelings, though I have feelings in me. I
know I am arrested for murder, I know what murder is; I know that
I have been tried and convicted for murder, but I do not realize the
position I am in."

He wrote that the jury system was "a disgrace to the country,"
and wondered if the members of his jury were not "fitter to die than

the prisoner." He acknowledged that his life had not unfolded as "I expected it to be."

The *Boston Globe* reacted to his confessional by writing: "What he says about the whereabouts on the day of the Millen murder, though showing an excellent memory for details, bears evidence of having been prepared for the purpose, and is unnatural, and no boy would minutely notice so many objects as he had and describe them except by way of afterthought, in order to make out his alibi."

One person who was stunned by Jesse's words was Charles Robinson Jr., one of the his attorneys. Robinson did not know the paper was publishing such a thing, and if he had, he would have tried to stop it, or at least to stall it. He did not believe the series was a good idea now or at any other time. Robinson knew Jesse had written it in the hope of soliciting sympathy toward his commutation. He also believed that Ruth Ann Pomeroy had a hand in it, because he recognized a heavy whiff of her rhetoric lacing the pages. Most of all, Robinson was unconvinced that Jesse's words would do anything to change the public's sentiments, which were still leaning toward execution.

Robinson was often asked about Jesse, and with the trial over and Jesse's words now published, Robinson had some liberty to respond with more honesty than he had before. He had been heavily criticized for attempting an insanity plea, which many felt was a ploy to let Jesse get away with murder. But Robinson disagreed, believing the boy not of "sound mind." "I would not have tried the case if I had thought that I would get a clear verdict of acquittal, for I do not believe the boy should be turned loose upon the world, as he is not in a measure—responsible for his acts," Robinson said.

Then he admitted that Jesse was a very "peculiar boy, with tendencies of the most morbid nature. . . . It was evident to me—strangely so—that he was unlike any boy of his age I had ever come across before. . . . Although I was engaged to defend the boy, I did not deem it my duty to endeavor to have him thrown loose upon the community again."

His strongly held opinion was that Jesse Pomeroy was thoroughly insane.

A MONTH AFTER JESSE'S articles were published, Ruth Ann had her own sour words splashed across the *Boston Globe*. In her letter she complained, as her son had done, about the justice system in Massachusetts. She believed Jesse had been convicted because he came from a poor family. Had he been a rich boy, she concluded, the outcome would have been different. Although her outburst was motivated by rancor, her insights were not altogether wrong. She also believed that without the stain in his eye he would have been merely a strapping youth hawking papers to make a living; the blotch in his eye, and especially the whiteness of it, had marked him not only as an outsider but as an evil one at that.

In detailing the crimes, her letter echoed Jesse's, but whether she had taken a cue from him or, as was most likely the case, he had reshaped his mother's words, they both contended the same thing. She believed Katie Curran was placed in the basement after they left it. Didn't she help Officer Adams and his colleague search the area? Didn't she hold up the lamp in order for them to get a better view? Didn't she remove rocks with her own bare hands from the spot near the water closet only to prove that there was nothing there? Hadn't a neighbor gone there to explore herself and found nothing? Ruth Ann said the lack of blood on the walls and floor meant only one thing: Katie had not been killed in the cellar. And the same could be said for the smell that had not been noticed for months. Rotting bodies were known to stink up a place, and this would be especially true as summer approached.

What Mrs. Pomeroy didn't know, and what wouldn't be recognized for many more decades, was that placing Katie Curran's body beneath the coal and ash heap prevented the smell of decomposition from rising. Coal is a natural odor absorbent; its properties have now been studied for years; it helped the perpetrator to hide the crime for many months. Only when the summer heat arrived did the smell accelerate and reveal itself to the tenants.

Mrs. Pomeroy and a few of the detectives also agreed that no blood was found at the scene. But they all neglected to mention that the basement was awfully cluttered and the blood spatter projected by Katie's body as her throat was cut would have been lost in the mess and the ash and coal on the ground. Even if there had been any indication of *something* having occurred, the simple truth was that the detectives would not have been able to distinguish blood from anything else. The formal study of bloodstain pattern analysis didn't begin until the mid-1890s in Europe; thus South Boston detectives, through no fault of their own, would have been unable to detect what remained of possible "arterial gushing."

"But I do declare that the time will come when this great injustice will be undone," Ruth Ann Pomeroy ended. "Mark what I say. Massachusetts will bow in shame for murdering my boy, for murder it will surely be. I have no fear for my boy, God will take care of him. 'Remember, Vengeance is mine, I will repay it, saith the Lord.'"

JESSE'S CELL IN THE Massachusetts State Prison was located in the "second tier" of the South Wing, the stronghold of the prison, facing the Charles River, though he could not see it. It was equipped with a bed frame and a mattress, a wooden chair, two buckets—one to hold water for personal hygiene and one for personal waste—and an iron spoon. Each cell across the wing held these same objects. Prison officials did not believe anything in the cells could be fashioned in any way to assist a prisoner in escaping.

On his first day, Jesse looked at every object and noticed that the outer strip of wire rounding the washbasin could be ripped and uncoiled. He did so, breaking it into smaller pieces. He was also given a sardine can for a snack. When he removed its cover, he saw it was as sharp as any knife he had ever seen. There were endless possibilities in both the iron spoon and the bow-legged chair, whose legs could be twisted off as easily as a child's neck, its uses limited only by one's imagination.

Jesse immediately unspooled the wire from the washbasin and began picking at the bricks, inserting it deep within the mortar. He twisted it back and forth, back and forth, with a tedious efficiency and patience he had already cultivated at the reform school and in his brother's shop, a continuous turning of the wrist that allowed the wire to penetrate deeper into the mortar, eventually exposing and loosening the bricks. A domino effect occurred: when a brick shifted, so did the ones next to it. He used one of the chair's legs to assist him with this. With the spoon he cleared the debris, stashing everything underneath his bed.

Not long after Jesse arrived, a guard named Bradley was told that Jesse had smuggled letters out of the prison and into the outside world. He could not imagine how he had done so. Bradley realized that Jesse had not accepted the prison rules and surprised him with an unannounced visit. As Bradley entered the cell, he noticed a brick sitting on the floor, which Jesse had not had time to hide.

Jesse was placed with his back to the wall while guards searched the small perimeter. Right away a large piece of paper affixed to the wall unfurled itself and fluttered to the floor, revealing a large hole in the wall. A number of bricks had been removed and several others were ready to come undone. The hole was not large enough for Jesse to pass through, but significant progress had been made. He had labored on it for weeks, digging each of the bricks with the spoon and disposing of the mortar under his bed.

The bricks had been loosened on the right-hand side of the cell, to the right also of the tall porthole and above Jesse's bed frame. At that particular section the wall was about two feet in depth, and Jesse must have somehow known that once the bricks were exposed, the officials walking the outside perimeters would not notice them. That the cell was covered with books and poster boards gave him additional security: no one would imagine, or could imagine, that a hole was being dug behind a white sheet of paper.

Officials believed he needed to remove only another half dozen more bricks before he could have plucked out one of the bars and made a hole large enough to fit through. If he had actually gotten outside his cell, he could have found a way to "lower himself from the iron gallery to the rotunda, by many cords taken out of the window." Officials reasoned he would have waited for midnight or thereabouts because that's when the guards changed shifts. Jesse must have thought no one would notice him during all the comings and goings. He then would have been able to "clear the jail building and scale the outside wall," Bradley surmised.

Bradley agreed that while success seemed far-fetched, it was not implausible. But Jesse may have intended another plan altogether. Bradley said: "Another way was to reach the ladder outside the building, and in that way reach the roof of the jail, from which position it would be an easy matter to reach the ground by means of the water spout and then scale the wall and gain his liberty."

IN 1877 THE MASSACHUSETTS State Prison began an extension project, which involved tearing down the section where Jesse was housed. It was believed that the new material used for construction would make escape impossible. The material was heavier, and stronger iron was engaged for the gratings in each cell. In addition, each cell would be completely within the sight of the officers on guard. They could watch Jesse for hours on end.

That these extreme measures wouldn't work became apparent right away. For months Jesse had been cutting away at the bars of his cell, which turned out to be accomplished with such ease, he also decided to employ his talents at the bars of his small upper window by jumping on his cot, now offering him a view of the yard. It was by sheer fortune on the officers' part, and misfortune on Jesse's, that the next escape plot was discovered.

During one of the guards' regular Friday-night rounds, the guard happened to lean accidentally against Pomeroy's cell door. As he did so, he felt one of the bars give way. The rod fell to the ground with a loud clank. The guard also noticed that two more rods had been cut away, and it was believed that Jesse needed only a few more hours, perhaps that very night, to wrench out the entire set.

More officers were called, and they discovered that the bars on the grating had also been meddled with, although they were not entirely cut yet. Jesse was searched, and guards discovered contraband items including "a couple of very fine sews of sterling silver," although they had no idea how he had gotten them. Jesse hinted that someone had been waiting for him on the outside world, and a meeting time had been set up.

Suspicions immediately fell on Mrs. Pomeroy. Perhaps Ruth Ann had been assisting her son and furnishing him with the tools he needed. She was not surprised to hear her son had tried to escape, nor was she surprised that newspapers and wagging tongues were pointing at her as his possible accomplice. She denied it, of course, though once, on one of her routine visits, mother and son had acted suspiciously, and the warden ordered that the fruit she had brought for Jesse be cut open and searched. Inside a banana was a small sharp file. From then on, the two had been watched "as a cat watches a mouse."

Other inmates had, of course, tried to escape, but no one was as problematic as Pomeroy. "It's a sort of satisfaction to realize that you are getting the best of your superiors," a paroled inmate told a journalist some years later, with not only a fondness for those days but obvious pride in his actions. "It's fun if you don't get caught, I tell you."

After one failed attempt, Jesse told the warden he hoped he would get paroled, though even he knew it was increasingly unlikely. The warden agreed. "Pomeroy, were it known that you were to be pardoned," the warden told him, "that day that should see you walk out of this institution would be the day that would hurtle you into eternity. . . . I do not think you could go 300 yards from this prison without being shot, so strong and intense is the feeling against you."

One of Jesse's schoolmates also confirmed the warden's warning, when many years later he stated in an interview for a South Boston newspaper: "If he ever escapes, he won't be caught," the unnamed man volunteered. "He killed for pleasure then; he will kill, if he ever again has a chance, for revenge. . . . Revenge upon society, I feel sure, is his dream now."

WHILE JESSE KEPT OCCUPIED trying to find ways to breech the security of the prison, in the years following his entombment a rush of crimes perpetrated by juveniles upon other juveniles spread across the country like a vile pestilence, so much so that it made people wonder if Jesse's malignant condition had become contagious, like the measles.

On August 29, 1878, a six-year-old boy named J. Howard Butterfield was vacationing with his family on Squirrel Island, a resort area near Augusta, Maine. He stepped away from his parents for a moment and began to play in a field where an old outhouse was located, abutting a small lake. He was found there several hours later by nearby vacationers. His clothes had been cut, ripped, and pulled apart, and the skin over his entire body was covered with cuts and bruises, blood oozing from beneath his arms and from his chest. He was near death.

Howard eventually recovered, and was able to tell a tale eerily similar to one older folks had heard before. While playing in the field, he had been approached by an older and larger boy he had never seen before. The boy seemed friendly, and he lured Butterfield near the outhouse with the promise of rock candy. There the older boy punched the younger one to the ground and dragged him behind the old outhouse, where he removed his clothes and threatened to kill him if he screamed or even whispered. Then the older boy beat him mercilessly with a strong stick, particularly near the groin and the genitals, drawing blood. When satisfied, the boy ran off, leaving Butterfield for dead.

When reporters learned of the attack, it did not take them long to draw parallels between this case and Jesse Pomeroy's crimes. But despite the similarities, concrete answers could not be found. Why were they seeing more crimes committed by children? Why was such an epidemic of childhood violence making its way across the country? Had children always been inclined to violence, and only after the Pomeroy story did adults pay attention to them?

And while Maine struggled to find the answers, New Jersey also contended with its own fiend.

"A ten-year-old boy . . . of late has developed a depravity and viciousness as great as that of the famous, or infamous, boy murderer of Massachusetts, Jesse Pomeroy," a local paper wrote. The boy in question, Freddy Reiley, was a resident of the Home of the Sisters of the Peace. A nun on her way to morning confession had found nine-year-old Freddy about to burn a three-year-old boy over an open stove. The little boy was gagged and bruised, but somehow he had managed to spit out a portion of the fabric that had been inserted into his mouth and utter a scream that was loud enough to alert the nun passing by.

When Freddy was asked why he had done those things to the little boy, he merely laughed and walked away. According to the Sisters of Peace, this was only the latest in Freddy's fiendish acts. He had also been stealing, hitting other children, and swearing crudely. What was worse, the nuns said, the boy was very calm and cool, especially after he had committed the vicious acts.

As the country reckoned with this new wave of criminality in children, Jesse grew into his sentence; his mother, whom he saw once a month, was his only connection to the outside world. In a letter she wrote in 1878, one of many delivered to him every two months, Ruth Ann advised him: "Jesse, my dear boy, be courageous. Do not be downhearted. The day will come when you will be free and respected. Acquire knowledge." He heeded her advice, and by 1888, when he was twenty-eight years old, he had learned Latin and Greek, along with a good smattering of several Romance languages.

He had started reading voraciously, his favorite book being *Napoleon's Exile in St. Helen.* He was confident that each step he took in bettering himself would bring him closer to the outside world. Because he had also started perusing legal texts, particularly those relating to the state of Massachusetts, he learned that since 1883 the governor of the state had pardoned at least a dozen prisoners who like him had been given life sentences. Eight had been sentenced for murder, spending on average twelve years behind bars before regaining their freedom. Given what he was finding out, Jesse felt secure in the knowledge that he would be going home soon. What he didn't know was that his crimes were still considered unusually atrocious, and the general public still believed he was a very dangerous individual. More important, the parole board shared these feelings as well.

He also took to reading books on mechanics, which did not please his jailors because they feared he would put that knowledge to practice; for their part, aside from his books, the guards allowed the very basic necessities to be available in his cell.

ON DECEMBER 31, 1889, the guards on duty at the Massachusetts State Prison heard the faint mewing of a cat. They believed it was Buster, Officer Thomas E. Brassel's cat, who freely roamed the hallways at night. The first to become aware of the suspicious purring was Officer Brassel himself, who was on his nightly rounds. He followed the cat's mewing down the dark hall toward the Cherry Hill section, the route that led toward solitary confinement. As he walked on, he realized the cat's purring came from a location near Jesse Pomeroy's cell, where Brassel also heard a rustling in a corner. He shined a light toward the farther end of the corridor, where he spotted Pomeroy crouched "near an electric switch box in the jail corridor." Jesse had inched his way out of the cell and against the wall, where he now squatted trying to avert the pool of light from Officer Brassel's flashlight.

Pomeroy had nearly succeeded in breaking free, if not for the cat. For weeks, without anyone noticing it, Jesse had been cutting away at the bars of his cell, three of which he had removed, allowing for enough space to stretch through. This had brought him into the corridor, where Buster had spotted him and started rubbing against his legs, purring in apparent delight.

Brassel called to his fellow guards that they had a "runner," meaning someone trying to make a break, and instructed Jesse to crawl from his spot and put his hands up. Jesse did so, and was directed toward the "Blue Room," a lone room in Cherry Hill where prisoners were taken for misbehaving. The guards searched him and discovered an assortment of crudely constructed tools: "two small pieces of steel . . . one was fashioned into a drill and with this he had drilled three of the steel bars on his cell gate." When he was caught, Jesse was in the process of removing several contraband cutting instruments, including a screwdriver, from a cabinet in the corridor to use in the outside world.

Jesse must have known that his actual chances of making it out of the prison were slim, but that didn't stop him from trying.

"Pomeroy is a digger," said one of the wardens, aware of the inmate's propensities, "and he will never give up until he escapes or is dead." His chances of doing so were far-fetched, and the guards did not believe he would ever make it any farther than he already had; however they were "constantly on the watch orders by the warden, and we half fear that he will."

AS THE YEARS PASSED, there was never a hint that Jesse had become remorseful, nor was there any reason to think he had engaged in any self-examination to discover why he had committed his crimes. He was often heard whistling so loudly that it could be easily heard in the cells of the other inmates. "Home, Sweet Home" was his favorite tune, the same one he had heard other inmates whistle in the Suffolk County Jail while awaiting his trial. The officers found his whistling especially irritating.

Jesse's two main goals were escaping or gaining a pardon. Insensitive, the warden said, he took "kindness as a matter of cause." This show of insensitivity was displayed also, and most especially, toward his mother, with whom he talked of nothing else other than what steps she was taking to secure his pardon or release. He never asked about her life, nor did he inquire about his brother, Charles, and the life he had forged for himself or the way his days were progressing. Had he done so, Jesse would have learned that on Christmas Day, 1877, Charles had married a lovely New Hampshire girl named Inez J. Durrell, and that a year later they had had a baby girl named Mable. He would have learned that Inez had died not too long after, and that despite his pain, Charles had soon married a girl named Emma, a very fertile girl who would birth six more children, none of whom would be named for their uncle, Jesse Pomeroy. He would also have learned that Charles had embarked on a career as a cook, eventually becoming the proprietor of a restaurant in Roxbury, Massachusetts, named Pomeroy and Farrenkopf.

Instead, Jesse was interested in exploring the legal loopholes in his case that might benefit him. "His main employment," the warden wrote, was "an unremitting effort to prove that he was illegally sentenced." He focused on the idea that he had been found guilty "as charged." In his mind, this meant he had been unlawfully tried, convicted, and sentenced. His contentions, according to his writings in the pardon papers, were that "murder committed with circumstances of extreme atrocity and cruelty," which was "one of the statutory ways in which murder in the first degree may consist and be proved as charged by the court was not established at the trial." Pomeroy argued that atrocity and cruelty had not occurred because the numerous wounds inflicted on Horace Millen were mortal and therefore did not cause suffering, a by-product of which would have been cruelty.

But the Prison Committee's response to these self-serving theories pointed out that "[Jesse] ignores the fact that none of the wounds were superficial, and the evidence that although death was caused by hemorrhage from the severed vessels of the neck, blood also flowed from some of the less severe wounds, showing that the boy was alive when they were inflicted." This "has no weight on his mind as at least a presumptive of torture."

Although nearly two decades had gone by since his incarceration, reporters had not forgotten about Jesse Pomeroy, and from the confines of his cell he kept abreast of what was written about him. And not surprisingly, he felt his name was being taken in vain, and money and notoriety that should have been rightly his were being earned by hacks. Unscrupulous reporters not only delighted in telling his story, he said, but each retelling was gorier and more despicable.

"I found an extremely insulting and misleading article in reference to myself," he wrote in July 1889, addressing the editor of the *World*. He explained that he had never hurt animals, as the article stated and his former neighbors implied, nor had he "decoyed little boys to lonely spots to apply a whip or club to their shrinking bodies, or using a knife." He denied everything, but said "they [the children] were more scared than hurt."

IN OCTOBER 1909, WHEN he was fifty-three years old, Jesse strove for freedom again. This time it was Officer L. F. Burk who found him, and he wrote in his report a few days later: "Found Jesse H. Pomeroy working in a corner of the cell and saw something on the table that looked suspicious. Waited until Officer Wood came on relief and accompanied by him entered Pomeroy's cell. Saw Pomeroy conceal something in his mouth as he rushed toward water-closet, asked Pomeroy to open his mouth, he refused, whereupon, I seized hold of him, and took from his mouth a small drill," a rudimentary tool meant to provide freedom.

Wood wrote a similar report: "On Wednesday, Oct. 13, Officer Burk with myself went into Jesse's Pomeroy's cell at Cherry Hill, for the purpose of taking some instruments, with which Officer Burk had reason to believe Pomeroy was using to dig. As we went in Pomeroy made an attempt to reach the toilet, evidently to throw the instruments in, but failed. He had them into his mouth and refused to give them up. He fought us, so we put him on his back on the floor, and kept him there till he gave up one of the instruments, which was a small, chisel-shaped tool. He was not hurt or handled in a rough way, and we told him he could get up if he would give us what he had in his mouth, but he refused."

A week or so after the incident, Warden General Benjamin E. Bridges wrote a letter to F. G. Pettigrove, chairman of the Prison Commission, describing the troubles Jesse was causing. "It is so seldom that I find any truth in his statements," he wrote. Apparently Jesse had been complaining that the officers had been "interfering" with his ability to get his due judicial process, though the warden denied such accusations. He also informed the commissioner, "Lately we have had reason to believe that he was trying to get back to his old line of digging. He has been found several times on the table, evidently trying to communicate with those in other cells."

Bridges also detailed certain discoveries Officers Burk and Wood made: "A few days since when he was out of his room, Officer Burk found his butter looking very suspicious, and upon investigation found that he had some twenty feet of braided twine which he had evidently torn from the book binding and made a very substantial cord as a weight so that it might be thrown into some other room. Pomeroy objected to his butter being interfered with and said there was nothing in it. He said there was no rope or cord and the officer said there was sufficient for him to hang himself with. . . . Also in the butter were concealed several steel pens which were evidently for the purpose of making instruments for his use, they being more effective than most he has ever worked with."

Though he was never successful in his escape attempts, Jesse did manage to keep his jailers on their toes.

CHAPTER 11

MADNESS UNLEASHED

All men tragically great are made so through a certain morbidness. Be sure of this, O young ambition, all mortal greatness is but disease.

—HERMAN MELVILLE, *MOBY-DICK*

Many times over the decades, reporters dug deeply into Jesse Pomeroy's genealogy to find strands of mental illness that might explain, if not excuse, the deeds he had committed, and though they found clues that were tantalizing, nothing concrete came of it. Whatever he was suffering from, it could not be directly linked to his family. Mental illness was also a topic of conversation that for years had obsessed the Melvilles, particularly Herman, whose relatives had become convinced of his insanity. The publication of *Moby-Dick* in particular seemed to solidify their belief that something was amiss with the author's mind. Many of the critiques of Melville's work often tied him to the character of mad Ahab, making the two indistinguishable.

The *Southern Quarterly Review* of January 1852 wrote: "His ravings [Ahab] . . . and the ravings of Mr. Melville himself, meant for eloquent declaration, are such as would justify a writ de *lunatics* against all." Or, as the *New York Day* put it more bluntly, HERMAN MELVILLE CRAZY.

The publication of *Moby-Dick* in 1851 had hinted at flights of fancy many of his readers did not understand and did not wish to explore. But the next year, Melville's *Pierre* caused an even greater sensation. In a psychosexual text, the titular character, Pierre, is caught between two women, representing good and evil. The idea of such sexual morbidity had not been encountered before in recent literature, and readers weren't certain what to make of it. The book immensely disturbed the family, and his wife and mother immediately thought that a more benign occupation away from the literary one, perhaps in government, should be found for him.

Despite every effort made by his relatives, they were never able to find Melville the desired job. In 1853 Melville's daughter Bessie was born, and in 1855 his last child, Frances, arrived. His brother Allan was now a successful lawyer, but he too was unable to find a proper post for Herman. Elizabeth confided in her father that she felt "great anxiety" over her husband's mental health and not surprisingly, Judge Shaw agreed to finance a new trip abroad to calm Herman's nerves.

"I suppose you have been informed by some of the family, how very ill Herman has been," Judge Shaw wrote to his son Samuel in September 1856. "When he is deeply engaged in one of his literary works, he confines him[self] to hard study many hours in the day, with little or no exercise & this especially in winter for a great many days together. He probably thus overworks himself & brings on severe nervous afflictions." Melville sailed for England on October 11, 1856.

By this time, Nathaniel Hawthorne was serving as American consul to Liverpool, having been appointed by President Franklin Pierce. As soon as Melville landed in England on November 10, he visited the Hawthornes. Though happy to see him, Hawthorne was surprised by Melville's appearance: there was a newfound pallor on Herman's skin, and a sadness that seemed to issue from every pore. He wore a heavy coat, which not only added bulk to his frame, but also gave him a kind of heaviness that hadn't been there before. He simply didn't look well. True, his bad eyesight and constant bouts of rheumatism were somewhat responsible, but Hawthorne surmised that part of this change was due to the "constant literary occupation," which he said Melville "pursued without much success." Hawthorne had read Melville's latest books and believed they "indicated a morbid state of mind."

The writers reminisced about their time in Pittsfield, outings with their New York and Boston friends, and their shared summer. Also, Hawthorne wrote in his journal, they spoke "of Providence and futurity, and everything that lives beyond human kin." Melville also told Hawthorne he had "pretty much made up his mind to be annihilated," though Hawthorne did not understand the meaning of those words.

Still, Hawthorne went on, "he does not seem to rest in that anticipation and, I think, will never rest until he gets hold of a definite belief. It is strange how he persists . . . to wonder to and forever these deserts, as dismal and monotonous as the sand hills amid which we were sitting. He can neither believe, nor be comfortable in his disbelief; and he is too honest and courageous not to try to do one or the other."

Hawthorne had always been aware of Melville's struggle to come to terms with a higher power, with his idea of God and the fact that he was unable to make peace with Him or wage war against Him.

The two parted by an intersection on the streets of Liverpool, and Hawthorne watched Melville walk on as a heavy downpour beat upon his oversize coat. It was a pitiful sight, he decided.

When Melville returned to Pittsfield, the family rallied to find work for him that would require dexterity of hands but not much mental strain. On April 7, 1857, his sister Augusta wrote to their uncle Peter Gansevoort, asking whether he might help Herman find the right job. She said it was of the "outmost importance that something should be done to prevent the necessity of Herman's writing." The family blamed his sedentary life, the hours spent in solitude with characters of ugly reputations and finicky minds; they blamed Melville's farmwork, which he had come to despise, and the responsibility of too many children, to whom he had become abrupt and often even cold. In Augusta's letter, she reiterated her belief that if he returned to writing, "he would risk the loss of all the benefit to his health which he gained by his tour, & possibly become an invalid. Of this his physicians have warned him."

But Uncle Peter was not helpful. As winter came tumbling down in the Berkshires, Melville received a letter from his friend George L. Duyckinck, brother of Evert, asking if he would be interested in joining the lecture circuit. Melville said yes, that he would "be glad to lecture . . . anywhere," as long as "they will pay expenses and gave a reasonable fee." He needed to make money so desperately he did not care whether the lectures were held in "Labrador or on the Isle of Desolation in Patagonia." Duyckinck assumed the masterly storytelling talents Melville demonstrated on paper would go on to enrapture a live audience in an auditorium. Melville agreed that he would use his adventures in the South Seas for his lectures.

The first lecture was set for February 24, 1859, at the Metropolitan Hall in Chicago, and was scheduled by the Young Men's Association, which had lately been sponsoring lectures by very prominent individuals, such as writers and philosophers. Despite the rainy evening, Melville had a very large audience who seemed happy to hear his tales of the South Seas.

Two days later, he spoke in Wisconsin, and the *Daily Wisconsin* wrote a very appreciative review: "The lecture of Herman Melville last night was attended by a very large and appreciative audience, who seemed greatly to admire his fascinating pictures of the different features characteristic of the South Seas Island. It was a pleasant, richly colored story, as it were (rather than a stilled lecture) of what the great Pacific is . . . while it was entertaining, too, it was also instructive."

Unfortunately, this was one of the few positive reviews he received throughout the tour. For the most part, he was thought of as a lousy lecturer, boring and without charisma. Most reporters disapproved of his methods, and on March 3, Illinois's *Rockford Register* declared that he was "without such qualities" to make him a success on the circuit. Two days later, on March 5, the same paper curtly concluded that "lecturing is evidently not Mr. Melville's sphere," adding, "It has rarely been our lot to witness a more painful infliction upon an audience." His last lecture was in Quincy, Illinois, and when done he was happy to return to the toils of Arrowhead and the familial worries of his brood.

The disappointments of *Moby-Dick* and *Pierre*, his farmwork, which brought him little or no satisfaction, his failed attempt at lecturing, a growing family he could barely provide for, and the continual needling of his family added to his mental fatigue. He had also begun to drink more heavily. He was a broken man, and those who met him became aware of it right away.

By December 1861 the Melville family decided to leave Arrowhead and return to New York City.

EACH MORNING AT DAWN, Melville made his way from his brownstone on East Twenty-Sixth Street to the corner of Wall Street and William Street, the large granite building that had formerly been the Merchant's Exchange Building and now served as the New York Custom House.

He had hoped for a government position, but in the end being employed at the Custom House felt like the better fit. The Custom House maintained most of the waters in the state of New York, as well as "the counties of Hudson and Bergen in the state of New Jersey." Nearly a thousand people worked there, making it one of the "largest Federal offices in the United States."

The top position during Melville's time there was held by a man named Henry A. Smighty, whose title was Collector of Customs. He was also in charge of a professional gang of intimidators who operated within the house and was commonly referred to by the uninspiring name the "Custom House Gang." With so many people employed there, delinquency and corruption were almost unavoidable.

Normally a person would acquire a position in the Custom House through the recommendation of friends or acquaintances in high places, but Melville had simply applied directly to Smighty, who had received his own appointment decades before from President Andrew Jackson. Smighty endorsed Melville's application for inspector, and Melville started on December 5, 1866, at the wage of four dollars per day.

Though a pittance, the job pacified those around him who worried that if he returned to writing books, his health would deteriorate again. "Herman's health is much better since he had been compelled to go out daily to attend to his business," Maria Melville wrote to her cousin Kate Gansevoort on March 11, 1867. "He is one of the District Officers in the Custom House. He has been in office about three months."

Each morning Herman made his way to the North River District #4, where as a district inspector part of his job entailed meeting a ship as it docked in the harbor and checking all of its paperwork to make certain they "had been properly boarded." With his tall figure stooping and a long shaggy beard, his badge affixed to his coat, it was easy to see how Melville's life had changed since moving from Arrowhead. He was no longer in the deep valleys of the countryside, but in New York City, which was now more crowded than ever, not only with the local populace but with the tide of immigrants that landed in ports every day along with those who were moving into the city from other parts of the country. Melville became a part of that crowd, moving to and fro with the same ease, or unease, as the others did, becoming one of those people James Gordon Bennett from the *Herald* strove to entertain with his publication.

"The city is a great school for studying human nature, and its people are proficient in the art of discerning character," wrote Edward Winslow Martin in his book *The Secrets of the Great City: A Work Descriptive of the Virtues and the Vices, of the Mysteries, Miseries and Crimes of New York City.* Martin determined that they cared only for themselves and no one else—so much so that it was possible to occupy an apartment for decades and never know who lived next door. He wrote that this attitude didn't mean that New Yorkers were mean-spirited; they were just very eager to make a good life for themselves. Jumping to socioeconomics, he noted that the city contained only two classes of people: the very rich and the very poor.

Now that he was living in New York, Melville received his daily share of the news from the local newsboys, who were as rampant as the plague. And just like a pestilence, scores of them swarmed about the ladies and the gentlemen passing by, urging them to buy the papers by thrusting the publications into their faces. Pedestrians often shelled out a penny or two just to get the boys out of their way.

Melville didn't mind these boys and from them he bought James Gordon Bennett's *Herald*, which allowed him to indulge in his daily dose of mayhem, tales of murders and gore, of young victims and young killers occupying the pages of newspapers across the country, which in turn made their way into his books. This was the sort of news that came from these newsboys, those filthy little boys who made their homes on the streets or in the tenement houses now sprouting across what had been the better parts of the city.

Many New Yorkers felt these homes for the immigrants and the poor had devalued the city. They were convinced that morality was lost within those tenement houses. "The walls were so dark . . . filled with wretched inmates," Martin wrote. "Rum, gin, whiskey and other liquors of the vilest kind, are used in here . . . thousands of children are born in these foul places every year. They never see the light of day until they are able to crawl in the streets."

But more than anything else about New York, Melville was drawn in by the area's waters, as he had been in his youth. In winter, when the temperature dipped and the snows fell, New York's rivers became inundated with large chunks of ice floating every which way, paralyzing the ferries and preventing them from working. But during summer, the sun struck the water just so, making it luminescent, its rippling bringing him memories of bygone days. Standing at the docks and looking out, it was even possible to feign being on a ship, the salty spray of a wave crashing against the port reminiscent of a whale's loud blow.

The New York waters were occupied by ships, boats, and ferries, and the harbor patrol looked not only for those running into problems or causing havoc, but for the dead bodies that all too often floated by. Drowning was as common as the parasols women used to shield the sun, as were murders and bodies dumped into the waters. It was also the job of the harbor patrol to retrieve these victims from the rivers and ports and take them to one of the dreariest places ever erected on the East River: the morgue.

Called the Dead House, it had been modeled on the one located in Paris. New Yorkers knew the unfortunates found along the waterways and riverbanks were sent to the Dead House in the hope that their loved ones would identify them. Clothing and personal trinkets were collected to help relatives claim the bodies, though when none came, the deceased were buried in a potter's field.

Melville watched the living and the dead, the corrupted and the incorruptible, the young and the old, moving about the city like ghosts. He performed his job at the Custom House judiciously but without much enthusiasm. He obeyed the rules imposed by his status like the perfect civil servant, but he never strove to move ahead. He never rose from his position, never earned more than he did on his first day, never distinguished himself in any way that made much of a difference, lapsing instead into indifference.

Oddly enough, on a previous visit to Nantucket, with his father-in-law, he had met Captain George Pollard, who had manned the *Essex* on its faithful journey when a whale rammed and sunk the ship. At the time of their meeting, Pollard had given up the sea and become a neighborhood night watchman. He had retreated into what he considered a life of oblivion and indifference. Melville wrote that "to the islanders he was a nobody." But Melville saw Pollard as "the most impressive man . . . that I ever considered." Whether Melville thought of Pollard as he patrolled the Custom House is unknown, although he never tried to avoid a similar fate.

Soon after Melville began working at the Custom House, word began to circulate that the inspectors' wages would be cut, and that several of them would lose their jobs. The Melville family worried that Herman, a relative newcomer, would see the job that had been so long in coming taken away from him. But a man named John Hoadley wrote to George S. Bartwell, an official at the Revenue Service, to speak on Melville's behalf and of his character, all done in order to keep him on staff. As it turned out, the letter was probably a little more revealing than he had intended.

"Proud, shy, sensitively honorable—he had much to overcome and has much to endure," Hoadley wrote. "But he tries earnestly to perform his duties as to make the slightest censure, reprimand, or even remainder—impossible for any superior . . . quietly declining offers of money for special services, quietly returning money which had been thrust into his pocket behind his back . . . quietly steadfastly doing his duty. . . . Advancement or promotion he does not seek—nor would his friends seek it for him—the pittance he receives ekes out his slender income."

Though Melville was valued at work for his punctuality and servitude, his true nature came out at home. He had resumed drinking, and difficulties between him and Elizabeth that had been present in Pittsfield became even more pronounced in New York. Extended family members discussed this with Dr. Henry Whitney Bellows, the minister at the All Souls Unitarian Church, which the Melvilles attended.

Elizabeth's brother Samuel Shaw wrote to Bellows frequently and spoke of the difficulties Herman was causing the family. In one such letter from Samuel Shaw to Dr. Bellows, dated May 6, 1867, an odd and seemingly naïve plan to get Elizabeth away from Melville was discussed. Shaw wrote that Herman's issues had been the "cause of anxiety to all of us for years." For just as many years now they had been pushing Elizabeth to leave New York and Herman behind, and most recently even the Melvilles had decided to go along with the plan. While they agreed that doing so was a good idea, they had to make certain that these were Elizabeth's "real wishes," and not just hopes on their part.

Shaw then detailed the plan in the letter: "She should come to Boston as if on a visit," he said, allowing her plenty of time to prepare but without arising suspicion in anyone, least of all Herman. Then, while in Boston, she "should inform her husband that a separation, for

the present at least, has been decided on." No one would think this a
rash decision, as aside from the family and relations, the family physician, Dr. Gardner, would also help in her steps. The family would keep
her in Boston and bar her husband from seeing her. "I think that the
safest course is to let her real position became apparent from the start,"
Shaw wrote. "Namely that a wife, who, being convinced that her husband is insane *acts* as if she were so convinced and appears and applies
for aid and assistance to her friends and *acts* with them."

But Elizabeth, either bound by love, duty, or guilt, did none of
those things. She did not go to Boston but remained in New York, the
long-suffering wife of a man she thought had lost his mind.

HERMAN'S CHILDREN WERE GROWING and though still young,
they were forging ahead, revealing flaws and character traits that would
mark their identities. By 1865, Malcolm, the oldest, was seventeen years
old and had found work with the Great Western Maine Insurance
Company. He earned a steady two hundred dollars a year. Strangely
enough, the boy was able to gain employment much more easily than
his father ever had, with the assistance of his uncle Allan. Malcolm
was also a member of the New York Twenty-Second Regiment of the
National Guard, which allowed him to don a taut uniform and to
carry a firearm. He displayed such pride in those accomplishments that
he often wore the uniform while at home, and paraded in front of his
sisters, who teased him.

What they didn't tease him about was the pistol. Malcolm often
delighted in telling his friends and family that he slept with it under
his pillow. The boy had recently also taken to staying out late with his
friends, a new turn of events for an otherwise steady boy.

In early September 1867, Herman and Elizabeth discussed taking
Malcolm's house key away from him in the hope of curbing his late-
night escapades. The step was never taken. They decided that these
were the exploits of a young man testing his independence and "frol-

icking with his young friends." But one night in the middle of that month, Malcolm remained out until 3 A.M., his mother staying up late waiting for him. When he returned, he told Elizabeth he had been at an "entertainment" given by his friends. He didn't seem drunk but merely tired. She tried talking to him, but she didn't have the heart to scold him. As he always did, Malcolm kissed his mother good night and went to his own room.

He didn't get up for work the next morning, as he usually did. Despite repeated calls from his sisters to get up, he did not. As Herman left for his own job, he told Elizabeth to let Malcolm sleep late and take the punishment he would receive at his job. Elizabeth did so, but throughout the day, she knocked on Malcolm's door and called out his name. This wasn't so strange; given his recent nightly jaunts, he had taken to staying in bed more and more. When Herman returned home that night, Malcolm was still not responding, and they decided to break down the door. They found the boy sprawled on his bed, still wearing his nightclothes, dead for several hours, a bullet hole in his skull.

Dr. Gardner was called and he advised the family to summon the coroner, who came quickly. The report came a few days later, and it was not what the family wanted to hear. The death was ruled a suicide. "That the said child came to his death by suicide by shooting himself in the head with a pistol at said place while laboring under temporary insanity of the mind," it said. That streak of instability plaguing the family had resurfaced.

The newspapers learned of the tragedy right away. "The parents of the deceased could not assign any cause for the suicidal act, and the jury came to the conclusion that the deceased must have been suffering from a temporary aberration of the mind."

Elizabeth and Herman fought against the ruling. Everyone in the family knew Malcolm not only carried the gun but also cleaned it before going to bed, and he even sometimes slept with it; they came to think the gun could have gone off unintentionally and struck him.

They argued with the coroner, so much so that on the next day the ruling of suicide was changed to that of an accident. "We believe that his death was caused by his own hands," the new ruling read, "but that the act was not by premeditation or consciously done, no motive for it having appeared during the inquest or after." Nonetheless, the uncertainty of what had happened remained.

The suffering they all endured from Malcolm's death seemed to exaggerate Herman's ever-growing impatience with his family. His daughter Bessie slowly began to succumb to the rheumatism that would eventually lead her to become an invalid. Their son Stanwix was now the only boy. He was a sensitive youth, and he had great difficulty handling the grief he saw in his parents. Unlike Malcolm, Stanwix was not able to find a steady occupation, and by 1869 he decided to heed the call of the sea, just like his father had, yearning for a nautical adventure of his own. This was also an opportunity to leave home. Herman and Elizabeth were not happy about this, but they eventually consented to a trip to China to "cure him of the fancy."

By the time Stanwix left for his adventure, Herman was not well. "If you see Herman, please do not tell him that I said he was not well," Elizabeth wrote to Peter Gansevoort and his wife while they visited New York in October 1869. "But if you think he looks well, I hope you will tell him so."

Stanwix returned to New York the next year, after deserting his ship, also much like his father had done. He planned to stay in New York and find a position and settle down, but he was never able to find a job, and the next month he traveled to Kansas for work, only to return to New York in 1871, and to depart again in 1872. This pattern of coming and going disturbed the family, particularly Elizabeth, who in May 1873 wrote to her cousin Kate Gansevoort that her remaining son was infested by the "demon of restlessness."

Her worries continued when Stanwix left again for Kansas but then took off for Mississippi, and from there to Cuba and then to several South American countries. Eventually he made his way to California, where he found work on a cattle ranch. But it wasn't long before Herman and Elizabeth learned that their son had grown ill. He had visited them almost two years before, looking well, but he became sick when he returned to the ranch, and he was taken to a San Francisco hospital, where he died. He was only thirty-five.

Deeply affected by this new loss, Herman and Elizabeth unexpectedly grew closer. They bonded over their shared grief, which would take them into their last years together.

BY NOW HERMAN MELVILLE was also involved in what would be his last work, the novella *Billy Budd*.

His brownstone in New York City had become even more somber, particularly his study, where he secluded himself even when he was not working. Facing north, this was an enclave where a large mahogany desk took up the better part of the space, along with four bookcases filled to the edges. Melville's granddaughter, Eleanor, the daughter of Frances, would later recall standing at the threshold of that room and watching the plaster heads atop each bookcase looking down at her. An iron bed covered with a dark blanket also rested in the middle of the space, along with several tables crowded with papers and unfinished manuscripts no one dared to touch. Melville's portrait hung on the wall, adding to the air of mystery already wafting within the room.

The room was cool not just in the winter but also in the summer, because of a lack of sunlight. Elizabeth's worries had not ceased as time passed, nor had she given in to her family's desire to separate from Herman. She had actually grown more disinclined to leave him alone, even if only for a few weeks, fearing his mental health would be further damaged. This became obvious when her health grew more precarious. From a very young age, she had suffered from severe bouts of hay fever.

By the early 1870s, she had grown accustomed to spending part of the summer away from New York and in the White Mountains of New Hampshire. The fresh air and the tranquility there always relieved her. She usually packed her summer belongings, along with her daughters, and made the trek northward. But now Herman prevented her from enjoying herself entirely. In a letter she wrote on June 19, 1877, to her brother Samuel, she said: "Hope we shall be able to pass a six week absence from New York—the only doubt of which is being able to leave Herman alone for so long, in his state of mental health, with a free conscience."

Others had also taken notice of Herman's growing peculiarities. A young man named Henry Thomas began to frequent the household, intent on courting Melville's daughter Frances. Thomas knew about Herman's work at the Custom House, as well as of his past jaunts on whale ships, but he soon began accompanying Melville on what had become his frequent ferry rides and became even more aware of Melville's fascination with the water.

Though family members believed Herman's mind had finally come undone, Thomas indulged his future father-in-law on those travels, even if he was often made nervous by Herman's propensity to "never sit still in one seat for long" and to move "about trying every place of vantage on the ferry boat." Whatever Melville yearned to find on those rides, Thomas never found out.

Melville continued his job at the Custom House, though it brought him little satisfaction, either financially or mentally. He yearned instead for leisure, independence from his financial constraints. He made this known to his cousin Catherine Lansing on September 5, 1877: "Whoever is not in the possession of leisure can hardly be said to possess independence. They talk of the dignity of work. Bah. True work is the necessity of a poor humanity's earthly condition. The dignity is in leisure. Besides, 99 hundredth of all work done in the world is either foolish and unnecessary, or harmful and wicked."

By the early 1880s, when Herman was already an old man, Elizabeth received an inheritance of $10,000 from her aunt, alleviating some of the family's burdens. Then another relative, a Mrs. Gilford, left an additional $10,000 for Elizabeth and $5,000 for Herman, along with smaller funds for the children. The windfall allowed Herman to leave the Custom House after nineteen years of duty. As he prepared to do so in 1884, he was visited by an old acquaintance, Julian Hawthorne, son of Nathaniel Hawthorne. Julian wanted to publish some reminiscences about his father, who had died in 1864, and he felt that Melville had much to share. Julian visited Melville at his brownstone, where he found the old author "looking pale, somber, nervous, but little touched by age."

They spoke of years past and of Hawthorne, a man for whom Melville said he had "the highest admiration . . . and a deep affection." He told Julian he thought his father was remarkably handsome and auspiciously quiet, a man who held on to many secrets, "which had never been revealed, and which accounted for the gloomy passages in his books." Julian was not surprised to hear that, but despite the odd conversation, Julian couldn't help but realize that there were few "more lovable men than Herman Melville."

On December 31, 1885, Melville officially retired. He had not published a long work of fiction in decades, but he had been steadily printing poetry since the 1850s. For some time now a new project had been percolating in his mind, taking shape very slowly. He had imagined a story taking place aboard a man-of-war, where an older man would be charged with plotting murder and on being found guilty of mutiny, would suffer the ultimate punishment: death. But as the years passed, the story changed, the characters becoming younger and younger.

Billy Budd covered similar elements as the Jesse Pomeroy trial: loss of innocence, youth, madness, monomania, evil; but above all it emphasized the fiendishness of the perpetrator, in Melville's book the evil John Claggart. Although Melville took great creative liberties with the text, all of the issues came forth with this final novella.

Just as in the case of Mary Rogers in 1840, the New York papers, including the *New York Times,* had reveled in the Jesse Pomeroy trial, and on July 26, 1874, just days after Pomeroy's arrest, the *Times* had run one of the first editorials that appeared in its pages, calling the crime

"one not only of extraordinary atrocity in crime but of singular interest in psychology." To those who were indeed interested in psychology, not only on a professional level but a literary one, Pomeroy made
for a compelling character study: a very young boy seemingly without
provocation assaulting very young children on their way to school or
to a bakery. It had all the makings for an exploration of myths as old
as time: David versus Goliath; good versus evil; the angelic versus the
demonic. More than that, it was the singular depravity of the acts that
made the whole episode unsavory and compelling, the story of a boy
who felt no guilt for the crimes he had committed, or pity for the children he had hurt or the murders he had done. It was merely, the *Times*
concluded in 1874, an "Exhibition of the fiendish capacity of human
nature." This fiendish capacity for evil could only be squashed by the
death penalty.

Capital punishment had been at the forefront across the country for
a long time, especially as it related to youthful offenders, as in the case
of Jesse Pomeroy, and from 1886 into the early 1890s, New York City
became the battleground for the debate over the death penalty. The
questions being raised in real life were the same ones Herman Melville
was grappling with, the same ones that would leak into his writing, the
same ones that had been asked at the Pomeroy trial by Oliver Wendell
Holmes and others like him: Does the death penalty deter others from
committing similar or even worse crimes? How does one determine
which crimes should be eligible for the death penalty? What about the
executions themselves—should they remain public or should they be
done in private? And if they are kept public, do they work more as a
spectacle than as an actual call for justice? If they are done in private,
is the state saying it is actually ashamed of what it is doing? What is
the nature of the death penalty, anyway? Is it a biblical and religious
act? An act of revenge? A show of power? All of these questions were
an integral part of the conversations occurring around Melville, and he
soaked them up and imbued his works with the answers.

Executions in America were nothing new. For centuries, public hangings had been viewed by the thousands with a sort of fanatical fervor. But by the time Melville began work on his new novel, executions had evolved with the times and, more important, with technology. It was actually in Melville's own backyard that the so-called battle of the century was being waged, bringing to light those moral questions that had been put aside for centuries.

In the early 1880s, Thomas Edison pushed the New York State Commission to attend one of his experimental displays with AC electricity. There he could show the attendees how "humanely" he had electrocuted dogs found in his neighborhood, not only as a very practical means of ridding oneself of the mongrels but, he thought, as a way for the commissioners to handle the state's own brand of executions. Unknown to him, a competitor, Harold C. Brown, was also talking to New York State prison officials about using AC generators, which he could hook up to what he called an "electric chair." He already knew this would work. Very quietly he had gone about the dispatching of a Newfoundland dog, all before the eyes of horrified crowds and animal lovers.

Given all the hoopla surrounding the humane way of executing criminals, on August 6, 1890, William Kimmler became the first victim of the electric chair. It was supposed to be very simple: with a flick of a switch, the spectacle and struggles of the gallows, the gurgling of the victim, and the jeering from the crowds attending the ordeal would come to an end. Its simplicity and speed would also allow little time to ponder whether what was being witnessed was truly humane. Everyone knew it was immoral to leave a man hanging and struggling to die, regardless of his past acts; the electric chair, in its swiftness, would prevent all of that.

But, as predicted by some, the execution did not go so easily. The *New York Times* described it as one of "the most revolting circumstances." Those who attended were "men eminent in science and medicine"; yet they were also "nauseated" by all they saw and felt that the new law allowing such ordeals should have been repealed. Those in attendance said they "had taken part in a science that would be told to the world."

Melville intended to tackle these pesky morality questions while at the same time returning to a favorite subject of his: mental illness.

Billy Budd tells the story of three characters: Billy, the young and naïve shipmate; Captain Vere, the obtuse and overall practical captain aboard the man-of-war; and John Claggart, the monomaniacal and evil master-at-arms, whose hatred for the boy simmers beneath the surface.

Billy was a nineteen-year-old boy, and though he had lived nearly two decades, he had no tangible life experience. He was ignorant of how the world worked, and more than that, he was ignorant of humanity at large. No one on the ship feared him, and most of Billy's shipmates were willing to do almost everything for him. He was also called Baby Budd, because of not only his delicate features but also his modesty and innocence. Nothing about him was masculine, nor was anything frightening that would put off those who came in contact with him.

John Claggart was in charge of keeping order aboard the ship. In his mid-thirties, he was tall and lean, and his well-manicured hands indicated a lack of practical manual labor. His chin stood out a bit haughtily, but more than that, to his shipmates the shape of his eyes and his head did not seem ordinary. Dark curls rounded his head, but it was the man's pallor that people spoke of, a sort of pasty hue that brought to mind "time-tinted marbles." Although his pallor was not entirely displeasing, it "seemed to hint at something defective or abnormal in the constitution and blood." There was a not-too-subtle hint at something satanic in Claggart, of which all were aware.

Melville revealed little about Claggart's past, though it was suggested that he was highly educated. Those on board believed he was an Englishman, although the faint trace of his accent indicated lands farther away and more mysterious than England. Despite these rumors, Claggart appeared to ignore them all and be offended by none, doing his job well and laughing on occasion, even when he heard what people were saying about him.

Yet few people on board realized that John Claggart had developed an incessant hatred for Billy Budd. Billy, too, was unaware of this because he had never experienced it in his short life and had no way of recognizing the situation developing with the master-at-arms.

Why did Claggart dislike Billy? The answer was as simple as it was complicated: it was easy for someone's apparent innocence, grace, youth, and beauty to instigate hatred in others, Melville said, along with jealousy, hostility, and a desire to do harm that had been hidden all along.

In explaining John Claggart, Melville referred to Plato's definition of "Natural Depravity: a depravity according to nature." This depravity rested underneath a person's façade of what Melville called "respectability." Even though in appearance, the person seemed calm, collected, and even content, on the inside hate was their only intent.

"These men are true madmen of the most dangerous sort," Melville wrote. "For their lunacy is not continuous but occasional, awakened by some special object . . . it is to the average mind not distinguishable from sanity." Claggart was a person with "the mania of an evil nature, not confounded by vigorous training or corrupting books or lascivious living but born with," in short, "a depravity according to nature." These men were *marked* from birth to suffer from their depravity, much like reporters had believed Jesse Pomeroy had been revealing his mark when committing his deeds.

On meeting Billy Budd, Claggart's main ambition became to destroy him. He would denounce Billy to Captain Vere, accusing Billy of plotting mutiny. Vere liked the young Billy, but his duties rested with the men on the ship. He could not take such an accusation lightly, especially when coming from the master-at-arms.

The captain summoned Billy to the cabin and told him that charges of mutiny had been brought against him. Billy did not respond, until Vere urged him to defend himself. Only then did Captain Vere understand the boy's stillness: Billy suffered from a stutter, an impediment of speech, which became more pronounced, causing Billy to act before thinking. Just then, he lifted his right hand and struck his superior Claggart, hitting him on the forehead. Claggart's body fell "like a heavy plank ticked from erectness" on the floor, where he remained motionless.

Vere remained dumbfounded for a moment, then, in reaching toward Claggart's body it seemed to him as if he "were handling a dead snake." Billy was left shaken by the ordeal. "Struck down by an angel of God," Vere whispered toward Billy. "Yet the angel must hang," he added. Billy had been given a death sentence. Vere uttered this with such urgency and rapidity that the surgeon on board who had been summoned to the cabin wondered if perhaps Vere was not "suddenly affected in his mind, or was it but a transient excitement . . . Was he unhinged?"

Many on board believed that Billy was innocent and disagreed with Vere's decision. But innocent of what? The writer C. B. Ives, who studied the text of *Billy Budd*, asked, "Is innocence applied to Billy's act or to Billy himself? Billy is innocent because he lacks experience, like Adam before the fall, but he is not innocent in that he is guilty of a crime. . . . Indeed, if Billy is innocent, why not Claggart? Is it just to blame Claggart for evil that was not his choice but was innate to inborn? His nature 'for which, the Creator alone is responsible,' must 'act out to the end the part allotted to it.' His antipathy was no more within his control than Billy's fits were under Billy's control. Billy's very existence and nearness was an excruciating, unbearable provocation to Claggart."

THE TALE SHIFTED AND took on more nuances as Melville worked on it. He was still writing it in July 1891, when he took ill and was placed under a doctor's care. On September 28 of that year, Herman Melville passed away, leaving *Billy Budd* unfinished. The text was stashed inside a bread box, where it remained for three decades, taken along on the family's various moves in New York, Massachusetts, and New Jersey.

Eleanor Melville, Herman's granddaughter, remembered the text and the perilous life it led prior to its publication in 1924 and wrote about it in her book, *Herman Melville: Cycle and Epicycle:* "Among the most cherished girlhood memories were the visits made to my grandmother's apartment—most especially when my grandmother, in the early years of the twentieth century, invited for the evening our mutual friend, the Reverend Samuel Henry Bishop, a man of unusual integrity, good mind, and more than sensitivity, . . . in order to enlist his interest in her husband's manuscripts. We would sit in the library surrounded by the remaining books of Melville's collection, himself looking down on us from his place over the white marble mantelpiece on the same table where he used to write while *Billy Budd* and fugitive, discarded, or rewritten pieces were inspected."

A Columbia University student named Raymond Weaver approached Eleanor in 1919 for information. He was writing a Melville biography and thought she could offer some assistance and insights. She arranged to meet him outside Boston during a very hot day in August that same year and brought with her various materials, among them the manuscript for *Billy Budd*.

By 1924, Melville was undergoing a transformation, with scholars and readers alike appreciating his books, particularly *Moby-Dick*, as they had not done during his life.

This lack of appreciation was evident in the obituaries when Melville passed away. "Death of a once popular author," read one in the *New York Times*. "There died yesterday at his quiet home in the city a man who although he had done almost no literary work during the past sixteen years, was once one of the most popular writers in the United States. Herman Melville probably reached the height of his fame about 1852, his first novel having been printed about 1847 . . . of late Mr. Melville—probably because he had ceased his literary activity—had fallen into a literary decline, as the result of which his books are now little known. Probably, if the truth were known, even his own generation has long thought him dead, so quiet have been the later years of his life."

His family expressed sadness at his death but also a hint of relief.

"You have doubtlessly learned of Uncle Herman's death at an early hour this morning," wrote Catherine Lansing. "The poor man is out of his suffering, and we cannot but rejoice for him. Poor aunt Lizzie must be about worn out with her long and constant care of him."

As Melville had been seen as almost an invalid and his mental suffering caused such strain on the family, his death was now seen almost as a blessing.

But had he actually been mad? Had he suffered from those familial mental aberrations his relatives had long suspected and accused him of, and which he had also feared he would succumb to? Had Melville been insane at any time during his life? As Melville wrote in *Billy Budd*, such a thing as mental illness was difficult to decipher: "Who in the rainbow can show the line where the violet tint ends and the orange tint begins? Distinctly we see the difference of the colors, but when exactly does the first blending enter into the other? So with sanity and insanity. In pronounced cases, in various degrees supposedly less pronounced, to draw the exact line of demarcation few will undertake."

CHAPTER 12

UNEARTHED

Every man's life ends the same way. It is only the details of how he lived and how he died that distinguishes one man from another.

—ERNEST HEMINGWAY

Nearly twenty years after Pomeroy was jailed, a reporter visiting the Massachusetts State Prison to interview another inmate found himself in the solitary confinement section and arranged a visit with Jesse, a feat no one had ever achieved. The reporter, a very young man feeling a little too full of himself, asked Jesse whether he would now take his "punishment and with no complaint," given that he had been caught several times trying to escape. The reporter was suggesting that the escape attempts had only made things worse.

Jesse didn't take kindly to this and merely stared pointedly at the reporter, who was so frightened by this he later wrote: "An evil look came into his eye. . . . It was fierce, and for a second, it seemed that the old-time fire which had been smoldering in his veins for so long had again been kindled, and he would make trouble."

But Jesse was able to keep those fires under control, telling the reporter, "I don't complain. It does no good." When asked about the crimes he committed while a youth, Jesse said briskly, "I don't want to talk about it. Don't ask me."

The years had marched on slowly, yet Jesse still hoped for freedom. On the one hand, he often wished the governor would simply make him part of a long tradition of pardoning a handful of prisoners on Thanksgiving Day. On that particular holiday two or three prisoners were chosen to be pardoned by the governor and the Governor's Council upon recommendation from the prison officials and the warden, those moves made known to the public on that very same day.

To Jesse's chagrin the tradition would soon be done away with. General Benjamin E. Bridges, the warden of the prison, agreed that it was good to discontinue this routine because he had seen long-term prisoners filled with hope go back to the outside world expecting to restart their lives anew and be sorely disappointed: "They never seem to realize that the world has undergone a great change during the period of his imprisonment. He expects to find it as he left it, perhaps a half a lifetime ago, and joyfully anticipates his stepping out among his old companions and fitting easily into the scenes of his youth again . . . those hopes are sadly disappointed," the warden said. "The old and familiar haunts of his youth have undergone startling changes and he finds himself a stranger amid strange people and new surroundings. . . . He comes back a veritable Rip Van Winkle, being as completely out of touch with the world as if his confinement had been a long sleep or a journey into a far country where only vague rumors reached him . . . time has, as it were, been annihilated. The clock of the prisoner's existence has been stopped at the hours of his conviction and has been started again exactly at the same hours on the day of his pardon."

Though the tradition would be discontinued during Jesse's time in jail, he had begun to work toward a pardon based on a loophole he found regarding solitary confinement. As early as 1888, he had learned of an arcane and discarded statute that indicated that no man should be kept in solitary confinement for more than twenty days. He had clearly served longer than that and reasoned that he had grounds for a dismissal. He began to pester officials with letters, vowing that the authorities would "not be able to keep him in prison until he dies."

His first petition for a pardon reached the Executive Department at the State House in the mid-1880s. Jesse's language was formal and described in great detail why he should leave the state prison. "I, Jesse H. Pomeroy, being now confined under sentence in the solitary cells over 28 years at the State Prison, Boston, on conviction of the crime of murder (capital sentence commuted) do petition for a pardon." He had obviously done his homework, studying the law judiciously. His reasons for granting a pardon were: "the youth of the prisoner, who was 14 years of age when arrested, April 1874; the exceedingly severity of his sentence—solitary imprisonment at hard labor for life . . . the jury recommended the prisoner to mercy because of his youth. Such a sentence as this has no parallel among the many thousands who have been confined in this prison. Four or more commutations have been granted by the executives, but they were not children, not one has suffered as this young life."

He told the council he had been reformed and, continuing to refer to himself in the third person, said, "he has shown no disposition to lead a criminal life," not mentioning his many attempts to scale the prison walls or that he had been found with contraband tools secreted in his cell and on his person. But those reading the application papers were already well aware of those matters.

"The prisoner hopes, it may be agreeable to permit him to go to Maine. On a farm there, with cheerful labor and perseverance," he wrote, hoping he could fade into obscurity. But he included a line that perhaps ruined any chance of a pardon. "Should a life be thrown away because of the unfounded stories told of him?" The charges against him were not unfounded. That he could not grasp that and still blamed society at large for his incarceration clearly showed, the council felt, that he had not repented, nor had he taken responsibility for his actions.

Such deep-seated hostility seemed normal and even justifiable to some, given that Jesse had in essence grown into manhood behind bars. On November 12, 1900, a Dr. Hale, in criticizing the Massachusetts prison system, spoke of its lack of classification: "Old and young, beginners in crime and hardened criminals, men guilty of petty offenses and those who have devoted their lives to crime, are herded together," he said. "We warn our children of the peril of bad company, we try to guard them from evil companionship, but if they fall into the hands of the state, it fences them into the closest contact with the worst men in the community."

IN SEPTEMBER 1907 JESSE marked his thirty-first year in solitary confinement. He was in surprisingly good physical health, and it showed. Many prisoners swiftly deteriorate, but doctors said Jesse paid very few visits to the infirmary and was never sick. He had grown a long beard, of which he was immensely proud; long and fine, it covered the better part of his face, and he groomed it daily.

He had also taken to pacing his cell for hours on end, aware that he needed to be fit for that day when he would be released. Officials who arrived in his cell unannounced often found him walking the small space back and forth, back and forth, for hours upon hours.

Years later, studies about the pacing engaged in by inmates revealed that it had nothing to do with wishing to be fit. David Morris, author of a book *The Sense of Space*, compared the pacing of inmates to what a caged lion does: "The lion does not first take the measure of its cage in objective units and then, finding it small, pace its confines; its elliptical, perpetual stride already is the 'measure' of its environments, the 'measure' of an environment in which there is no striking distance, no safe remove; correlatively, one caged lion's stride is the 'measure' of an animal warped by its confinement."

By now Jesse's case had been taken up by the American Society for the Promotion of Criminal Anthropology. Its secretary, Fred H. Gale, in petitioning the governor for Jesse's release, called Jesse's treatment a "relic of the past." Without ever visiting Jesse or talking to him, Gale described Pomeroy's conditions: "quite pitiful, wasting away, confined in a cell no larger than a closet, deprived of opportunity for getting in the open air, of attending divine services, etc."

Like others before him, Governor Curtis Guild Jr., who had been elected in 1906, didn't take well to outsiders questioning how the state was handling Pomeroy and replied that he wasn't even considering changing the situation. And even if the council agreed to a bit of freedom, he would veto it.

On March 24, 1914, a letter was sent to Warden Bridges, asking him to allow Jesse to perform more meaningful work, despite his solitary condition. A knitting machine was placed in Jesse's cell, which he used to make socks and mittens. Jesse was also told the commissioners had decided to allow his new application for a pardon to be forwarded to the governor.

Articles about this new development appeared in the press, and the commissioner, who always tried to solve such matters privately, was irked. With the ball now in motion an "alienist" (psychiatrist) visited Jesse, though Jesse refused to talk to him.

On June 12, 1914, the chairman of the Prison Commission, following a visit by the alienist, who had not been able to talk to Jesse, wrote a letter to Jesse that was marked by irritation. The letter read: "It was my request that some physicians visited you in order that they might be in a position to aid the board in determining what action, if any, would be proper for the board to take. It was done with the approval of the board. We have not yet received from the Attorney General his opinion as to your request for legal counsel as submitted to question to him in May. I understand you to complain last year because you had no work. I understand now you to complain because it is offered to you. I wish that you were able to drop the past, and things that, on examination, have been found to amount to little or nothing, and turn your face to the future, and co-operate with those who, in good faith, and with impartiality and kindly motive, are trying to determine what steps they may properly take, looking to the amelioration of your present condition. My advice to you is to make a strong effort to do so, and to attribute to those in authority a good and commendable purpose."

Many of those complaints the commissioner spoke of were trivial, as usual. Jesse accused Warden Bridges of being unkind to him and of keeping his cell in "poor light," which did not allow him to read his papers and magazine. He said he could not see the yard from where his cell was located—even though it had been in the same place for decades now, and even though the warden had nothing to do with the way the prison was structured. He charged that newspapers were being denied him and so were paper and pencils, making it therefore impossible for him to write. This charge was ironic because many people in authority were the unhappy recipients of dozens of his letters. The governor had told Jesse he disapproved of this letter writing, but Jesse appeared not to hear him.

Jesse's actions, although irritating, were the normal reactions of someone who had been forced to live in isolation for as long as he had. In 1913 Frank L. Randall, then commissioner of corrections, enlisted the aid of Dr. William Healey, a well-known Boston psychiatrist, to study Jesse. Healey's assessment was similar to earlier ones: he was not defective in the standard term, nor was he entirely insane. "The habits he displays, such as 'querulousness' . . . are nothing more than might be regarded as a pretty normal reaction to his long confinement." The more he remained in jail, particularly in isolation, the more his keepers would have to grow accustomed to his quirks.

On August 12, 1914, following a battery of examinations by physicians and alienists, the board sent the governor a letter on behalf of Jesse Pomeroy. It spoke of the crime he had committed and the length of time he had been in solitary, and while it did not specifically ask for a pardon, the board did recommend a "commutation of his commuted sentence."

Another statement, on November 10, asked for an amelioration of his conditions. And so it was that in November of that year, the result was "a lessening of the severity of the terms of his imprisonment."

On November 26, Jesse Pomeroy was allowed to attend services in the prison chapel. This occurred on his fifty-fifth birthday. The papers, of course, had a field day with it. "Jesse Pomeroy . . . celebrated his 55th birthday yesterday by attending the services in the chapel . . . for the first time in 33 years," the Boston Globe reported. "He was accompanied to the chapel by prison officials, both of whom occupied seats in the rear of the congregation."

This was odd because Jesse had always scoffed at the idea of redemption and laughed when the chaplain entered his cell. There were some inmates, the reverend always said, whose need for God was so profound that they always bowed their heads when they saw him approach. Jesse was not one of them. Jesse never wanted to hear prayers or any notions of salvation. To him the Bible was full of lies and, moreover, he had done nothing he needed salvation for.

Going to the service was only a small victory. Once again the governor had ignored his petition for a full pardon.

BY 1915 COMMISSIONERS WERE trying to determine whether or not more privileges should be granted to Jesse Pomeroy. At a hearing the late Katie Curran's brother spoke up. "I have no desire to make Pomeroy suffer unnecessarily," he told the prison committee, "but I feel it would be extremely dangerous to allow Pomeroy any liberty whatever. He is ingenious and probably would make his escape and no one knows what the consequences would be." No privileges were extended.

On January 10, 1915, Ruth Ann Pomeroy succumbed to complications of pneumonia. She had been sick for several days, and an earlier bout of the same illness in 1909 had significantly weakened her constitution. Though she had grown older and tired, she had not been dejected, and in 1911 she had made one last effort on Jesse's behalf with Governor Eugene Foss, which had proven fruitless. "Aged and weakened with sorrows," her obituary read, "she could not fight the disease." By the time of her death, her unwavering support for her son had come to be seen as something more than just maternal love: it had become nearly an obsession. And now it was over.

On the next day Warden Nathan D. Allen told Jesse about his mother's passing, which deeply "affected" him and even caused him to burst into tears. Jesse's only link to the outside world was now dead, and she would no longer fight for him. But despite her death, Jesse felt she was better off. She had aged so much since her last bout of illness,

Jesse told the warden, it had pained him to watch her struggle up the long flight of stairs toward the visiting area.

Rumors swirled about Jesse attending the funeral, but the governor quickly put an end to them. He had not received an official request for Jesse to do so, and he would not have allowed it.

IN SEPTEMBER 1916 JESSE marked his fortieth year behind solitary confinement, and that November he turned fifty-eight. On December 8, 1916, as was his custom, he wrote a new request for a pardon. And again it was denied. But a small victory had come his way earlier in the year. In late June he had been granted permission to view his first "moving picture." He was delighted with *The Battle of Peace*, for a time even forgetting the presence of burly Officer Anderson, situated next to him and ready to tackle him should he try to run.

On January 3, 1917, District Attorney Pelletier took up his cause, pleading to Governor Samuel Walker McCall to institute some better treatment for Jesse, who had now become "the only example in the nation of a person being inhumanly treated," and who was slowly suc-cumbing "to death of insanity." "The homicidal insane are allowed every possible minute of freedom with their associates in insane asy-lums. Men who have committed the most vicious crimes are sentenced for life, but permitted freedom with the other prisoners and reasonable opportunity to talk with other human beings," Pelletier went on. Why should people continue to think of Pomeroy a fiend, a demon who needed to be kept alone even behind bars?

Finally in 1918, after Jesse had spent forty-three years in isolation, a councilman led by Colonel Cyrus B. Adams, director of the Prisons Bureau, reviewed Jesse Pomeroy's sentence and agreed to commute it to life imprisonment, which meant he would have all the privileges given to criminals immured for life. But something odd happened: by partially giving in to some of the demands Jesse had made, the council was ending Jesse's reign as the state prison's "star boarder." He would no longer be special. He would no longer be the longest-serving man in solitary confinement, waging a battle against the system for what he believed was justice.

He was now just an aging common criminal imprisoned for life without a chance for parole, doomed to die behind the walls of the Bastille. He would have to do his share of labor; he would have to stand in line with the rest of the prisoners for his meals; he would have to exercise with the rest of the inmates in the courtyard and take his air like everyone else.

Solitary confinement had had its privileges, even though he hadn't recognized them: meals had been brought to him at specific and regular times; he hadn't had to wait for extra rations, when those had been allotted to him; he had exercised in his cell and paced it as often and for as long as he had wished; he hadn't had to work, but for decades had indulged in reading, writing, learning languages, studying poetry, hunting down historical facts, laws, and government rules. There had been no kitchen duty for him; there had been no washing of dirty dishes and filthy pots, nor had there been the mending of socks or the fixing of shoes or the laundering of linens. And, most important, his cell had been his own.

Now he would be required to work like the rest, however menial a job that would be, given that his age was somewhat advanced and his eyesight nearly failing. He would no longer be able to read and write to his heart's content. As it stood, his special status had disappeared in favor of the freedoms he had craved. And he had unremittingly asked for those freedoms himself.

More than anything, he wished to keep his cell on Cherry Hill, his home for decades now, one he did not want to share with anyone. No one knew if a new inmate would be made to come in and stay with him, or worse still, if he would be moved to another cell altogether, but either way, getting a cellmate meant he would have to deal with the gasps, moans, curses, sweats, farts, belches, arguments, and fights of others.

He soon realized the state he had fallen into. Just as in his youth, when Governor Rice and the council had commuted his sentence of hanging to solitary confinement, all believing they were doing him a favor, someone had now commuted his sentence from solitary to life imprisonment, believing they were easing his situation.

When Warden Allen lifted the steel bars to Jesse's cell and opened the door, he was met by a stone-faced prisoner reclining on his bunk, his blue eye suspiciously cast in Allen's direction. Jesse Pomeroy was no longer a frightening man: he was slightly below medium height and weighed just over 140 pounds. His hair was thinning and his beard and mustache were leaning toward the gray. The white spot in his eye no longer seemed so unnerving. Still, something in the way his good eye shifted, in his peculiarly quiet stance, was unnerving.

Allen told Jesse about his new requirements: the new meal times and his place in line, the formation of which would begin at the same time every day, and that any deviation from it would not be tolerated. The warden also informed him that a tin mug and a plate would be issued to him, and that as part of his new status he would also be required to do some kind of work. This had not been assigned yet, but it would be soon, and after work he would be returned to his cell.

There was no word yet about accommodations, meaning whether he would be allowed to remain on Cherry Hill, but that would come soon. It was a drastic change after so many years, Allen agreed, but that was what you had been fighting for, wasn't it? he asked Jesse.

Rather than expressing gratitude for what was essentially a victory, Jesse looked calmly toward the warden and told him firmly that he objected to this new ruling and did not intend to accept any of the changes, and certainly was not going to comply with any of the rules the warden had just put forth. He preferred to go on living under the old sentence, Jesse said, in Cherry Hill, under isolated conditions. He had asked, wanted, demanded, and deserved a full pardon from the state, not an amelioration of his current conditions. Nothing less would do. "I asked Governor McCall for a pardon, not for a change in my sentence," Pomeroy declared indignantly. "If I can't have what I asked for, then I don't want it." His objections were in vain. The governor had instructed Allen to enforce the sentence, whether Jesse agreed to it or not. As the papers reported, "He (Pomeroy) was peevish and cross at what had been done for him, or rather, from his own viewpoint, what had not been done for him."

Although relieved of solitary, he felt entitled to a pardon, and wrote the governor about it. He gave two reasons that in his opinion had been overlooked: his good record while incarcerated, which truthfully, had not been that good at all, and there was the "illegal conviction . . . the attorney general neglecting to prove . . . atrocity." He felt he had been imprisoned more for the crimes he had committed on the boys in Chelsea and South Boston, rather than the ones on the two murdered victims. His new efforts were in vain. The new ruling stood.

He was given work in the prison yard, where a patch of earth had been dug out for the planting of potatoes. Officers knew he would be useless anywhere else; he had not been engaged in any actual meaningful physical tasks for decades. The simple actions of lifting a shovel and bending over to dig a hole were all he could manage. But manipulative as always, he refused to form a line or go to work, and was punished by being returned to solitary in Cherry Hill, which was what he wanted. This placed prison officials in a very awkward position.

Soon thereafter, Pomeroy contributed an article to the prison's newspaper the Mentor titled, "Segregation—In Truth," which explained his near devotion not only to his cell but also to solitude in general. The article was eventually reprinted in part in the Boston Daily Globe, on June 30, 1919. "I cannot say it has been my good fortune to live a solitary life, but it has been my experience almost 43 years, from 1874, when I was 14 years old, up to 1917," he wrote. "I have been often asked, 'How could you live apart from others?' My answer has been, 'I was so young, not realizing or knowing anything of life except as I lived it, it became, as it were, a natural way of living. Though in truth, it is a most unnatural life. The passing of years flowed without a change, and I grew up in boyhood, to be a young man, and then, as manhood arrived, and middle life and finally elderly life, solitude became my second nature, without on my part any noticeable change that I could remark."

On February 21, 1924, Jesse once again sought a full pardon, which was denied, and on November 29, 1926, he turned sixty-seven, marking a half century behind bars. By now those people who had been there when he first entered the prison were no longer present, either as inmates or officers. Fifteen administrators had come and gone, an undisputed record. Yet, despite time passing and what he deemed uncontrollable adversities, he still relished the thought of freedom.

By 1927 many newspapers, particularly the *New York Times,* were reporting that Clarence Darrow, the famed attorney, had decided to take on Pomeroy's case. The *Times* article of March 17, 1927, headlined the few paragraphs with the enticing lines: "DARROW MAY HELP LIFER: TALKS OF INTERVENING FOR JESSE POMEROY, 50 YEARS IN PRISON."

Darrow had recently gained notoriety for defending a pair of teenage killers in Chicago, Nathan Leopold and Richard Loeb. During the summer of 1924, nineteen-year-old Leopold and eighteen-year-old Loeb were arrested and put on trial for the murder of fourteen-year-old Robert "Bobby" Franks. Their backgrounds could not have been more different from Pomeroy's. Leopold was a law student at the University of Chicago, ready to transfer to Harvard Law School. Loeb held the distinction of being the University of Michigan's youngest graduate. Despite all of their advantages in life and apparent intelligence, it became obvious right away that the murder they had committed had not been given much planning.

When a motorist found Robert Franks's body by the side of a secluded road outside the city, Leopold's eyeglasses were also spotted nearby. The boys were tracked down and arrested and soon gave a full confession. When asked why they had committed such a deed, Leopold said, "The thing that prompted Dick to want to do the thing and prompted me to want to do this thing was a sort of pure love of excitement . . . the . . . love of thrill, doing something different . . . the satisfaction of the ego of putting something over."

Darrow took the job of defending the two, the case being dubbed in the press "the trial of the century." To the astonishment of many, Darrow convinced the boys to plead guilty, thus avoiding a trial. The gist of it became a sentencing hearing in which he declared that Leopold and Loeb were mentally ill. The hearing lasted twelve hours. The two were sentenced to life in prison with an additional ninety-nine years added to that. Darrow's summation was printed and became an immediate bestseller.

It surprised no one that the Pomeroy case interested Darrow, though in the end he did not take it on, despite feeling strongly about it. In *The Story of My Life*, published in 1932, Darrow stated, "I know one man who was sentenced to death when he was in his early teens who is now a helpless, tottering, garrulous old man. He killed a little girl at fifteen, and yet the Commonwealth of Massachusetts still keeps him inside his prison walls. I once thought I would try to get him out. When it was discovered I was informed that it had been attempted before; that they put a cat in Jesse Pomeroy's cell, and he carved it to pieces while it was still alive. I went to the warden with the story, to investigate; he told me that he had been a warden there for more than twenty years, that he had often heard the tale and he had asked other wardens and guards who had been there before his time, and the story was absolutely false and unfounded, without one scrap of evidence to support it. Then the warden added: 'I have been here a long time. I will guarantee that you can put any animal, even a rat, in a convict's cell and he will pet it and treat it with the greatest kindness, he is so anxious to have its companionship.' If there ever was a reason for sending a man to prison, that reason no longer exists today after he becomes old and harmless; or at any other time when it is fairly sure that he can live outside."

In July 1929 Pomeroy was placed on a list with several other inmates to be transferred to the State Farm Infirmary at Bridgewater.

Warden James L. Hogsett had sent a request to Governor Frank G. Allen for a transfer so as to relieve the prison of its overcrowded conditions, and because Jesse was now suffering from an enlarged hernia, a condition that made him a good candidate for a medical facility. At long last, Jesse H. Pomeroy would leave the Massachusetts Bastille.

BUILT IN THE EARLY 1850s, the Bridgewater State Farm was situated among wide and rolling fields. One of its primary missions had been to house paupers whose families could no longer care for them at home. Set up as a self-sufficient institution, it had a four-story barn as well as a chapel and a granary on its grounds. As time passed, the facility also began to take in the mentally unstable, criminals, and those who were generally unwanted by society. It became a virtual dumping ground of sorts for everyone who did not fit in elsewhere.

By the time of Pomeroy's arrival, many experts agreed that those hills would likely be the last images Jesse Pomeroy would see before he died.

A committee of thirty-five members presided over by Lieutenant Governor William S. Youngman convened to determine whether Pomeroy would be a good fit for the Farm. The meeting lasted all of thirty-five minutes, and Jesse Pomeroy's health was addressed in particular. It was known that he suffered from a very large and painful hernia, for which he had declined care and examination by the prison's physician for years. He was also growing older, and aside from puttering around the yard, he held no other job at Charlestown. In the end, all agreed that Pomeroy would benefit from the environment afforded at Bridgewater.

Pomeroy's attorney, John Daly, petitioned to halt what he considered the unconstitutional machinery that had allowed Pomeroy's paperwork to be filed. He told reporters, "If they get him to Bridgewater before I can start action," which they were about to do, "I will petition for a writ of habeas corpus which will open up the question of the

constitutionality of the removal statute. . . . The statutes specifically
stipulate the sort of misdemeanors for which persons may be committed to Bridgewater. These include drunkenness, abandonment . . . but
no person convicted of a felony can be committed there unless insane."
Although Jesse's insanity pleas had failed when he was on trial as a boy,
Daly had argued to the governor, and continued to do so, that Jesse had
indeed been insane in his youth and deserved a full pardon.

At the trial in 1874 many people had refuted Jesse's insanity plea,
but no one now argued that he had become insane as an adult. "That
his mind is officially shattered to justify his classification among the
criminal insane during his last years, no one will doubt," the *Boston
Globe* stated, the assumption being that incarceration had rendered him
so. "Few people now living can remember the murder Pomeroy committed . . . in a feat of adolescent blood lust."

Sentiment in Boston had also shifted, and there appeared to be a
certain amount of understanding, and yes, even sympathy that people
were willing to extend toward him at this moment in time, and understanding that had not been there when a boy.

"Old people cling tenaciously to their homes, to every article of
furniture, every valueless knickknack, every creaking floorboard. Thus
they maintain their identity in a world that has forgotten them. Trans-
plant them and they wither and die," the *Holyoke Transcript* wrote on
August 1, 1929, of Jesse's reluctance to leave the prison. "Jesse Pomeroy's original crime is probably to him no more than the half remembered dream of some former existence. But his Charlestown cell is his
life, vivid to him through a hundred little habits of the daily round.
One need not descend to pathos to wish that he might be permitted to
die where he has lived."

The warden had received a request from a Hollywood production
company to film the transfer, but he said no because he felt the move
would bring about even more publicity than an inmate was entitled to,
or deserving of. Pomeroy had already garnered too much of that.

Upon Jesse's transfer, his walk down the long corridor was no more than a shuffled glide over the concrete he had tried to flee so many times before. He slowly and carefully made his way toward the court-yard, where he was treated to his first automobile ride, which startled and amused him. The *New Britain Record*, from Connecticut, wondered whether Jesse philosophized about his life now as he rode along: "If he was philosophical, he might have consoled himself with the reflection that if he hadn't been jailed he probably would have been killed by a hit and run driver long ago."

The overwhelming colors—the various shades of blue in the sky and the rivers, the verdant valleys, the orange sun, and the colorful pastel garments on the passersby—were loud and vibrant after the ste-rility of Jesse's cell. A crowd had gathered in each town they passed through. They wanted to look at the car, to catch a glimpse of the old man behind the glass. Many of the onlookers were children, and as they stared, Jesse pulled his cap low over his eyes.

After leaving Prison Point over the Prison Point Bridge, they trav-eled across Charles Street, Beacon Street, Brookline Avenue, and the Riverway, admiring the modern construction along the riverbanks and growing tall by the sidewalks. This brought the entourage toward Franklin Park and across Blue Hill Avenue to Mattapan Square, Thatcher Street, and toward Milton and Quincy, where modernity had not caught up yet, and the sparsely settled countryside still yielded its summer beauty. With the windows now rolled down, a warm breeze entered the car as it made its way toward Avon and Brockton, and caught by a traffic light, Jesse glanced toward a corner store, which was displaying that day's newspaper in its window. The cover captured his own aging face with the headline screaming, POMEROY TAKEN TO THE STATE FARM.

Jesse didn't say anything throughout the ride, but those in the car later reported that they heard him grunting every so often under his breath. Not far from Bridgewater, the guards stopped for a few mo-ments and got out of the car at a corner store, and one of them went inside. He returned soon, holding ice creams and ginger ales that he handed to the prisoners. The guard watched as Jesse, much like a delighted schoolboy, alternated between sips from the carbonated soda bottle and licks from the melting ice cream, eager to taste them both.

When they reached the Farm, Jesse was the last to step out of the sedan, and, still clutching his newspaper-wrapped package, he staggered up the staircase and into his new home. He was met by Joseph Pullen, the receiving clerk, and was once again made to undergo an admission routine akin to those he had experienced as a youth when he first entered the Westborough State Reform School and the Massachusetts State Prison: he was questioned about his life, to which he gave short and curt replies that did not invite any further questions. When Pullen had enough information, he let the orderlies lead Jesse to the washroom for the bath and later to receive his regulation haircut and shave. A new uniform was assigned to him, as well as a new room in the infirmary.

This room was large and bright, and he had it all to himself, providing him with a great deal of space and liberty. He was placed under the care of Dr. John H. Weller, who did not seem tremendously put off by Jesse's sullenness. It was all part of the adjustment period, Weller told reporters.

Back at the state prison his life had been coordinated by the ding of the breakfast, lunch, and dinner plates in which his grub had been served, the hours in between spent mainly reading, or writing endless letters to judges and attorneys who might have been willing to hear his many complaints. Now he could rest.

When Jesse was seventy-one years old, officials discovered he had not given up his old ways. An inspection revealed that he was in possession of a selection of knives, some sharp files, and several little cutting instruments. Dr. Weller and other officials assured everyone that Jesse was too physically impaired at this point to get anywhere in an escape attempt. Still, it was clear that his mind was as sharp as ever.

On September 29, 1932, after being at the Farm for three years, Jesse Pomeroy died while playing cards with a few of the other inmates. The estate he left behind was appraised at nearly one thousand dollars.

The superintendent of the Bridgewater State Farm, Robert C. Sherman, put out a notice: "The aged inmate died last night at the State Farm camp which he had been transferred to several years ago after many years in the State Prison at Boston. Heart disease was given as the cause of death."

On October 3, his body was cremated at Forest Hills Crematory, without a religious ceremony. The small casket containing his ashes was buried in the North Weymouth Cemetery, beside his mother's body. Present were only a few of his relatives and William Finn, a former altar boy at the state prison to whom Jesse had bequeathed all of his possessions.

Reports of his passing filled the papers alongside other headlines: Cuban students were rioting and clashing with the police in front of the home of Senator Wilfredo Fernandez. In Cleveland special investigators were examining the Bureau of Prohibition Department. In North Dakota a bank had been robbed and hostages used as shields by the robbers. Massachusetts had voted in favor of repealing the Eighteenth Amendment. Still, all over the country obituaries were reserved for Pomeroy, his deeds summarized once again for those who fifty years later had either forgotten or never heard of them.

Louis Lyons, of the *Boston Daily Globe*, managed to find some medical reports that had been filed about fifteen years before, several paragraphs of which he included in an article dated October 2, 1932, titled "Records Show Jesse Pomeroy Never Did Deserve Sympathy." It revealed that a handful of well-known doctors had studied Jesse Pomeroy and reported their findings to Frank L. Randall, corrections commissioner, who was looking into whether or not Jesse Pomeroy deserved to be paroled. The most revealing one came in 1914, when Dr. Henry R. Stedman, state expert on insane criminals; Dr. Walter E. Fernald, of the Waverly School for the Feebleminded; Dr. Joseph I. McLaughlin,

prison physician at Charlestown; and Dr. Gregg C. Fernald, physician
for the Concord Reformatory, got together and examined Pomeroy.

Their report included a recap of Jesse's history, but also addressed
who he had become as an older man, and of his chances for rehabilitation should he live in the outside world. "Criminals of this type are
the bane of prison management," the report said. "[T]he history of
pronounced cases of mental or moral defectiveness is that they fail to
show any radical improvement. Always they are unable to control their
innate propensities, as these are the results of rooted congenital arrest
or faulty development of the mind. If taken early their lives can be reg-
ulated, better habits and more self-control constituted and a different
outlook engendered by constant supervision and special treatment. But
they are sure to deteriorate unless kept under constant guidance and
control." They added: "This is especially true of the moral degenerate,
of which Pomeroy is an extreme example. To properly safeguard the
community, their close and continual custody is absolutely necessary."

The *New York Times* also printed an obituary. Unlike many other
newspapers across the country, the *Times* didn't bother to give extensive
background, nor much evidence from experts explaining why Pomeroy
had done what he did. Instead, in a few short words, the paper boiled
the man down to what many believed he had always been: "He was a
psychopath."

EPILOGUE

Don't let it end like this.
Tell them I said something.

—PANCHO VILLA

By the time Jesse Pomeroy died, the men who had been involved in his case, either directly or indirectly, had already died as well. Detective James R. Wood retired from the Boston Police Department shortly after the Pomeroy ordeal, back in 1879, and opened the first detective agency in New England, the James R. Wood Detective Agency. He became involved in and solved many famous cases throughout New England, but besides increasing his status as a sleuth, he also became something of a scribe. He contributed a series of articles to a crime magazine, one of the many so popular toward the end of the nineteenth century. In one of these articles, he mentioned Pomeroy, showing a certain fondness for his jailhouse antics, of which he had obviously been keeping track throughout the years. "But there was one thing they could not break," Wood wrote. "That was Pomeroy's *Indomitable* spirit."

Chief of Police Edward Hartwell Savage also took to literature. He published *Police Records and Recollections, or, Boston by Daylight and Gaslight*, a large book totaling more than four hundred pages and detailing the history of Boston from the late 1600s to the late 1800s. He described all he felt was important for the average citizen to know, as well as for those outsiders coming into the city to learn about: Storms large and small that had battered the city he recounted with gusto. Fires were detailed with the same heat one would feel if standing near the scorching logs and buildings. The hanging of alleged witches and the stoning of fortune-tellers also made their appearance, as did the legends of the sea, these tales brought forth by those lucky mariners who survived ocean disasters.

For the year of 1872, Savage mentioned and detailed all he believed was relevant: William Gaston was then mayor of Boston and Savage the chief of police. There were 468 men on the police force, and on January 23 of that year they all assembled at the city's Music Hall for their annual assembly. By June the force had increased by nearly one hundred men, and by October the first notice of the epizootic in the horses was mentioned. Savage also recounted the gruesome murder of the merchant Abijah Ellis, which occurred that November and whose body was found in the Charles, causing such uproar in the city. The Great Fire, of course, with all of the calamities that followed, also took the better part of the entry for 1872.

But oddly enough, nowhere was there a sign, a glimpse, or even a hint that during that time and for several months before and after, a very young and very dangerous juvenile delinquent had been making his rounds in Boston and the vicinity. There was no mention of Jesse Pomeroy, Katie Curran, Horace Millen, or any of the other children who were involved in the Pomeroy saga either in Chelsea or South Boston. As 1872 rolled into 1873 and then 1874 came about, other matters occupied Savage's writings and attention: telegraph lines were set up by May 1873, which certainly deserved a mention, as did the spectacular fireworks that lit up the night sky on the Fourth of July 1874. Still, no notion that Jesse Pomeroy had existed then, or of the deeds he had committed, of his trial, of his incarceration; no mention of his victims, not for that year, the two preceding it, or the ones that followed. Despite having had such a hand in capturing him, it seemed as if Savage refused to mention him or acknowledge him. Perhaps he did so believing that the boy would simply be erased from history as a whole.

BY 1903 FIRE CHIEF John Damrell was seventy-five and still in very good health. He was also still involved with city affairs, working as inspector of buildings, though the current mayor, Patrick Collins, had grown tired of Damrell's presence and was seeking to oust him. Collins didn't care how he accomplished this task: force or resignation would do, and if all else failed, he reckoned, he would simply fire him. In Damrell's place it was believed Collins wanted to place Hugh Montague, who was then working as superintendent of public works.

By the turn of the century, Bostonians were more forgiving of Damrell regarding the fire. He was now well liked, and in his new position bequeathed and received many favors, from locals and politicians alike. This was not always a very good thing, for these favors often led to allegations of illegal activities. To that end, evidence had been stacking up against him, further fueling Collins's desire to have him ousted.

Following the 1872 fire, fire building codes and regulations had become stricter and rigid, inflexible by many standards. But many in government had come to believe that Damrell had grown lax with the regulations depending on who the builder was, which was odd, considering what he knew about building construction. This had happened more than once: by allowing certain construction workers to outbid their competition and weave their way through the city bureaucracy, he was putting people at risk and allowing legitimate builders to be out of the running for lucrative contracts. Damrell was using and abusing those same laws that he had fought so hard to implement.

"This favoritism brought about jealousy," the *Boston Daily Globe* of February 26, 1903, declared. "The Department naturally gets into many disputes with builders. This is inevitable, but they do say there are some favored builders who seem to be able to do anything they wish, while others obliged to live strictly by the letter of the law."

The topic of insanity and psychopathy was also gaining more popularity as the century rolled on, and there was a deeper understanding of the disease. In 1941, American psychiatrist Harvey M. Cleckley published *The Mask of Sanity: An Attempt to Clarify Some Issues About So-Called Psychopathic Personality*. The book was based on a series of interviews Cleckley conducted with patients in a mental institution. Cleckley described psychopaths as "hot headed, manipulative, irresponsible, self-centered, shallow, lacking in empathy or anxiety, and more likely to commit more types of crimes than other offenders. They are also more violent, more likely to recidivate, and less likely to respond to treatment."

His description became the most influential and most quoted in regard to psychopaths throughout the century, and would have benefited those studying and dealing with Pomeroy had the information been available to them then.

Jesse Pomeroy's mental faculties were also scrutinized, and a better picture of who he had been as a boy was possible to develop. Mark E. Safarik, a retired member of the FBI's elite Behavioral Analysis Unit, placed Jesse in the category of sexual sadists, that small group of killers who are often the most difficult to catch, unless they make a mistake. Jesse had been young when he committed his murders, his skills undeveloped, which allowed detectives to quickly home in on him. Had he not been caught and jailed then, Safarik agreed, he most likely would have continued his murderous spree.

When asked whether environment or genetics had created Jesse Pomeroy, Safarik noted that this basic question has stumped experts for centuries. Certainly, his father's beatings might have caused Jesse's latent propensities toward sadistic murder to reveal themselves. It was during those beatings that Jesse might have learned to fuse violence, sex, and arousal, and he had no control over the situations and how he reacted to them. He was later able to reconstruct the scenarios with children, on whom he could impose his cruelty.

Jesse appeared to display all the hallmark signs of psychopathy: he was cold, calculating, narcissistic, and lacking empathy. Children were merely objects to be used by him. Safarik surmised that Pomeroy's satisfaction didn't come from the injuries he inflicted on the kids, but instead from the responses he got. This was obvious even while he was incarcerated in the reformatory school in Westborough.

NOTHING MUCH REMAINS FROM the life or the era surrounding Jesse Harding Pomeroy. The neighborhood on Bunker Hill Avenue in Charlestown has undergone a remarkable change, and the home where he lived with his family has become one of the many over-priced condominiums standing in the shadow of the Bunker Hill Monument. Those living in the community are, for the most part, blissfully unaware that a boy murderer roamed their streets in the 1800s. Nowadays they are more concerned with the price of real estate, the traffic jams created by tourists on their way to view the famous monument, and specials at the newly opened Whole Foods Market.

Similar redevelopment happened in South Boston. While in the 1870s this was a spot where the less-well-to-do sought financial relief, it is now a location for those on the up-and-up, luxurious town houses sharing the space with ethnic restaurants and bakeries offering lattes and cappuccinos. Where Mrs. Pomeroy's shop used to stand, at last check an Edible Arrangements store had sprung up.

Massachusetts State Prison was demolished and the land is now home to Bunker Hill Community College, which is surrounded by highways and other roads. The Charles River flows as lazily as it has always done, taking its righteous place between Boston and Cambridge, while the Mystic River leads a similar existence between Charlestown and Chelsea.

The only structure that can still be viewed and is similar to what it was in the 1870s is the Suffolk County Jail, or Charles Street Jail, where Jesse Pomeroy spent time prior to his trial, and then the subsequent years awaiting the execution that never came. It remained a jail well into the 1900s, and in 1973 its prisoners rioted, a move that prompted federal judge W. Arthur Garrity Jr. to visit the institution and spend a night within its walls. That visit caused him to rule that many of the prisoners' constitutional rights had been violated, and soon it was deemed too old and unsafe to stay in operation. Over its many years, it held many infamous and famous inmates, including anarchists

Sacco and Vanzetti, who spent months there prior to their execution on August 23, 1927.

In 1990 the jail closed its doors permanently. Fifteen years later, it was bought by developers who, rather than demolishing it, renovated the building and reopened it as, of all things, a world-class hotel. The Liberty Hotel opened its doors in 2007 and soon became a prime destination for visitors to Boston. It boasts internationally renowned restaurants such as Clink, Alibi, the Liberty Bar, and Scampo, which in Italian means "to escape." The common areas still offer historical views of the jail, as well as a faraway glimpse of what life must have been for those imprisoned within it.

It is a far cry from the environment that greeted Jesse Pomeroy and the other inmates. Marble floors now don the reception area, and plush, oversized, and very expensive leather chairs and sofas are scattered about. A short hallway leads to a gallery full of historical artifacts, and an escalator carries patrons to the restaurants on the mezzanine level. The voices of its guests, many of them in foreign tongues, are delightful, especially on a crisp October morning and while waiting for a Sunday breakfast to begin.

But within the clamor of this fancy hotel, while sitting in one of their sofas or chairs sipping a Bloody Mary or cappuccino, it is possible to remember those who came before. If imagination is on your side, it is also still possible to believe that besides the voices, the music, the cell phone ringtones, and the chipper chants of the children, one can make out the strands of a harmonica emanating from somewhere down a hall, within the bowels of this place, along with the voices of night guards rattling their sticks against the iron bars, trying to still the wailings of those crying out, "Home, Sweet Home."

ACKNOWLEDGMENTS

I came across Jesse Pomeroy's story while researching my earlier book, *The Lady and Her Monsters*. One of the first people who heard me talk about Jesse Pomeroy was my agent, Rob Weisbach, at Rob Weisbach Creative Management. A great debt of gratitude goes out to him for reading many, many drafts of my proposal. His insights, keen eye, humor, and support, not to mention expertise, made the work infinitely better, and I am always in awe of him.

The remarkable Henry Ferris, at William Morrow, continues to show why he is the editor most writers dream of and few ever get to work with. His dedication, compassion, firm hand, and kindness allowed the book, through various incarnations, to take the shape that it did. A thank-you also to Henry's assistant, Nick Amphlett, whose kindness in answering many of my questions was second to none.

Heidi Richter, William Morrow's senior publicity manager, is to be applauded for her tenacity, creativity, and intelligence, not to mention the time she spent working with me. I am, and always will be, grateful for her dedication to my work.

A number of organizations and individuals contributed their time in the quest to find material on the lives of Herman Melville, his family, and the ones related to his story, including that of Oliver

Wendell Holmes. Those people include: Brian Yothers at the Melville Society; Kathleen Reilly, supervisor at the Berkshire Anthenaeum; Will Garrison, curator at the Berkshire Historical Society at Arrowhead; Beth Joress, assistant director for information services, Iwasaki Library; Caleb Smith, Yale University; Betsy Boyle, Massachusetts Historical Society.

The life of Jesse Pomeroy and his family, his deeds, and his time in prison, both as a youngster and as an adult, is well recorded in many files kept in various offices throughout the state. In that regard, my deepest gratitude goes out to the individuals who facilitated the research. These people include: Lisa Kulyk-Bourque, reference librarian for the Lynn Public Library; Helena Hirshman-Seidel at the Lynn Museum and Historical Society; David Hennessey and Carl Zellner at the Charlestown Historical Society; the Weymouth Historical Society; Suzanne Stewart at the New England Historic Genealogical Society; Mary O'Connell, reference Librarian at the Bridgewater Public Library; Michael Hannon at the University of Minnesota, Clarence Darrow Collection; Martha Crilly, City Archives; Jose Mejia of the Chelsea Public Library; Abigail Cramer, librarian and archivist at Historic New England; Edward Gordon of the Victorian Society; Nancy Odell, local history librarian, Westborough Public Library; Maureen Ambrosino, library director of the Westborough Public Library; Edwin Moloy, curator of modern manuscripts and archives, Historical and Special Collections, Harvard Law School Library; Kathryn Swiniarski of the General Counsel's Office, Department of Youth Services; Elizabeth Bouvier, judicial archivist at the Massachusetts Judicial Archives; Jennifer Fauxsmith, reference supervisor at the Massachusetts Archives; Diane Wiffin, of the Department of Corrections.

For a psychologial profile on Jesse Pomeroy, I'd like to thank Mark E. Safarik, president of Forensic Behavioral Services Inc., who taught me quite a bit about what may have driven Pomeroy to commit his crimes, as well as Gina Santoro, Ph.D., director of Santoro Psychological Services, with whom I had quite an eye-opening conversation about child serial murderers that left me shaken for days. Their expertise was welcomed, albeit frightening.

John Paolucci, president of Forensic 4 Real, Inc., helped me to understand why the police may have been unable to discover Katie Curran's body in the cellar upon her murder, and how weather conditions and the properties of ash aided Pomeroy in getting away with murder for several months. He was also kind enough to point out the difference between blood spatter and blood splatter.

A great thank-you also to Michael Gerry, of the Boston Fire Historical Society for all the information about the fire, and for directing me toward additional information and archives. To Vivien Li, president of the Boston Harbor Association, for information on the history on McCay's Wharf, and to Sean Reardon, director of sales and marketing at the Liberty Hotel, formerly the Charles Street Jail, for allowing me to visit and roam the area freely.

Thank you also to my family, to my mother, Celeste, and my sister, Francesca, who had to deal with me talking repeatedly about the deeds of this young boy, and who were very happy when I finally decided to just put them down on paper. To my family abroad, who, somehow, also had to hear about Jesse Pomeroy, and to my extended family at Emerson College, my colleagues and students, who continue to be a font of inspiration.

Thank you to all!

NOTES

PROLOGUE

Newspapers across the country and even abroad followed with interest the transfer of Jesse Pomeroy from the state prison in Charlestown to the Bridgewater State Farm. Newspapers in Massachusetts, especially, which had followed the case for decades, saw this as an epilogue to a long and drawn-out drama. As seen in the bibliography, the *Boston Sunday Post, Boston Post, Boston Daily Globe, Boston Evening Globe, Boston Globe, Boston Herald*, and *Lowell Sun* devoted many articles to the event, printing stories days before and immediately after his transfer. Many reporters also came from large metropolitan newspapers from across the country, such as the *New York Times* and *Stanford Advocate*, as well as the smaller publication such as the *San Mateo Times* and the *Zaneville Times*. The *London Standard* also printed stories about Pomeroy.

Information on the Massachusetts State Prison, not only its history but its physical layout, can be found in archival material located in the files of the Charlestown Historical Society; the Charlestown Public Library, which is a branch of the Boston Public Library; as well as the Boston City Archives, which holds numerous files also on Jesse Pomeroy and his time in the prison.

Information on the Bridgewater State Farm is located in the archives of the Bridgewater Public Library. They have followed the history of the farm from its inception to its more recent issues, including its history of abuse and neglect. The Boston Public Library also has an extensive collection on the subject.

CHAPTER I: THE INHUMAN SCAMP

The early history of Jesse Pomeroy's criminal career is traced not only in the extensive newspaper archives, such as the *Boston Daily Globe, Boston Globe*, and *Charlestown Advertiser*, who dedicated more than fifty years to him, but in the detailed files archived in the Massachusetts Supreme Judicial Court, files that can be viewed only by special permission and only at the Massachusetts State Archives. The extensive records, including the official indictment for murder, trace Pomeroy's history by compiling the Chelsea Police Records, those portions of his medical records that have not been redacted, police searches, both in Chelsea and South Boston, autopsy files, jury indictments, and official testimonies and transcripts from the trial. Its pages number in the hundreds.

Information on his early deeds can also be viewed at the Boston City Archives, the Boston Public Library, the Chelsea Public Library, and the Massachusetts Historical Society.

The physical details pertaining to Charlestown, as well as its history, are available in the Charlestown Public Library, as well as the Charlestown Historical Society. These include records of the battles fought in Charlestown, the various fires that plagued the city as it developed, the history of its bridges, the street layout, and the history of the Navy Yard.

The National Peace Jubilee was followed greedily by many of the local papers, such as the *Boston Post* and *Boston Daily Advertiser*. William Dean Howells published a series of articles in the *Atlantic*, while Patrick Gilmore published a history of it titled *History of the National Peace Jubilee and Great Music Festival*. All of the articles gave a day-by-day account of the event, detailing balloon rides, speeches, and band celebrations, as well as the darker side of the jubilee, including thievery, salaciousness, and petty crimes.

Information on the life and career of Mayor William Gaston can be found at the State House Library, the Boston Public Library, and the Boston City Archives, as well as an extensive publication titled *A Memorial of William Gaston*, from the city of Boston, which was published after his death. It details his youth, his development into a lawyer, and his rise within the commonwealth's political machine.

The doings of Chief of Police Edward Hartwell Savage were also of interest to many Bostonians. Information on his life and work is found included in the records of the City Police in the Boston City Archives, the Boston Public Library, and the Massachusetts Historical Society.

CHAPTER 2: THE BRIDGE

The development of the local bridges that linked Charlestown to the city proper, as well as to the smaller towns that surrounded it, gave a tremendous boost to Charlestown, both morally and financially. The history of these bridges is detailed in the files at the Charlestown Public Library and the Charlestown Historical Society, repositories for all that relates to Charlestown's history.

The background for the Pomeroy family, including marriage and divorce records, genealogical records, and financial information, was gathered from records and reports done by the New England Genealogical Society, as well as the Massachusetts State Archives and the Massachusetts Supreme Judicial Court.

Newspaper accounts from the early 1870s, including the ones published during Jesse Pomeroy's trial, offer additional information on the family, especially coming from those neighbors who lived in the vicinity of the Pomeroys, and Jesse's teachers. These retellings included episodes of misconduct while at school, information on the family dynamics inside the Pomeroys' apartment, including the fights between Jesse and his father, Thomas Pomeroy, and the incidents relating to the butchered cat and Mrs. Pomeroy's canaries.

Information on Fire Chief John Damrell and his dealings with the Boston Fire Department is held in the files contained in the Boston City Archives. There much of what relates to the fire of 1872 is located. Information on his life can also be found in the Boston Fire Museum. Additional archival material on the blaze is also located in the Massachusetts Historical Society, as well as in the diaries of Harold Murdock, the Charles Pelham Curtis Diary, and the Higginson Family Papers, also in the Massachusetts Historical Society. In addition, they hold the *Report from the Commission on the Fire*, material in which relates to John Damrell.

The Chicago History Museum holds extensive material on Chicago's history of fires, particularly the one that struck the city in 1871.

CHAPTER 3: THE MARBLE EYE

The history of Savin Hill and its development can be found in the Boston City Archives, the Boston Public Library, the Dorchester Athenaeum, and the Massachusetts Historical Society. Historical information in these files includes the history of the Tuttle House and the development of the surrounding railroad system.

The details of Jesse Pomeroy's crimes on George Pratt, Robert Gould, and Joseph Kennedy can be reviewed in even further detail in the files provided by the Massachusetts Supreme Judicial Court records. Along with the gruesome list of injuries he inflicted on the boys, there are details on the deeds he committed on the boys in Chelsea, and how he came to choose them and eventually hurt them. By following the chronology of the crimes and of the injuries, it is also possible to trace not only a pattern of his deeds but also his mental development.

The Dime Novel Collection at the Library of Congress is a good place to begin for those who wish to delve even deeper into the history of dime novels, their influence, and their beginnings and rise to success. Stanford University also holds an extensive collection on the subject, as does the University of Florida, in its Dime Novel Collection.

Friends and acquaintances of Jesse Pomeroy spoke to reporters about his love for dime novels and how he preferred to spend his time delving in books rather than playing. Teachers also worried that his behavior was directly linked to the criminality described in these books. These concerns were aired during the trial; the transcripts are available to read from the Massachusetts Supreme Judicial Court Records at the State Archives.

The history of Jesse Pomeroy's grandfather, his namesake, was gleaned from the files of the New England Genealogical Society. There the elder Pomeroy's history on the Canadian border, his move to Massachusetts, his marriage and abuse of his wife, and subsequent divorce and new marriage, are detailed.

Information on the Old Colony Railroad is found in the Boston Public Library, as well as the State Transportation Library, which holds files and records on the railroad system's development throughout Massachusetts and the rest of New England.

Joseph Kennedy's ordeal at the hands of Jesse Pomeroy is detailed in the records of the Massachusetts Supreme Judicial Court. These records also include details on Jesse's new life in South Boston, his schooling information, the hunt that ensued upon the children being found maltreated, Officer Bragdon's testimony, and his recollections on seeing Jesse Pomeroy entering his police station. Also, the testimonies of the children who came to court and spoke of being assaulted by Pomeroy are included. The judge's sentence to the reform school can also be studied.

The history of the House of Reformation at Westborough, later called the Lyman School for Boys, can be explored through various sources. The best places to begin are the Westborough Historical Society and the Westborough Public Library. Both of these institutions hold extensive records detailing the school's geographical location, how the site was chosen, the school's structural development, and the progress it made through the decades. They also hold an extensive historical collection related to the city of Westborough itself.

The Boston Public Library, the Massachusetts Historical Society, and the Massachusetts State Archives also hold case files for the school, but the most valuable resource on the subject is *The History of the Internal Organization of the State Reform School for Boys at Westborough, Massachusetts (1846–1974)*, by James Gillespie Leaf. Leaf worked on the project for years as part of his thesis for Harvard University, class of 1988. He not only offers a chronology of the school but also writes about the many incidents of abuse the boys underwent, as well as the methods the officers and guards used to discipline the boys.

Jesse Pomeroy's desire for a life at sea can be read in the *Autobiography of Jesse H. Pomeroy*, which
he wrote and published in the *Boston Sunday Times* in July 1875. There he spoke of his
grandfather's life at sea, and his own wish that his parents had allowed him to board a
ship. Other details of his young life are also included in the autobiography.

CHAPTER 4: THE BOUNDLESS SEA

There have been thousands of books written on the life of Herman Melville, whether they
relate to his youth, his time at sea, his personal life with his wife, or his works. These
books have dissected Melville's texts, trying to find meaning in every one of his sentences.
His letters and correspondence with others in his circle have also been cause for speculations. One of the most extensive biographies is *Herman Melville: A Biography*, by Hershel
Parker. Spanning nearly two thousand pages, it leaves no stone unturned. *Herman Melville:
Cycle and Epicycle*, written by his granddaughter, Eleanor Melville Metcalf, also offers intimate views of the author, albeit biased ones. Eleanor was Frances's daughter, and Frances
often talked to her daughter about Melville's perceived shortcomings and reasons for
embarrassment.

From an archival standpoint, the Berkshire Athenaeum, in Pittsfield, Massachusetts, and the
Berkshire Museum, also in Pittsfield, offer a starting point. Melville spent a great many
years there, particularly those years surrounding the writing and publishing of *Moby-Dick*.
The Athenaeum offers not only an extensive collection on Melville, but also archival
material on Melville's friendship with Nathaniel Hawthorne, as Hawthorne lived nearby
for a period of time. They also hold material on Oliver Wendell Holmes, another of the
area's residents.

Extensive letters and other correspondence to and from Melville can be found in various
collections at the Massachusetts Historical Society, beginning with the Lemuel Shaw
Papers. These record not only Shaw's judicial life, but his personal one, including letters
to and from Herman Melville, Maria Melville, and other members of the Melville and
Shaw families, particularly after Allan Melville passed away. These letters relate, more
often than not, to financial matters.

The Samuel P. Savage Shaw Papers, of the son of Judge Shaw and Melville's brother-in-law,
also held at the Massachusetts Historical Society, hold correspondence between Samuel
and Herman, Samuel and his father, his sister, Elizabeth, and many people and friends
they all had in common. Oftentimes these letters reveal thoughts on Melville's writings,
Samuel's worry for his sister, and their belief that Herman was suffering from some kind
of mental malady and needed help, aside from his interminable financial woes.

The Hope Savage Shaw Diaries, while a part of the Lemuel Shaw Collection, reveal correspondence between Elizabeth and her stepmother. Elizabeth's introduction to married
life is displayed, her new and overcrowded house in New York is depicted, and Herman
Melville's writing habits are also described.

The Melville Collection at Harvard University includes many notes, letters, pamphlets,
books, personal information, and financial records on the Melvilles. A lot of material
can be accessed directly from personal computers, as a lot of it has been digitized, though
for more extensive research, visiting the library is necessary. The library also holds the
original text of *Billy Budd*, including notes and marginalia.

The Melville Society records all that relates to Herman Melville, including private letters
and notes on his private life and circle of friends, such as his friendship with Oliver
Wendell Holmes.

The New Bedford Historical Society and the New Bedford Whaling Museum are a must for those studying not only Herman Melville, but also the history of whaling in general, and especially in Massachusetts, with its rise and decline through the decades. The New Bedford Whaling Museum, in particular, holds an abundance of artifacts and photographs, along with thousands of books, personal diaries, logbooks, and everything else that relates to the lives of mariners and the whaling business, as well as the physical characteristics of the whales themselves.

CHAPTER 5: THE GREAT FIRE

Records of the life, times, and accomplishments of Dr. Oliver Wendell Holmes can be found in various repositories, beginning with the Massachusetts Historical Society, whose Quincy, Wendell, Holmes, and Upham family papers hold numerous references to the doctor. The Berkshire Athenaeum also has information on Holmes's life in the Berkshires, and the impact he had on the area.

The Oliver Wendell Holmes Jr. Collection at Harvard Law School also holds considerable material on Oliver Wendell Holmes Sr. In fact, correspondence between father and son, notes on Dr. Holmes, and letters related to him are located in this large collection.

The Oliver Wendell Holmes Library, in the Book and Print Collection of the Holmes Family, located in the Library of Congress, is also a font of information, and resources for research are also available from the National Library of Medicine, which recently became the recipient of a bulk of material related to Holmes.

The Oliver Wendell Holmes Library at Phillips Andover Academy, and the Oliver Wendell Holmes Collection at the University of Virginia, also offer additional material for the scholar and curious alike, as does the New England Historical Society.

The history of Boston and its development and various historical depictions of its neighborhoods can be traced in the Boston Public Library, the Boston Athenaeum, the Massachusetts Historical Society, and the State House Library. All of them hold information relating to the various districts of Boston, including the area of Beacon Hill, Mount Vernon Street, and what was known as Mount Whoredom Street.

There are many good references for the history of the Great Fire of 1872, beginning with the Boston City Archives, where reports from and for Fire Chief John Darrell to the aldermen are housed, as well as the city's plans, and the reports that followed the spark and the fire.

At the Massachusetts Historical Society, references to the fire are found in the Lemuel Shaw Papers, the Higginson Family Papers, and the Murdock Diaries, along with many other collections.

The Boston Fire Museum, Boston Fire Historical Society, Boston Fire Society, and Boston Public Library all hold extensive material related to the fire, including photographs, journals, personal diaries, and collections of newspaper articles.

The history of the epizootic, which the local horses suffered from at the time of the fire, is detailed in many newspaper articles published around that time, as well as in-depth reports held in the Boston City Archives.

The history of the Trinity Church in Boston is detailed in the church's archives themselves, the Trinity Boston Preservation Trust, and the extensive records of its burning and rebuilding located in the Boston Public Library.

CHAPTER 6: LOSS OF INNOCENCE

The history of Katie Curran, her life in Boston, her family, the path she took to school, and her disappearance are all detailed in the Massachusetts Supreme Judicial Court Records, to be viewed at the Massachusetts State Archives. These records also include extensive autopsy reports relating the many wounds she received, the cause of her death, and the condition of her body when she was discovered beneath the ash heap. The Boston City Archives hold a poster that displays the reward and her personal statistics, a poster that was printed at her family's and neighborhood's insistence after she went missing.

The Massachusetts Supreme Judicial Court Records also provide details relating to Horace Millen, his family and their days in South Boston, his disappearance, and his eventual discovery on the beach. These papers also include all the transcripts of eyewitness testimony, the eventual trial, and even the burial information.

The history of South Boston as a location for those of lesser means is detailed in archival material found at the Boston Public Library. These papers talk about South Boston's geographical location, its history, its financial importance, and its development.

Information on the life of Chief of Police Edward Hartwell Savage and the history of the Boston Police Department can be found in several sources, beginning with the Boston Police Museum. The Police News Collection and Scrapbooks, located in the Northeastern University Libraries, Archives, and Special Collection Departments, also offer a wealth of information, as do the Justice George Lewis Ruffins Society Records, also held in the Northeastern University Libraries. The Bostonian Society, the Boston Public Library, the State House Library, and the Massachusetts Historical Society also hold information.

Information on the life and work of Detective James "Revolver" Wood is held almost entirely in the Wood Detective Agency Records, located in the Harvard University Law Library and Special Collections. The collection is enormous, spanning from the 1870s to the late 1930s. It not only details the life and times of Detective Wood and the extensive reports on nearly all the cases that he worked on and assisted with, but holds additional information on other cases throughout the country and the world that he was interested in. The detective liked to study the history of crimes, the methodology his colleagues across the country used in solving those crimes, and keep abreast about the evolving field of criminology. His son, James Wood Jr., inherited not only the detective agency but also all of his father's records. He added more material to it, and when the agency closed, he donated all of the records to the library.

Information regarding Gardiner Tufts and the State Board of Charities can be found in the Massachusetts Supreme Judicial Court Records, as well as the State House Library.

The details on Jesse Pomeroy's physical scratches, his clothing, his interview with the police at the police station, his visit to the undertaker, his confession, and the visit from Stephen A. Dublois are also included in the Massachusetts Supreme Judicial Court Records, as well as in the Detective Wood Files. In the Judicial Court Records, one can also find the eyewitness testimony from those who saw Jesse and Horace together by the beach.

CHAPTER 7: KATIE

The details of Mrs. Pomeroy's life in South Boston, along with how the children were growing up, and Jesse's new life at the reform school and immediately following it are detailed in the files kept at the Massachusetts State Archives and the Massachusetts Supreme Judicial Court Records.

Those papers, which are several hundreds of pages long, also note Katie's discovery, along with the autopsy reports on her remains and transcripts from the two workers who were hired to clean up the Pomeroys' former basement, as well as William Kohr's testimony.

The whole neighborhood was aware of Captain Dyer's feelings for Mrs. Pomeroy, and neighbors spoke of this turn of events with not only the mayor but the papers. The *Boston Post*, *Boston Globe*, *Boston Daily Globe*, and others wrote articles on this relationship.

The history of James Nash's purchase of Mrs. Pomeroy's former store is given in documents in the Massachusetts Supreme Judicial Court Records, where one can also find Detective Wood's thoughts on the case and his ideas as to how Jesse might have gotten away with this murder for so long.

The debate over what to do with Jesse Pomeroy took center stage not only in court but primarily in the newspapers: the *Charlestown Advertiser*, *Boston Daily Globe*, *Boston Post*, *Boston Sunday Post*, *New York Times*, and dozens of others published not only reportage but also dozens of pieces submitted by anyone who had an opinion on the case, and it appeared that everybody did. The consensus was that Jesse should hang.

Details on the history of Massachusetts State Prison, aside from the written records included in the bibliography, can be found in the Charlestown Public Library, the Charlestown Historical Society, the State House Library, and the Boston City Archives.

CHAPTER 8: THE WOLF AND THE LAMB

The report on the interview between Dr. John E. Tyler and Jesse Pomeroy is found in the Massachusetts Supreme Judicial Court Records, where additional medical reports are also located. Jesse Pomeroy also speaks of these encounters in the *Autobiography of Jesse H. Pomeroy*, where he makes it clear that he lied to the doctors and that he had read widely on his case and prepared to answer those questions posed to him based on the knowledge he gained from reading stories on other famous cases. He believed his answers were going to help him get convicted by reason of insanity.

Information on the entire trial of Jesse Pomeroy can be found in the Massachusetts Supreme Judicial Court Records and the Massachusetts State Archives. Jesse Pomeroy also wrote at length about the trial in his *Autobiography of Jesse H. Pomeroy*, as well as in the parole request papers that he sent to the State Parole Board. These papers are in the Massachusetts State Archives. The newspapers also detailed the trial to no end, and a detailed bibliography is given.

The information on William Baxter, the young juvenile delinquent also arrested and placed in a jail cell next to Jesse Pomeroy, is to be found at the Massachusetts Historical Society.

Not surprisingly, Harvard Law School, particularly its libraries, holds quite a bit of material on the Webster-Parkman murder trial. It is a great place to begin for those who wish to find additional reference material. The Bostonian Society, Massachusetts Historical Society, and Victorian Society of America, New England Chapter, also hold information.

The record of the James Thomas Fields interview with Jesse Pomeroy is located in the Annie Fields Papers at the Massachusetts Historical Society. The overall Fields collection is quite large, more than seventy volumes, and consists primarily of Mrs. Fields's interactions with the literary society in Boston, her social life, descriptions of trips abroad, and her social life. Her husband's contributions to the collection include a diary from a tour to Europe, and his interview with Pomeroy. In addition to the interview that has been quoted in the book, there are notes on the case and thoughts on dime novels and the readership of young people in general.

The decision of Governor Rice to commute Jesse Pomeroy's sentence and the papers pertaining to that decision are included in the records of the Massachusetts Supreme Judicial Court.

CHAPTER 9: THE TWISTED MIND

Dr. Oliver Wendell Holmes, like several others, believed Jesse Pomeroy should be studied in order to learn from him, rather than executed. His letters to Governor Gaston went unanswered; on the other hand, his article in the April 1875 issue of the *Atlantic* was read throughout the country and received a lot of attention. The Berkshire Athenaeum alerted me very early on to this publication and its connection between Holmes and Pomeroy.

In addition, the Berkshire Athenaeum holds relevant material on the lives of Herman Melville, Dr. Oliver Wendell Holmes, and Nathaniel Hawthorne during their stay in the Berkshires. This period coincided with Melville's writing of *Moby-Dick*, as well as the height of the Melville family's worries that he might have been suffering from some kind of mental imbalance.

The Berkshire Historical Society at Arrowhead, former home of Herman Melville in Pittsfield, has a lot of information not only on the author himself, but the area's history and culture, helping visitors and researchers alike understand the author a bit better.

The life and times of Elizabeth Shaw Melville can be traced in the Lemuel Shaw Papers, Hope Savage Shaw Diaries, and Samuel P. Savage Shaw Papers at the Massachusetts Historical Society.

CHAPTER 10: PATIENCE PERSONIFIED POMEROY

While all were surprised by the publication of Jesse Pomeroy's words in the July 1875 issue of the *Boston Sunday Globe*, none was more so than his lawyer Charles Robinson Jr., who believed Jesse was doing more harm than good with his words. Robinson agreed to an interview, and his responses appeared also in the *Boston Sunday Globe* a week after Jesse Pomeroy's autobiography did.

The details of Katie's burial under the ash heap were included in the records of the Massachusetts Supreme Judicial Court case, and they were revealed during the trial. For additional details on blood spatter, John Paolucci, president of Forensics 4 Real, revealed arterial gushing, bloodstain pattern analysis, and the coal and ash properties.

Details on the location, size, and structure of Jesse's cell were all provided by the Charlestown Historical Society and the Charlestown Public Library, as well as the Boston City Archives, which holds the structural plans for the prison. Jesse Pomeroy also wrote articles, which he contributed to the prison's newspapers, describing in minute details the condition of his cell.

The Charlestown Prison Punishing Books, held at the Massachusetts State Archives, and the Charlestown Prison Warden's Memorandum of Prisoners, 1858–1902, also at the State Archives, hold all the records of the escape attempts Jesse made. The books also include the responses from the part of the officers, detailing where and how Jesse was found, and how he was disciplined. The local papers always got wind of these attempts and wrote widely on them. A list of these articles is provided in the bibliography.

Information on the Massachusetts State Prison extension plans can be found in the Massachusetts State Archives.

CHAPTER 11: MADNESS UNLEASHED

Details on the trips Herman Melville took abroad can be found in the Lemuel Shaw Papers at the Massachusetts Historical Society. There are letters between the judge and several family members, and many of them show concern for Herman. Additional information is found in the Melville Collection at Harvard University.

Information related to New York City during the 1800s, its history, its people, culture, geography, and vices, can be found in the New-York Historical Society, the New York Public Library, the New York Municipal Archives, and the New York Genealogical and Biographical Society. Information on newsboys, the newspapers of the age, crimes, and criminals are found in all of these repositories.

The letters written by Samuel Shaw, Elizabeth's brother, to Dr. Henry Whitney Bellows were discovered in the archives of the Massachusetts Historical Society, and there they still reside.

The information on Malcolm Melville's death is also found in the Samuel P. Savage Shaw Papers at the Massachusetts Historical Society; the death was reported in all the newspapers of the time, including the *New York Times*.

Melville's granddaughter, Eleanor Melville Metcalf, who included it in her book, *Herman Melville: Cycle and Epicycle*, reported the information on Herman's last years. The book spoke extensively, and favorably, of her grandmother Elizabeth, and less so of Herman.

Articles on the significance of *Billy Budd* have been published in spades, and a detailed bibliography is offered. The original text is kept in the Harvard University Archives.

CHAPTER 12: UNEARTHED

The information on Jesse's last years in the state prison comes from several sources. The Charlestown Prison Punishing Books and the Charlestown Prison Warden's Memorandum of Prisoners, both held at the Massachusetts State Archives, detail not only Jesse's attempts at escape but the evolution of those attempts and the sophistication of his planning while incarcerated. They also speak of the conditions of his cell, the books he read, the letters he wrote and sent, and the studies he was indulging in. Although the majority of the medical records are redacted, those portions that aren't give a glimpse of his physical condition, which was, for the most part, excellent. Newspapers followed his story, and one can trace his aging through the newspaper articles as well.

The pardon papers are also held by the Massachusetts Supreme Judicial Court Records and in them it is possible to read and detect not only Jesse's intelligence—he used legal jargon freely and made arguments that at a certain level made perfect sense—but also the fact that he had not taken responsibility for his actions.

The papers related to the amelioration of his conditions, as well as the end of his stay in solitary confinement, are in the records held in the Massachusetts Supreme Judicial Court. There, one can find the petitions and the transfer papers related to the Bridgewater State Farm.

A detailed history of the Bridgewater State Farm can be traced from the files held at the Bridgewater Public Library. They have followed its progress from its beginning to the more current events pertaining to its guards, and it is possible to trace a linear, albeit painful history of the institution.

Pomeroy's death was covered by virtually every newspaper in the country, and a more detailed bibliography is given for those who wish to read the obituaries printed about Pomeroy, though after a time they tend to become a little repetitious.

EPILOGUE

Detective James R. Wood's departure from the Boston Police Department, his opening of the first detective agency in New England, his writings, and the eventual handing over of its cases to his son, are all detailed in the Wood Detective Agency Records located in the Harvard University Law Library.

Information on Chief of Police Edward Hartwell Savage and his later years can be found in the Boston City Archives, the Boston Public Library, and to some extent, the Massachusetts Historical Society. As it happens, these institutions also hold quite a lot of material on Fire Chief John Damrell, though in his case, the Bostonian Society and the Boston Fire Museum also are great places to go.

The mental makeup of Jesse Pomeroy has been of great interest to forensic psychiatrists for many years, despite the events having taken place so long ago. Mark Safarik, formerly of the FBI Behavioral Analysis Unit, provided a detailed profile, as did Gina Santoro, a forensic psychiatrist specializing in treating youths.

The evolution of Charlestown in the past one hundred years or more can be traced by visiting the Charlestown Public Library and Charlestown Historical Society, which hold not only written records but also many photographs.

Information on the Charles Street Jail can be found in the Boston Public Library, though a better place is the Liberty Hotel itself. They have reserved a space for photographs displaying the jail as it was, giving visitors a sense of what might have been during Jesse Pomeroy's reign.

BIBLIOGRAPHY

BOOKS

An Account of the Massachusetts State Prison: Containing a Description and Plan of the Edifice: the Laws, Regulations, Rules and Orders: with a View of the Present State of the Institution. Board of Visitors, 1806.

Baron-Cohen, Simon. *The Science of Evil: On Empathy and the Origins of Cruelty.* New York: Basic Books, 2011.

Bates, Edward Craig, and Herman Packard DeForest. *History of Westborough, Massachusetts: The Early History.* 1891.

Beale, Thomas. *The Natural History of the Sperm Whale, to Which Is Added a Sketch of a South-Sea Whaling Voyage.* London: John Von Voorst, 1838.

Bingham, Nathaniel. *Observations on the Religious Delusions of Insane Persons, and on the Practicability, Safety, and Expediency of Imparting to the Christian Instructions.* London: J. Hatchard & Son, 1841.

Blair, James, Dereck Mitchell, and Karina Blair. *The Psychopath: Emotion and the Brain.* Malden, MA: Blackwell, 2005.

Browne, J. Ross. *Etchings of a Whale Cruise, with Notes of A Sojourn on the Island of Zanzibar, to Which Is Appended a Brief History of the Whale Fishery, Its Past and Present Condition.* New York: Harper & Brothers, 1850.

Chase, Frederic Hathaway. *Lemuel Shaw: Chief Justice of the Supreme Judicial Court of Massachusetts 1830–1860.* Boston and New York: Houghton Mifflin, 1918.

Clarke, Margaret Harriman. *Images of America: Chelsea.* Charleston, SC: Arcadia, 1998.

———. *Images of America: Chelsea in the 20th Century.* Charleston, SC: Arcadia, 2004.

Clarke, Ted. *Beacon Hill, Back Bay, and the Building of Boston's Golden Age.* Charleston, SC: History Press, 2010.

Cleckley, Harvey. *The Mask of Sanity: An Attempt to Clarify Some Issues About the So-Called Psychopathic Personality.* St. Louis: C. U. Mosby, 1955.

Coffin, Charles Carleton. *The Story of the Great Fire.* Boston: Shepard & Gil, 1872.

Denning, Michael. *Mechanic Accents: Dime Novels and Working-Class Culture in America.* New York: Verso, 1987.

Eissler, K. R. *Searchlights on Delinquency.* New York: International Universities Press, [1949].

Esquirol, E. *Mental Maladies: Treatise on Insanity.* Translated from the French, with additions, by E. K. Hunt, M.D. Philadelphia: Lea & Blanchard, 1845.

Fenichel, Otto. *The Psychoanalytical Theory of Neurosis.* New York: Norton, 1945.

Foucault, Michel. *Discipline & Punish: The Birth of the Prison.* 2nd ed. New York: Vintage Books, 1995.

———. *History of Madness.* London: Routledge, 2006.

Guenther, Lisa. *Solitary Confinement: Social Death and Its Afterlives.* Minneapolis: University of Minnesota Press, 2013.

Gura, Philip F., ed. *Buried from the World: Inside the Massachusetts State Prison, 1829–1831.* Boston: Massachusetts Historical Society, 2001.

Hare, Robert D. *Psychopathy: Theory and Research.* New York: John Wiley & Sons, 1970.

———. *Without Conscience: The Disturbing World of the Psychopaths Among Us.* New York: Guilford Press, 1993.

Hart, Colonel Joseph C. *Miriam Coffin, or the Whale Fishermen: A Tale.* New ed. 2 vols. in one. San Francisco: A. L. Bancroft, 1872.

Hawthorne, Julian. *Hawthorne and His Circle.* New York and London, Harper & Brothers, 1903.

Haynes, Warden Gideon. *Pictures from Prison Life: An Historical Sketch of the Massachusetts State Prison, with Narratives and Incidents, and Suggestions on Discipline.* Boston: Lee & Shepard, 1871.

Hermann, Donald H. J. *The Insanity Defense: Philosophical, Historical, and Legal Perspectives.* Springfield, IL: Charles C. Thomas, 1983.

Holmes, Dr. Oliver Wendell. *The Benefactors of the Medical School of Harvard University, with a Biographical Sketch of the Late Dr. George Parkman, an Introductory Lecture.* Delivered at the Massachusetts Medical College, November 7, 1850. Boston: Ticknor, Reed, & Fields, 1850.

Howe, M. A. DeWolfe. *Memories of a Hostess: A Chronicle of Eminent Friendships Drawn Chiefly from the Diaries of Mrs. James T. Fields.* Reprinted from the Collections of the University of California Libraries, 1922.

Howells, William Dean, and Augustus Hoppin. *Jubilee Days: An Illustrated Daily Record of the Humorous Features of the World's Peace Jubilee.* Boston: James R. Osgood, 1872.

Hunnewell, James. F. *A Century of Town Life: A History of Charlestown, Massachusetts, 1775–1887, with Surveys, Records, and Twenty-Eight Pages of Plans and Views.* Boston: Little, Brown, 1888.

Ingram, Allan, ed. *Patterns of Madness in the Eighteenth Century: A Reader.* Liverpool: Liverpool University Press, 1998.

Jacobs, Thomas Jefferson. *Scenes, Incidents, and Adventures in the Pacific Ocean, on the Islands of the Australian Seas, During the Cruise of the Clipper Margaret Oakley, under Capt. Benjamin Marrell.* New York: Harper & Brothers, 1844.

Leaf, James G. *A History of the Internal Organization of the State Reform Boys at Westborough, Massachusetts (1846–1974).* Ann Arbor: UMI Research Press, 1988.

Lehuu, Isabelle. *Carnival on the Page: Popular Print Media in Antebellum America.* Chapel Hill and London: University of North Carolina Press, 2000.

Lunt, Mrs. George. *Behind the Bars.* Boston: Lee & Shepard, 1871.

Macy, Obed. *The History of Nantucket, Being a Compendious Account of the First Settlement of the Island by the English, Together with the Rise and Progress of the Whale Fishery; and Other Historical Facts Relative to Said Island and Its Inhabitants. In Two Parts.* 2nd ed. Mansfield, MA: Macy & Pratt, 1880.

Magid, Dr. Ken, and Carole A. McKelvey. *High Risk: Children Without Conscience.* Lakewood, CO: K&M, 1987.

Martin, Edward Winslow [James Dobney McCabe]. *The Secrets of the Great City: A Work Descriptive of the Virtues and the Vices, Mysteries, Miseries and Crimes of New York City.* Philadelphia: National, 1868.

McGovern, Constance M. *Masters of Madness: Social Origins of the American Psychiatric Profession.* Hanover, NH: University Press of New England, 1985.

Meloy, J. Reid. *The Psychopathic Mind: Origins, Dynamics, and Treatment.* Northvale, NJ: Jason Aronson, 1998.

Melville, Herman. *Moby-Dick, or, the Whale.* Chicago: Northwestern University Press and the Newberry Library, 1988.

———. *Pierre, or, the Ambiguities.* Digireads.com, 2012.

———. *Redburn: His First Voyage.* Digireads.com, 2009.

———. *Typee, or a Peep at Polynesian Life.* New York: Modern Library, 2001.

A Memorial of William Gaston, from the City of Boston. City Council Press of Rockwell and Churchill, June 25, 1894.

Milder, Robert. *Critical Essays on Melville's Billy Budd, Sailor.* Boston: G. K. Hall, 1989.

Miller, Perry. *The Raven and the Whale: Poe, Melville, and the New York Literary Scene.* New York: Harcourt, Brace, 1956.

Morse, Robin Karr, and Meredith S. Wiley. *Ghosts from the Nursery: Tracing the Roots of Violence.* New York: Atlantic Monthly Press, 1997.

Murdock, Harold. *Letters Written by a Gentleman in Boston to His Friend in Paris Describing the Great Fire: With Introductory Chapters and Notes.* Boston and New York: Houghton Mifflin, 1873.

Otto, Samuel. *Melville's Anatomies.* Berkeley: University of California Press, 1999.

Porter, Roy. *Madness: A Brief History.* New York: Oxford University Press, 2002.

Prichard, James Cowles. *Treaties on Insanity and Other Disorders Affecting the Mind.* London: Sherwood, Gilbert, & Piper, 1835.

Ray, Isaac. *Mental Hygiene.* Boston: Ticknor & Fields, 1863.

———. *A Treatise on the Medical Jurisprudence of Insanity.* Boston: Little, Brown, 1853.

Reiss, Benjamin. *Theaters of Madness: Insane Asylums & Nineteenth-Century American Culture.* Chicago: University of Chicago Press, 2008.

Renker, Elizabeth. *Herman Melville and the Scene of Writing: Strike Through the Mask.* Baltimore: Johns Hopkins University Press, 1996.

Report of the Commissioners Appointed to Investigate the Cause and Management of the Great Fire in Boston. City Printers, Rockwell & Churchill, 1873.

Reynolds, David S. *Beneath the American Renaissance: The Subversive Imagination and the Age of Emerson and Melville.* Cambridge, MA: Harvard University Press, 1988.

Ryan, Tim, with Bob Casey. *Screw: A Guard's View of Bridgewater State Hospital.* Boston: South End Press, 1981.

Sammarco, Anthony Mitchell. *Images of America: Boston's Back Bay.* Charleston, SC: Arcadia, 1997.

———. *Images of America: Charlestown.* Charleston, SC: Arcadia, 1996.

———. *Images of America: Dorchester.* Charleston, SC: Arcadia, 1995.

———. *Images of America: The Great Boston Fire of 1872.* Charleston, SC: Arcadia, 1997.

———. *Then & Now: Boston's South End.* Charleston, SC: Arcadia, 2005.

Sammarco, Anthony, and Paul Buchanan. *Images of America: New Bedford.* Charleston, SC: Arcadia, 1997.

Savage, Edward H. *Police Records and Recollections, or Boston by Daylight and Gaslight for Two Hundred and Forty Years.* Boston: John P. Dale, 1878.

Schechter, Harold. *Fiend.* New York: Pocket Books, 2000.

Schorow, Stephanie. *Boston on Fire: A History of Fires and Firefighting in Boston.* Beverly, MA: Commonwealth Editions, 2003.

Sedgwick, William Ellery. *Herman Melville: The Tragedy of the Mind.* New York: Russell & Russell, 1962.

Sereny, Gitta. *Cries Unheard: Why Children Kill: The Story of Mary Bell.* New York: Henry Holt, 1998.

Tanenhaus, David S. *Juvenile Justice in the Making.* New York: Oxford University Press, 2004.

Tuke, Daniel Hack. *Chapters in the History of the Insane in the British Isles.* London: Kegan Paul, Trench, 1882.

Upham, Thomas C. *Outlines of Imperfect and Disordered Mental Actions.* New York: Harper & Brothers, 1840.

Wells, Donna M. *Images of America: Boston Police Department.* Charleston, SC: Arcadia, 2003.

Wilkes, Charles, U.S.N. *Narrative of the United States' Exploring Expedition, During the Years 1838, 1839, 1840, 1841, 1842.* Condensed and abridged ed. London: Whittaker, 1845.

JOURNAL ARTICLES

Beer, M. Dominic. "Psychosis: A History of the Concept." *Comprehensive Psychiatry* 37, no. 4 (July/August 1996): 273–91.

———. "Psychosis: From Mental Disorder to Disease Concept." *History of Psychiatry* 6, no. 22 (June 1995): 177–200.

Bell, Millicent. "Pierre, Boyle and Moby Dick." *PMLA* 66, no. 5 (September 1951): 626–48.

Berrios, G. E. "Historical Aspects of Psychosis: 19th Century Numbers." *British Medical Bulletin* 43, no. 3 (1987): 484–98.

Bilnes, Murray. "Delinquent's Escape from Conscience." *American Journal of Psychotherapy* 19, no. 4: 633–40.

Blackburn, R. "On Moral Judgments and Personality Disorders: The Myth of Psychopathic Personality Revisited." *British Journal of Psychiatry* 153 (1998): 505–12.

Blair, James, et al. "Theory of Mind in the Psychopath." *Journal of Forensic Psychiatry* 7, no. 1 (May 1996): 15–25.

Braswell, William. "Melville's *Billy Budd* as an Inside Narrative." *American Literature* 29, no. 2 (May 1957): 133–46.

Bromberg, Walter. "A Psychological Study of Murder." *International Journal of Psychoanalysis* 32 (1951): 117–27.

Brown, Harold P. "The New Instrument of Execution." *North American Review* 149, no. 369 (November 1889): 586–93.

Brown, Willard. "Civil Service Reform in the New York Custom House." Published for the Civil Service Reform Association by G. P. Putnam's Sons, New York, 1882.

Bryant, R. H. "Discussions of the Constitutional Psychopathic Inferior." *American Journal of Psychiatry* 6 (1927): 683–89.

Camus, Albert. "Reflections on the Guillotine." *Evergreen Review* 1, no. 3 (1957): 5–55.

Carlton, Eric T. "Benjamin Rush and His Insane Son." Paper presented at a meeting of the New York Psychiatric Society held by the Century Association, New York, NY, January 6, 1975.

———. "The Unfortunate Dr. Parkman." *American Journal of Psychiatry* 123 (December 1966): 724–28.

Ciccone, J. Richard. "Murder, Insanity, and Medical Expert Witness." *Archives of Neurology* 49 (1992): 608–11.

Cohen, Daniel A. "In Defense of the Gallows: Justification of Capital Punishment in New England Execution Sermons, 1674–1825." *American Quarterly* 40, no. 2 (June 1988): 147–64.

Cook, Richard M. "Evolving the Inscrutable: The Grotesque in Melville's Fiction." *American Literature* 49, no. 4 (January 1974): 544–59.

Crowe, Raymond R. "An Adoption Study of Antisocial Personality." *Archives of General Psychiatry* 31, no. 6 (December 1974): 785–91.

Davis, Merrell. "Melville's Midwestern Lecture Tour, 1859." *Philological Quarterly* 20 (1941): 46–57.

Dinwiddie, Stephen H. "Dangerous Delusions? Misidentification Syndromes and Professional Negligence." *Bulletin of the American Academy of Psychiatric Law* 21, no. 4 (1993): 513–21.

———. "Genetics, Antisocial Personality, and Criminal Responsibility." *Bulletin of the American Academy of Psychiatry and Law* 24, no. 1 (1996): 95–108.

Dodge, Kenneth A., et al. "Mechanism in the Cycle of Violence." *Science* 250 (December 1990).

Dolan, Maired. "Psychopathic Personality in Young People." *Advances in Psychiatric Treatment* (2004): 466–73.

Easson, William M., et al. "Murderous Aggression by Children and Adolescents." *Archives of General Psychiatry* 4, no. 1 (January 1961): 1–9.

Finkel, Norman J., and Sharon F. Handel. "How Jurors Construct Insanity." *Law and Human Behavior* 13, no. 1 (March 1989): 41–59.

Fishbein, Diana H. "Biological Perspectives in Criminology." *Criminology* 28, no. 1 (1990).

Fisher, George Park. "The Madness of Ahab." *Yale Review* 66 (1976): 14–32.

Fogle, Richard. "*Billy Budd:* The Order of the Fall." *Nineteenth-Century Fiction* 15, no. 3 (December 1960): 189–205.

Franklin, H. Bruce. "*Billy Budd* and Capital Punishment: A Tale of Three Centuries." *American Literature* 69, no. 2 (June 1997): 337–59.

Frick, Paul J., et al. "Psychopathy and Conduct Problems in Children." *Journal of Abnormal Psychology* 103, no. 4 (1994): 700–707.

Friedlander, Kate. "Formation of Antisocial Character." *Psychoanalytical Study of the Child* 1 (1945): 189–203.

Gacono, Charles B., et al. "A Rorschach Investigation of Narcissism and Hysteria in Antisocial Personality." *Journal of Personality Assessment* 55, no. 182 (1990): 270–79.

Garn, Elliott J. "Good-bye Boys, I Die a True American: Homicide, Nativism, and Working-Class Culture in Antebellum New York City." *Journal of American History* 74, no. 2 (September 1987): 388–410.

Garner, Stanton. "Surviving the Gilded Age: Herman Melville in the Custom Service." *Essay in Arts and Sciences* 15 (June 1986): 1–13.

Gault, William Barry. "Some Remarks on Slaughter." *American Journal of Psychiatry* 128, no. 4 (October 1971).

Gibbs, Jack P. "The Death Penalty and Penal Policy." *Journal of Criminal Law and Criminology* 69, no. 3 (1978): 291–99.

Gilman, Amy. "The Death of Mary Rogers, the Public Prints, and the Violence of Representation." *Legal Studies Forum* 17, no. 2 (1993).

Goff, Brent G., and H. Wallace Goddard. "Terminal Care Values Associated with Adolescent Problem Behaviors." *Adolescence* 34, no. 133 (Spring 1999).

Goldsmith, Larry. "History from the Inside Out: Prison Life in Nineteenth Century Massachusetts." *Journal of Social History* 31, no. 1 (Winter 1997).

Goldstein, Joseph, and Jay Katz. "Abolish the Insanity Defense—Why Not?" *Yale Law School Legal Scholarship Repository* 72, no. 5 (1963).

Goldstein, Robert Lloyd, and Merril Potter. "The Psychiatrist's Guide to Right and Wrong: Judicial Standards of Wrongfulness Since M'Naghten." *Bulletin of the American Academy of Psychiatric Law* 16, no. 4 (1988): 359–67.

Gray, Sheila. "The Insanity Defense: Historical Development and Contemporary Relevance." *American Criminal Law Review* 10 (1972): 559–83.

Greenacre, Phyllis. "Conscience in the Psychopath." *American Journal of Orthopsychiatry* 15, no. 3 (July 1945): 495–509.

Guze, Samuel B. "Nature of Psychiatric Illness: Why Psychiatry Is a Branch of Medicine." *Comprehensive Psychiatry* 19, no. 4 (July/August 1978).

Guze, Samuel, et al. "Psychiatric Illness in Families Convicted of Convicted Criminals: A Study of 519 First Degree Relatives." *Diseases of the Nervous System* 28, no. 10 (October 1967): 651–59.

Halleck, Seymour L. "Clinical Assessment of the Voluntariness of Behavior." *Bulletin of American Academy of Psychiatry and Law* 20, no. 2 (1992).

———. "Which Patients Are Responsible for Their Illnesses?" *American Journal of Psychotherapy* 42, no. 3 (July 1988): 338–53.

Hallenbrand, Harold. "Behind Closed Doors: Ishmael's Dreams and Hypnagogic Trances in *Moby Dick*." *ATQ*, no. 61 (1986): 47–71.

Harpur, Timothy J., and D. Hare. "Assessment of Psychiatry as a Function of Age." *Journal of Abnormal Psychology* 103, no. 4 (1994): 604–9.

Harris, Grant T., et al. "Psychopathy as a Taxon: Evidence That Psychopaths Are a Discreet Class." *Journal of Consulting and Clinical Psychology* 62, no. 2 (1994): 387–97.

Harris, Neil. "The Gilded Age Revisited: Boston and the Museum Movement." *American Quarterly* 14, no. 4 (Winter 1962): 545–66.

Harvey, Charles M. "The Dime Novel in American Life." *Atlantic*, July 1907, 37–45.

Hayford, Harrison. "The Confidence-Man." *Nineteenth-Century Fiction* 14, no. 3 (December 1959): 207–18.

Hays, Peter L., and Richard Dilworth Rust. "Something Healing: Fathers and Sons in *Billy Budd*." *Nineteenth-Century Fiction* 34, no. 3 (December 1979): 326–36.

Hellman, Daniel S., and Nathan Blackman. "Enuresis, Firesetting and Cruelty to Animals: A Triad Predictive of Adult Crime." *American Journal of Psychiatry* 122, no. 12 (June 1966): 1431–35.

Hillway, Titus. "Melville and the Spirit of Science." *South Atlantic Quarterly* 18 (1948): 77–88.

———. "Melville's Use of Two Pseudo-Sciences." *Modern Language Notes* 64, no. 3 (March 1949): 145–50.

Holmes, Oliver Wendell. "Crime and Automatism." *Atlantic*, April 1875.

Howell, Andrew J., et al. "Immediate Antecedents to Adolescents' Offenders." *Journal of Clinical Psychology* 53, no. 4 (1997): 355–60.

Ives, C. B. "*Billy Budd* and the Articles of War." *American Literature* 34, no. 1 (March 1962): 31–39.

Jaffe, David. "Some Origins of *Moby Dick*: New Finds in an Old Source." *American Literature* 29, no. 3 (November 1957): 263–77.

Jester, Jean Catto. "The Abolitions of Public Executions: A Case Study." *International Journal of Criminology and Penology* 4, no. 1 (1976): 25–32.

Judson, Adoniram. "History and Cause of the Epizootic Among Horses upon the North American Continent, in 1872–1873." *Public Health Papers and Reports* 1 (1873); 88–109.

Kasson, David S. "Divided Visual Attention in Psychopathic and Non Psychopathic Offenders." *Personality Individual Differences* 24, no. 3 (1998): 373–91.

Kasson, David S., et al. "A New Method for Assessing the Interpersonal Behavior of Psychopathic Individuals: Preliminary Validation Studies." American Psychological Association, 1997.

Klinternberg, Britt A. F. "The Psychopathic Personality in a Longitudinal Perspective." *European Child & Adolescent Psychiatry* 5, Supplemental 1 (1996): 57–63.

Korpman, Ben. "On the Need of Separating Psychopathy in Two Distinct Clinical Types: Symptomatic and Idiopathic." *Journal of Criminal Psychopathology* 3 (1941): 112–37.

Kring, Walter, and Jonathan Carey. "Two Discoveries Concerning Herman Melville." *Proceedings of the Massachusetts Historical Society* 87 (1975): 137–41.

Law, James. "Influenza in Horses." In *Report of the Commissioner of Agriculture*, Washington, DC, 1872.

Lee, Dwight A. "Melville and George J. Adler." *American Notes & Queries* (May/June 1974).

Lilienfield, Scott O. "Methodological Advances and Developments in the Assessment of Psychopathy." *Behavior Research and Therapy* 36 (1998): 99–125.

Loeber, Rolf. "Development and Risk Factors of Juvenile Antisocial Behavior and Delinquency." *Clinical Psychology Review* 10 (1990): 1–41.

Lowry, Lowson G. "The Psychopathic Delinquent Child." *American Journal of Orthopsychiatry* 20, no. 2 (April 1950): 223–65.

Luntz, Barbara K. "Antisocial Personality Disorder in Abused and Neglected Children Grow Up." *American Journal of Psychiatry* 151, no. 5 (May 1994).

Lynam, Donald R. "Early Identification of Chronic Offenders: Who Is the Fledgling Psychopath?" *Psychological Bulletin* 120, no. 2 (1996): 209–34.

———. "Pursuing the Psychopath: Capturing the Fledgling Psychopath in a Nomo Logical Net." *Journal of Abnormal Psychology* 106, no. 3 (1997): 425–38.

McHoskey, John W., et al. "Machiavellianism and Psychopathy." *Journal of Personality and Social Psychology* 74, no. 1 (1998): 192–210.

McShane, Clay. "Gilded Age of Boston." *New England Quarterly* 74, no. 2 (June 2001): 274–302.

Milder, Robert. "An Arch Between Two Lives: Melville and the Mediterranean, 1856–57." *Arizona Quarterly* 55, no. 4 (Winter 1999): 21–47.

———. "The Ugly Socrates: Melville, Hawthorne, and Homoeroticism." *ESQ* 46 (2000).

Miller, Derek, and John Looney. "The Prediction of Adolescent Homicide: Episodic Dyscontrol and Dehumanization." *American Journal of Psychoanalysis* 34, no. 3 (Fall 1974): 187–98.

Miller, Linda Patterson. "Poe on the Beat: Doings of Gotham as Urban Penny Press Journalism." *Journal of the Early Republic* 7, no. 2 (Summer 1987): 147–65.

Mitchell, David T., and Sharon L. Snyder. "Masquerades of Impairment: Charity as a Confidence Game." *Journal of Melville Studies.*

Moore, Mitchell S. "Mental Ilness and Responsibility." *Bulletin of the Menninger Clinic* 39, no. 4 (July 1975): 308–28.

Morse, Stephen J. "Causation, Compulsion, and Involuntariness." *Bulletin of American Academy of Psychiatric Law* 22, no. 2 (1994).

———. "Excusing the Crazy: The Insanity Defense Reconsidered." *California Law Review* 58, no. 3 (March 1985): 777–836.

Murphy, Geraldine. "The Politics of Reading *Billy Budd.*" *American Literary History* 1, no. 2 (Summer 1989): 361–82.

Myers, Andrew B. "A Consideration of an Additional Source for Melville's *Moby Dick.*" *Penny Cyclopaedia of the Society for the Diffusion of Useful Knowledge* XXVIL.

Myers, Wade C. "Sexual Homicides by Adolescents." *Journal of American Academy of Child and Adolescent Psychiatry* 33, no. 7 (September 1994): 962–69.

Myers, Wade C., et al. "Psychopathology and Personality in Juvenile Sexual Homicide Offenders." Division of Child and Adolescent Psychiatry, Health Science Center.

Noone, John B., Jr. "*Billy Budd*: Two Concepts of Nature." *American Literature* 29, no. 3 (November 1957): 249–62.

O'Brien, Bridget S., and Paul J. Frick. "Reward Dominance: Associations with Anxiety Conduct Problems and Psychopathy in Children." *Journal of Abnormal Child Psychology* 24, no. 2 (1996).

Patrick, Christopher J. "Emotion in the Criminal Psychopath: Fear Image Processing." *Journal of Abnormal Psychology* 103, no. 3 (1994): 523–34.

Pauley, John J. "The Great Chicago Fire as a National Event." *American Quarterly* 36, no. 5 (Winter 1984): 668–83.

Pollock, Nathan L. "Accounting for Predictions of Dangerousness." *International Journal of Law and Psychiatry* 13 (1990): 207–15.

Putzell, Max. "The Source and the Symbols of Melville's *Benito Cereno*." *American Literature* 34, no. 2 (May 1962): 191–206.

Ramsey, William. "Melville's and Barnum's Man with a Weed." *American Literature* 51, no. 1 (March 1979): 101–4.

Reid, John. "Psychopathy—A Clinical and Legal Dilemma." *British Journal of Psychiatry* 168 (1996): 4–9.

Renker, Elizabeth. "Herman Melville, Wife Beating, and the Written Page." *American Literature* 66, no. 1 (March 1941): 123–50.

Reynolds, J. N. "Mocha Dick: Or, White Whale of the Pacific: A Leaf from a Manuscript Journal." *Knickerbocker, or New York Monthly Magazine* 13, no. 5 (May 1839): 377–92.

Richards, Robert J. "Rhapsodies on a Cat-Piano, or Johann Christian Reil and the Foundation of Romantic Psychiatry." *Critical Inquiry* 24 (Spring 1998).

Rogers, Richard. "Predictors of Adolescent Psychopathy: Oppositional and Conduct Disordered Symptoms." *Journal of the American Academy of Psychiatry and Law* 25, no. 4 (1997).

Runder, John P. "Columbia Grammar School: An Overlooked Year in the Lives of Gansevoort and Herman Melville." *Melville Society Extracts* 46, no. 1 (May 1981): 1–3.

Rygaard, Neils Peter. "Psychopathic Children: Indicators of Organic Dysfunction." In Theodore Millon et al., *Psychopathy: Antisocial, Criminal, and Violent Behavior*. New York: Guilford Press, 1998, 247–59.

Sadoff, Robert L. "Violence: Roots and Remedies: The Perspective of the Forensic Psychiatrist." *Bulletin of the American Academy of Psychiatry and the Law* 10, no. 2 (1988).

Sargent, Douglas. "Children Who Kill—A Family Conspiracy?" *Social Work*, January 1962.

Satten, Joseph, et al. "Murder Without Apparent Motive: A Study in Personality Disorganization." *American Journal of Psychiatry* 117 (July 1960): 48–53.

Schneck, Jerome. "Hypnagogic Hallucinations: Herman Melville's *Moby Dick*." *New York State Journal of Medicine* 77, no. 13 (1977): 2145–47.

———. "Karl Kahlbaum's Catatonia and Herman Melville's Bartleby the Scrivener." *Archives of General Psychiatry* 27, no. 1 (July 1972): 48–51.

———. "The Psychotherapeutic Statement and Psychosomatic Observation of Hawthorne in *The Scarlet Letter*." *Journal of the History of the Behavioral Sciences* 1, no. 3 (July 1965): 259–61.

Shepherd, Gerard W. "Pierre's Psyche and Melville's Art." *ESQ* 30 (1984): 83–98.

Shneidman, Edwin. "Some Psychological Reflections on Herman Melville." *Melville Society Extracts* 64, no. 19 (1985): 7–9.

Shroeder, John W. "Sources and Symbols for Melville's *Confidence-Man*." *PMLA* 66, no. 4 (June 1951): 363–80.

Smith, Sydney. "The Adolescent Murderer: A Psychodynamic Interpretation." *Archives of General Psychiatry* 13, no. 4 (October 1965): 310–19.

Steadman, Henry J. "A Situational Approach to Violence." *International Journal of Law and Psychiatry* 5, no. 2 (1982): 171–86.

Stebbins, Theodore E., Jr. "Richardson and Trinity Church: The Evolution of a Building." *Journal of the Society of Architectural Historians* 27, no. 4 (December 1998): 281–98.

Stewart, David M. "Cultural Work, City Crime, Reading, Pleasure." *American Literary History* 9, no. 4 (Winter 1997): 676–701.

Stewart, Mark, and Loida Leone. "A Family Study of Unsocialized Aggressive Boys." *Biological Psychiatry* 13, no. 1 (February 1978): 107–17.

Thorne, Frederick C. "Psychological Investigation of a Homicidal Youth." *Journal of Clinical Psychology* 5, no. 1 (January 1949): 88–93.

Titus, David K. "Herman Melville at the Albany Academy." *Melville Society Extracts* 42, no. 1 (May 1980): 4–10.

Vitelli, Romeo. "Childhood Disruptive Behavior Disorders and Adult Psychotherapy." *American Journal of Forensic Psychology* 16, no. 4 (1998).

Watters, R. E. "Melville's Metaphysics of Evil." *University of Toronto Quarterly* 9 (1940): 170–82.

Whipple, William. "Poe's Two-Edged Satiric Tale." *Nineteenth Century Fiction* 9, no. 2 (September 1954): 121–33.

Widner, Kingsley. "The Perplexed Myths of Melville: *Billy Budd*." *Novel: A Forum on Fiction* 2, no. 1 (Autumn 1968): 25–35.

Wightman, Richard. "Early American Murder Narratives: The Birth of Horror." In *The Power of Culture: Critical Essays in American History.* Chicago: University of Chicago Press, 1993, 671–701.

Willett, Ralph W. "Nelson and Vere: Hero and Victim in *Billy Budd, Sailor.*" *PMLA* 82, no. 5 (October 1967): 370–76.

Williams, Daniel E. "Behold a Tragic Scene Strangely Changed into a Theatre of Mercy: The Structure and Significance of Criminal Conversion Narratives in Early New England." *American Quarterly* 38, no. 5 (Winter 1986): 827–47.

Winnsatt, William Kurtz, Jr. "Poe and the Mystery of Mary Rogers." *PMLA* 56, no. 1 (March 1941): 230–48.

Young, Philip. "The Earlier Psychologists and Poe." *American Literature* 22, no. 4 (January 1951): 442–54.

NEWSPAPER ACCOUNTS

The story of Jesse Pomeroy was followed for many years by newspapers across the country and even across the world, starting early in the 1870s and continuing well into the 1930s. Occasionally articles appeared well after his passing. The list that follows by no means includes *everything* that was published in all newspapers, but it is a good place to begin for the reader who wants to learn more about how the story was dealt with in the media.

Albion Noble County Democrat: Wednesday, October 9, 1889.

Alton Telegraph: Thursday, July 30, 1874.

Ames Daily Tribune Times: Saturday, October 8, 1932.

Anglo American Times, London: Saturday, October 12, 1872; Friday, August 6, 1875.

Appleton Post Crescent: Friday, August 2, 1929; Friday, September 30, 1932.

Atlanta Constitution: Friday, April 3, 1914.

Attica Daily Ledger: Friday, April 9, 1909.

Austin Daily Herald: Wednesday, September 8, 1909.

Barre Times: August 1, 1929.

Bedford Weekly Mail: Friday, January 3, 1913.

Biloxi Daily Herald: Saturday, October 26, 1901; Friday, September 30, 1932.

Boston Daily Globe: June 8, 1872; October 8, 1873; October 27, 1873; April 24, 1874; April 27, 1874; April 28, 1874; July 20, 1874; July 22, 1874; July 24, 1874; September 29, 1874; November 5, 1874; December 9, 1874; December 10, 1874; December 14, 1874; April 1, 1875; April 3, 1875; May, 28, 1875; July 7, 1875; July 26, 1875; August 5, 1875; August 13, 1875; August 19, 1875; September 30, 1875; December 1, 1875; February 17, 1876; May 17, 1876; May 23, 1876; May 27, 1876; July 27, 1876; July 31, 1876; August 2, 1876; August 9, 1876; June 8, 1878; July 11, 1878; August 22, 1878; August 29, 1878; August 27, 1879; November 27, 1881; June 14, 1882; March 7, 1883; March 1, 1885; March 27, 1885; May 9, 1885; February 14, 1886; June 19, 1886; March 8, 1887; July 20, 1887; September 21, 1887; November 14, 1887; January 19, 1888; July 6, 1888; July 26, 1888; November 13, 1888; December 26, 1888; December 30, 1888; February 24, 1889; June 7, 1889; July 20, 1889; November 10, 1889; December 7, 1889; May 4, 1890; January 17, 1891; August 17, 1891; August 18, 1891; August 20, 1891; October 17, 1891; March 21, 1892; May 10, 1892; May 31, 1892; January 18, 1893; March 23, 1894; February 23, 1895; July 23, 1895; July 24, 1895; August 15, 1895; November 20, 1895; December 4, 1895; January 28, 1896; March 30, 1896; January 8, 1897; May 24, 1897; June 28, 1897; August 11, 1897; August 24, 1897; October 29, 1897; November 12, 1898; November 13, 1898; April 14, 1900; May 25, 1900; November 12, 1900; December 2, 1900; December 8, 1900; February 7, 1902; February 26, 1903; January 22, 1904; August 8, 1904; February 4, 1905; September 15, 1905; October 31, 1905; November 4, 1905; November 8, 1905; November 19, 1905; March 17, 1906; June 3, 1906; June 10, 1906; October 27, 1906; June 30, 1907; September 7, 1907; September 8, 1907; October 21, 1907; October 4, 1908; February 12, 1909; June 5, 1910; September 8, 1910; September 28, 1910; June 1, 1911; December 26, 1912; May 10, 1914; November 26, 1914; November 30, 1914; January 12, 1915; February 15, 1915; February 23, 1915; April 20, 1915; July 16, 1915; August 22, 1915; October 6, 1915; November 30, 1915; December 1, 1915; December 7, 1915; January 6, 1916; January 24, 1916; February 14, 1916; February 16, 1916; February 19, 1916; September 7, 1916; November 30, 1916; December 8, 1916; December 25, 1916; December 27, 1916; January 3, 1917; January 17, 1917; January 21, 1917; January 25, 1917; January 26, 1917; January 28, 1917; January 29, 1917; January 30, 1917; January 31, 1917; April 30, 1917; May 1, 1917; November 28, 1918; December 26, 1918; June 30, 1919; November 28, 1919; November 30, 1919; January 24, 1920; February 4, 1920; February 20, 1920; September 26, 1920; September 30, 1920; November 30, 1921; November 1, 1922; November 5, 1922; November 10, 1922; September 8, 1923; November 30, 1923; February 21, 1924; April 1, 1924; May 11, 1924; May 2, 1925; May 24, 1925; September 7, 1926; September 8, 1925; November 26, 1926; November 29, 1926; November 30, 1926; May 2, 1927; August 8, 1927; September 7, 1927; September 11, 1927; November 30, 1927; January 6, 1928; January 7, 1928; June 6, 1928; June 7, 1928; September 10, 1928; July 21, 1929; August 1, 1929; August 2, 1929; August 21, 1929; November 17, 1929; August 29, 1930; September 21, 1930; May 26, 1931; June 24, 1931; August 11, 1931; December 31, 1931; October 2, 1932; October 3, 1932; October 4, 1932; December 1, 1932; February 17, 1937; October 24, 1937; August 28, 1939; December 7, 1953; May 25, 1969.

Boston Evening Globe: January 11, 1915; April 19, 1915; November 19, 1915; February 10, 1915; January 29, 1917; January 30, 1917; November 29, 1919; November 30, 1919; June 4, 1920; August 1, 1929.

Boston Globe: November 4, 1872; August 19, 1874; September 5, 1874; January 12, 1875; January 26, 1875; August 3, 1875; January 28, 1917; June 28, 1917; November 30, 1919; November 5, 1961; September 24, 1965; November 12, 1972.

Boston Herald: March 21, 1873; March 25, 1873; April 1, 1925; April 10, 1925; May 9, 1925; September 5, 1926; August 27, 1929.

Boston Intelligencer & Evening Gazette: Monday, August 5, 1929; Monday, September 21, 1942.

Boston Post: July 2, 1874; July 20, 1874; July 21, 1874; July 22, 1874; July 23, 1874; July 30, 1874; December 12, 1874; July 22, 1875; December 21, 1877; December 20, 1884; July 30, 1886; August 29, 1887; November 12, 1887; May 27, 1891; April 18, 1892; January 1, 1896; January 8, 1897; August 12, 1897; March 24, 1904; April 1, 1904; April 15, 1904; April 16, 1904; February 22, 1905; February 24, 1905; March 13, 1905; August 18, 1905; October 21, 1905; March 26, 1906; March 29, 1906; September 14, 1907; June 6, 1908; September 12, 1908; September 24, 1909; November 24, 1910; May 19, 1911; December 26, 1911; November 29, 1912; December 26, 1912; December 31, 1912; May 31, 1913; December 26, 1913; March 30, 1914; July 31, 1914; November 30, 1914; December 7, 1914; January 11, 1915; January 22, 1915; February 9, 1915; February 23, 1915; April 20, 1915; November 29, 1915; April 24, 1916; December 1, 1916; December 26, 1916; January 15, 1917; January 25, 1917; January 27, 1917; February 1, 1917; May 5, 1917; May 7, 1917; June 30, 1917; July 5, 1917; January 18, 1918; July 9, 1919; November 16, 1923; August 1, 1929.

Boston Sunday Post: March 10, 1895; August 11, 1895; April 22, 1900; November 9, 1902; August 19, 1906; September 29, 1907; May 2, 1909; December 26, 1909; January 14, 1912; August 25, 1912; October 20, 1912; September 13, 1914; January 17, 1915; December 24, 1916; January 29, 1917; January 6, 1918; February 24, 1918; June 9, 1918; July 7, 1918; January 25, 1920; March 14, 1920.

Boston Transcript: August 1, 1929.

Boston Traveller: November 15, 1923; August 1, 1929.

Bradford Era: Wednesday, August 19, 1891; Saturday, May 20, 1911.

Bridgeport Post: August 1, 1929.

Bridgeport Telegram: Friday, March 18, 1927; Monday, October 18, 1954.

Brockton Times: July 31, 1929.

Burlington Gazette: Friday, September 30, 1932.

Cambridge City Tribune: Tuesday, June 10, 1890.

Centralia Daily Chronicle Examiner: Friday, February 5, 1915.

Chariton Patriot: Wednesday, June 14, 1882.

Charleston Daily Mail: Friday, October 25, 1929.

Charleston Gazette: Thursday, August 1, 1929; Sunday, September 27, 1953.

Charlestown Advertiser: Saturday evening, January 18, 1873; Saturday evening, March 1, 1873; July 12, 1873; November 8, 1873.

Charlestown Times: January 11, 1872; August 9, 1873; August 23, 1873; September 13, 1873.

Christian Science Monitor: July 31, 1929.

Chronicle: Charlestown: Saturday, July 5, 1873.

Circleville Herald: Tuesday, October 4, 1932.

Clearfield Progress: Friday, January 14, 1916; Friday, January 5, 1917; Monday, October 3, 1932.

Concord Enterprise: Tuesday, June 14, 1897.

Concord Monitor: August 1, 1929.

Connellsville Daily Courier: Thursday, September 7, 1911.

Corona Daily Independent: Thursday, April 9, 1914.

Corsicana Daily Sun: Friday, September 30, 1932.

Covington Friend: Friday, June 12, 1896.

Daily Globe, Michigan: Saturday, October 8, 1932.

Daily Leader: Saturday, February 3, 1917.

Daily Nevada State Journal: Wednesday, April 12, 1876.

Danville Gazette: Thursday, September 14, 1911.

Decatur Republican: Thursday, November 19, 1874.

Delphos Daily Herald: Monday, October 3, 1932.

Des Moines Daily News: Monday, April 5, 1905.

El Paso Herald Post: Friday, February 11, 1944.

Emporia Gazette: Tuesday, November 15, 1927.

Escanuba Daily Press: Saturday, October 1, 1932.

Evening Independent, Ohio: Tuesday, December 31, 1912; Wednesday, September 28, 1927.

Fall River News: April 8, 1925.

Fitchburg Daily Sentinel: Thursday, July 22, 1875; Tuesday, December 31, 1912; Monday, December 21, 1914; Thursday, June 30, 1921.

Fort Gibson New Era: Thursday, December 5, 1912.

Fort Wayne News: Tuesday, June 30, 1917.

Fort Wayne Journal Gazette: Tuesday, November 6, 1877; Sunday, December 1, 1895; Saturday, January 27, 1917.

Fort Wayne Sentinel: Saturday, March 20, 1875; Friday, August 20, 1886; Wednesday, August 25, 1897; Thursday, June 1, 1911; Monday, December 21, 1914; Thursday, May 4, 1916.

Galveston Daily News: Friday, September 3, 1875.

Gettysburg Times: Thursday, February 1, 1917.

Goshen Daily Democrat: Wednesday, August 11, 1875; Wednesday, June 5, 1881; Saturday, October 13, 1888; Friday, October 11, 1901.

Greensburg Standard: Wednesday, March 17, 1875; Wednesday, May 19, 1875; Wednesday, July 28, 1875; Wednesday, September 1, 1875; Friday, September 2, 1887.

Holyoke Transcript: August 1, 1929.

Huntingdon Daily News: Tuesday, October 13, 1891; Friday, September 30, 1932.

Independent: Wednesday, May 14, 1913; Sunday, August 11, 1929.

Indianapolis Indiana State Sentinel: Tuesday, April 28, 1874; Tuesday, July 28, 1874; Wednesday, March 20, 1878.

Indianapolis People: Sunday, July 26, 1874.

Iowa City Press Citizen: Tuesday, June 28, 1921.

Iowa State Reporter: Wednesday, August 5, 1875.

Jacksonville Daily Journal: Saturday, October 1, 1932.

Janesville Daily Gazette: Saturday, September 5, 1914.

Joplin News Herald: Thursday, August 8, 1929.

Kansas City Star: Friday, September 30, 1932.

Kingsport Times: Thursday, August 20, 1925.

Kokomo Tribune: Thursday, December 2, 1926.

Laredo Times: Sunday, October 9, 1932.

Lawrence Telegram: July 31, 1929.

Lebanon Weekly Pioneer: Friday, March 26, 1875.

Legrange Saturday Call: Saturday, April 23, 1910.

Lock Haven Gazette: Monday, November 21, 1927.

Logansport Daily Star: Friday, July 24, 1874; Saturday, February 25, 1905; Tuesday, February 28, 1905; Thursday, July 10, 1920.

Logansport Weekly Journal: Saturday, March 13, 1875; Thursday, April 8, 1909; Saturday, September 15, 1928.

London Magnet: Monday, March 15, 1875.

London Standard: Friday, March 17, 1911; Wednesday, March 22, 1911.

Lowell Sun: Wednesday, August 22, 1894; Thursday, March 24, 1904; Saturday, August 19, 1905; Tuesday, October 31, 1905; Saturday, June 6, 1908; Tuesday, December 16, 1911; Monday, January 11, 1915; Tuesday, December 7, 1915; Monday, January 31, 1916; Monday, June 24, 1916; Wednesday, January 3, 1917; Tuesday, June 30, 1917; Wednesday, November 30, 1921; Friday, September 30, 1932; Thursday, June 14, 1934; Thursday, October 23, 1941; Wednesday, August 4, 1943; Sunday, August 2, 1953.

Madison Daily Democrat: Wednesday, March 7, 1894.

Madison Daily Herald: Sunday, May 18, 1884; Friday, April 3, 1914.

Martinsville Republican: Thursday, July 8, 1875; Thursday, September 21, 1876.

Medicine Hat News: Thursday, September 7, 1911; Friday, September 30, 1932.

Middletown Times Press: Friday, June 26, 1917; August 1, 1929.

Milford Mail: Thursday, December 19, 1895; Thursday, April 21, 1910.

Monroe News Star: Friday, September 30, 1932.

Muscatine Journal and News Tribune: Friday, September 30, 1932.

New Albany Ledger: Thursday, October 23, 1890.

New Britain Herald: August 1, 1929; August 2, 1929.

New Castle News: Tuesday, September 12, 1911; Tuesday, November 15, 1927; Thursday, August 15, 1929; Friday, September 30, 1932.

New Oxford News: Friday, June 21, 1898; Thursday, September 12, 1907.

New York Herald: July 31, 1929.

New York Times: Saturday, August 4, 1883; August 1, 1929.

New York World: Sunday, March 13, 1888.

Newark Daily Advocate: Saturday, September 30, 1893.

Newport Daily News: Monday, April 28, 1879.

Newport Mercury: Saturday, June 4, 1913.

North Adams Transcript: Wednesday, November 25, 1914; Thursday, August 1, 1929.

Oakland Tribune: Monday, March 8, 1926; Sunday, August 2, 1953.

Ogden Standard Examiner: Monday, November 13, 1932.

Olean Times: Thursday, September 7, 1911; Thursday, September 13, 1928; Wednesday, August 14, 1929.

Oshkosh Daily Northwestern: Saturday, October 1, 1932.

Oskaloosa Evening Herald: Wednesday, July 19, 1893.

Peru Miami County Sentinel: Thursday, December 31, 1874.

Piqua Daily Call: Saturday, June 4, 1892; Tuesday, January 30, 1917; Saturday, September 29, 1928; Friday, August 2, 1929.

Pocahontas County Sun: Thursday, April 16, 1914.

Port Arthur News: Saturday, August 17, 1929.

Portland Press: August 1, 1929.

Portsmouth Herald: Thursday, February 9, 1911.

Portsmouth Times: Friday, September 30, 1932.

Providence Tribune: August 1, 1929.

Pulaski Southwest Times: Wednesday, November 2, 1932.

Raleigh Herald: Thursday, September 24, 1908; Friday, June 21, 1916.

Reno Evening Gazette: Friday, April 7, 1916; Tuesday, September 7, 1926.

Salem Daily News: Thursday, October 3, 1895.

San Antonio Gazette: Saturday, September 5, 1908.

San Antonio Light: Monday, May 10, 1909; Friday, June 6, 1928.

San Mateo Times: Monday, September 17, 1928; Friday, September 30, 1932.

Sandusky Star Journal: Thursday, September 7, 1911; Tuesday, September 13, 1928; Friday, September 30, 1932; Saturday, October 1, 1932.

Salt Lake Tribune: Tuesday, September 3, 1935.

Sheboygan Press: Saturday, December 14, 1912.

Shelbyville Democrat: Saturday, September 16, 1911.

Shelbyville Republican: Friday, September 8, 1911.

Stanford Advocate: August 1, 1929.

Syracuse Evening Herald: Friday, September 29, 1893; Thursday, January 25, 1917; Sunday, August 11, 1929; Monday, October 3, 1932.

Taunton Gazette: July 31, 1929.

Thomasville Daily Times Enterprise: Monday, January 29, 1917; Friday, September 30, 1932.

Times Evening Herald: Thursday, October 6, 1932.

Titusville Herald: Thursday, November 12, 1914.

Torrington Register: August 1, 1929.

Tyrone Daily Herald: Monday, June 17, 1898; Wednesday, January 31, 1917; Thursday, February 1, 1917; Monday, July 6, 1925.

Uniontown Morning Herald: Wednesday, March 30, 1927.

Warren Ledger: Friday, August 30, 1895.

Washington Post: Monday, July 17, 1911; Sunday, August 24, 1913; Tuesday, July 21, 1914; Friday, June 26, 1917.

Waterloo Daily Courier: Wednesday, October 4, 1893.

Ways of the World: January 5, 1918.

Wichita Daily Times: Friday, September 30, 1932.

Williamsport Warren Republican: Thursday, December 24, 1874.

Winchester Journal: Wednesday, June 22, 1881.

Winnipeg Free Press: Tuesday, January 5, 1932.

Winsted Citizen: August 1, 1929.

Worcester Telegram: August 1, 1929.

Zanesville Times Recorder: Friday, September 23, 1927.

INDEX